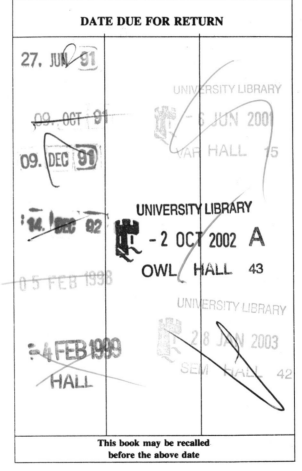

Housing Markets and Policies under Fiscal Austerity

Recent Titles in Contributions in Sociology
Series Editor: Don Martindale

Housing Markets and Policies under Fiscal Austerity

EDITED BY
Willem van Vliet—

Contributions in Sociology, Number 62

GREENWOOD PRESS

New York • Westport, Connecticut • London

344896

Library of Congress Cataloging-in-Publication Data

Housing markets and policies under fiscal austerity.

(Contributions in sociology, ISSN 0084-9278 ;
no. 62)
    Includes bibliographies and indexes.
    1. Housing. 2. Housing policy. I. Van Vliet,
Willem. II. Series.
HD7287.H67   1987   363.5   86-29603
ISBN 0-313-25409-5 (lib. bdg. : alk. paper)

Library of Congress Catalog Card Number: 86-29603
ISBN: 0-313-25409-5
ISSN: 0084-9278

First published in 1987

Greenwood Press, Inc.
88 Post Road West, Westport, Connecticut 06881

Printed in the United States of America

∞™

The paper used in this book complies with the
Permanent Paper Standard issued by the National
Information Standards Organization (Z39.48-1984).

10 9 8 7 6 5 4 3 2 1

Contents

Tables and Figures

TABLES

FIGURES

Preface

The chapters in this volume emanated from an international conference on "Housing Research and Policy Issues in a Era of Fiscal Austerity" held in Amsterdam, the Netherlands, in June 1986. The event was organized under the auspices of the Ad Hoc Group on Housing and the Built Environment of the International Sociological Association (ISA) and cosponsored by the Stichting Gestructureerde Samenwerking (G.S.; Foundation for Structured Collaboration), an institutional framework that coordinates housing research in the Netherlands. More than 120 researchers from 22 countries worldwide, representing diverse disciplines including sociology, political science, planning, geography, and policy analysis, participated in the discussion of about 70 papers that were presented during four days of sessions. The present version of the papers selected for this collection is often a substantial revision, which has benefited from those discussions and has also incorporated comments from subsequent reviews of the earlier version.

While it is impossible to provide comprehensive coverage of all the relevant issues in any single volume, the scope of the chapters in this book includes a number of widely different political economies as found in the United States, Canada, Australia, and various European countries. The relatively greater attention afforded to Britain reflects the notion that trends in that country (for example, regarding the sale of public housing) may be precursors of similar developments in other nations or, if not that, examples of policy responses that may inform alternative courses of action elsewhere.

Important to the success of the conference in Amsterdam has been the commitment of long-standing members of the ISA Ad Hoc Group on Housing and the Built Environment to international activities fostering exchange and collaboration. Among these is in the first place Elizabeth Huttman who has been a major driving force behind the ISA Group ever since its inception. Others with significant contributions include Harvey Choldin, Sylvia F. Fava, Herbert Gans, Suzanne Keller, William Michelson, and David Popenoe. Frans Grunfeld made the initial contact between the ISA Group and G.S., and Leon Deben and Dick van der Vaart took responsibility for the Dutch role in organizing the conference. Thanks to Raymond Studer, then head of the Department of Community Studies at Pennsylvania State University, for making available both expert clerical support and the considerable resources for postage and telephone which I needed for interactions first with participants of the conference and afterwards with contributors to this book. Monica Allebach provided indispensable and superb assistance in conducting the seemingly never abating correspondence, typing, and a miscellany of other essential activities. I am also grateful to Mary R. Sive, Editor for Social and Behavioral Sciences at Greenwood Press, for her unflagging enthusiasm in promoting this publication on housing (along with several others) and for her careful scrutiny and meticulous review of the manuscript.

The developments described and analyzed in this volume continue. When this appears in print, the ongoing changes may require the updating of details in some chapters. However, the value of this collection lies not in presenting the most recent statistics released yesterday afternoon, but rather in identifying and analyzing major structural developments that are transforming the housing markets and policies of many countries in this era of fiscal austerity.[1] It is hoped that this contribution will stimulate and inform needed further studies.

NOTE

1. A companion to this volume with a different focus is being published by Greenwood Press under the title *Housing and Neighborhoods: Theoretical and Empirical Contributions*, edited by W. van Vliet—, H. Choldin, W. Michelson, and D. Popenoe. The papers on housing in the Third World will appear in Spring 1987 in a thematic issue of *Environment and Behavior*.

Housing Markets
and Policies
under Fiscal Austerity

Introduction

WILLEM VAN VLIET—

This volume appears at a time of resurging interest among social science researchers in issues of housing policy. It might seem paradoxical that this interest should be increasing when in many countries there remain, in fact, fewer housing policies to be studied. Many existing national programs have been or are being eliminated, curtailed, or replaced by mechanisms that place greater reliance on local government and private initiative in the market for the provision of housing. These two processes of, respectively, decentralization and privatization are themselves the subject of various analyses in this book. Beyond that, however, many of the authors bring into focus both the antecedents an implications of these developments. While presenting perspectives from various disciplines and different housing systems, the chapters contain elements of certain common trends, albeit couched in the specific features that characterize particular national situations. This is not the place to add to the insightful commentaries offered in this regard by Michael Harloe in Chapter 1. The following limited observations regarding the context of current changes in housing policies and markets are intended to highlight salient points as background for the more detailed discussions and analyses that follow.

Fiscal austerity is a central theme in many of the chapters in this volume. Other chapters articulate contexts relevant to the interpretation of implications of austerity for housing markets and policies. Austerity in and of itself is not, however, a novel condition in housing. National and local governments as well as individual households have faced scarce housing resources in the past. What *is* new, is the growing realization that the ramifications of austerity for housing are not the outcome of some temporary aberration from prevailing trends but instead are inextricably intertwined with structural changes in national political economies evolving in a system of growing global interdependencies. Prominent in this regard, in Western countries in particular, are the greatly increased mobility of capital, changes in employment structure, disinvestment in traditional manufacturing industries, and concomitant large-scale unemployment. Tax evasion practices engaged in by proliferating multinational enterprises parallel a failure of nonsocialist governments to tax as much as one-third of their national wealth (Carlo 1983), further eroding the capacity of governments to sustain their previously established roles in the public welfare sector. Public policies in general, and particularly those in the domain of housing, formulated in conjunction with these developments have emphasized increasingly what has come to be known as privatization.

As is not uncommon in the social sciences, the frequency with which the descriptor is adopted is inversely related to the precision of its contents. Different authors appear to attach different meanings to the same term. Some analysts use privatization as a convenient label to suggest a withdrawal of government from involvement in established arenas of intervention (such as health care, education, social security, and housing) and a shifting of government's traditional responsibilities in these domains to the private sector. This description accords with political rhetoric and popular ideologies but, while ostensibly valid to an extent, it simplifies and obfuscates what is actually happening. Careful examination of the processes taking place reveals not so much a withdrawal of government as a transformation of its role and mode of intervention. Analyses of legislation, policy decisions, and budgetary data provided in this volume (for example, Forrest and Murie; Brindley and Stoker) and elsewhere in the literature (for example, Adams 1986; Robinson 1986) show, for example, that while direct housing expenditures have been reduced, indirect expenditures in the form of mortgage interest relief and other tax benefits have greatly increased. In contrast to capped production expenditures, the costs of automatic entitlements are much harder to predict and control. It is also difficult to arrive at precise figures because actual expenses may show up only in a longer time frame (see, for example, Chapter 4 by Hulchanski and Drover), or they may be transferred to other welfare programs (see, for example, Chapter 2 by Forrest and Murie) or be cloaked in the invisibility of off-budget financing mechanisms (Schwartz 1986).

The available evidence indicates that there has not been a significant cut in real housing expenditures. What has changed is the *way* in which money is spent (from direct expenditures to indirect expenditures; from object subsidies to subject subsidies), the *context* within which it is allocated (a shift to other policy programs), and the *recipients* (increasing emphasis on private home owners). At the same time, traditional roles of housing professionals and experts are in question and undergoing change (see Houlihan, Chapter 14; Choldin, Chapter 15). Privatization is, therefore, a more complex process than just the transfer of responsibilities from the public to the private sector.

The question of whether and to what extent privatization of housing is occurring is, however, in many ways a moot one. It seems more relevant to inquire about criteria that can be used as a yardstick to evaluate approaches pursued at present. Are they effective? Efficient? Equitable? Opinions vary. However, answers to these questions must be based on facts, not on opinion. Research reported in this volume contributes empirical insights required to make more informed judgments in this regard.

Readers will look in vain for unequivocal answers. Analysts bring with them different value commitments, selectively directing their attention to different issues or different facets of the same issue, or suggesting different interpretations of identical factual observations. In addition, the analyses reflect multiple extant contradictions. Such contradictions are found within housing policies, between housing policies and other public policies, and between housing policy objectives and housing market developments. Brindley and Stoker, in Chapter 3, examine such contradictions in Britain, as do Misztal and Misztal in Chapter 12 for Poland. Other examples include Wollmann's (1984) analysis of the West German situation, an examination by Van Vliet— (1985) of Israel's housing policy vis-à-vis national objectives of integration and dispersal of the population and a study by Flynn (1986) of budget cuts in Dutch housing policy. Studies of such internal and external contradictions are useful in revealing underlying competing interests that structure housing systems and in explicating how public policies outside the realm of housing have significant implications for housing.

The perspectives taken by the authors almost invariably situate housing in a broader framework. They tie housing in with other national policy concerns and include in their analyses linkages between housing, economic trends, and party politics. A question arising in this connection, one not explicitly addressed in this book, is whether problems of housing production, distribution, and management, such as examined here, are inherent in capitalist systems. On a general level, similarities noted in many Western countries might suggest that this is the case. On the other hand, trends of rising costs, declining output, and privatization have also been documented for collectivist economies such as Poland (Misztal and Misztal, Chapter 12), Hungary (Szelenyi 1983), and Cuba (Hamberg 1985). Likewise, inequities in access to housing opportunities have historically been found and continue to exist in capitalist countries, the Eastern bloc, the Third World.

The problem with such global observations is that they fail to bring into focus on a less aggregate level those aspects of housing provision that would explain the manner in which certain outcomes are being produced. Such outcomes depend on historically specific factors molding the relationships between stakeholders in the production and consumption of housing. The structure of housing provision is constituted by configurations of nationally (and internationally) interdependent economic, political, cultural, and other variables that take on different values and that, moreover, change over time. Comparative analyses have an important function here. Such comparison is a central concern in the chapters by Roistacher, and Ambrose and Barlow in this book. However, many more studies along these lines are needed with designs that go beyond cross-sectional analyses to include also consideration of the historical development of given housing systems. Recent empirical and theoretical work may effect a growing interest in this type of research and provides methodological guidance that should make such investigations more fruitful (see, for example, McGuire 1981; Harloe and Martens 1984; Barnett, Groth, and Ungson 1985; Environment and Planning 1984; Masser 1984; Pickvance 1986; Van Vliet—, forthcoming).

REFERENCES

Adams, Carolyn Teich
1986 "The Politics of Privatization." Presented at the International Research Conference on Housing Policy, Gävle, Sweden, June 1986.
Barnett, T., A. J. Groth, and C. Ungson
1985 "East-West Housing Policies: Some Contrasts and Implications." In *Public Policy Across Nations: Social Welfare in Industrial Settings*, edited by A. J. Groth and L. L. Wade, 129–51. Greenwich, Conn.: JAI Press.
Carlo, A.
1983 "Multinational Enterprises and National State: An Incurable Conflict." *International Journal of the Sociology of Law* 11, 105–21.
1984 *Environment and Planning, B: Planning and Design*, II, Special issue on cross-national research.
Flynn, Robert
1986 "Cutback Contradictions in Dutch Housing Policy." *Journal of Social Policy* 15, no. 2, 223–36.
Hamberg, Jill
1985 *Housing Policy in Revolutionary Cuba*. New York: Center for Cuban Studies.
Harloe, M., and M. Martens
1984 "Comparative Housing Research." *Journal of Social Policy* 13, no. 3, 255–77.
McGuire, Chester C.
1981 *International Housing Policies: An International Comparison*. Lexington, Mass.: D.C. Heath.
Masser, I.
1984 "Cross-national Comparative Planning Studies: A Review." *Town Planning Review* 55, no. 2, 137–49.
Pickvance, C. G.
1986 "Comparative Urban Analysis and Assumptions about Causality." *International Journal of Urban and Regional Research* 10, no. 2, 162–84.
Robinson, Ray
1986 "Restructuring the Welfare State: An Analysis of Public Expenditure, 1979/80–1984/85." *Journal of Social Policy* 15, no. 1, 1–21.
Schwartz, Nathan H.
1986 "The Relation of Politics to the Instruments of Housing Policy." Presented at the International Research Conference on Housing Policy, Gävle, Sweden, June 1986.
Szelenyi, I.
1983 *Urban Inequalities Under State Socialism*. New York: Oxford University Press.
Van Vliet—, Willem
1985 "Housing Policy as a Planning Tool." *Urban Studies* 22, 105–17.
n.d. "Cross-national Studies of Housing." In *International Handbook of Housing Policies and Practices*, edited by W. van Vliet—. Westport, Conn.: Greenwood Press. Forthcoming.
Wollmann, Hellmut
1984 "Housing Policy between State Intervention and Market Forces." In *Policy Making in the Federal Republic of Germany*, edited by Klaus von Beyme and Manfred Schmidt. London/Beverly Hills: Sage.

1

Housing in an Age of Austerity

MICHAEL HARLOE

One of the chapters in this collection contains an analysis of contemporary trends in housing provision in an advanced industrialized country that will be all too familiar to many analysts. It very clearly describes the impact on housing of economic austerity. This resulted in cuts in public expenditure, declining local authority resources and fiscal crisis, the selling off of public housing, the emergence of informal and spontaneous housing solutions—all leading to an increasing polarization, in terms of housing access and quality, between upper and lower income households.

What is striking about this chapter (by Misztal and Misztal) is not the uniqueness of the developments it analyzes, in whole or in part they are repeated in country after country, it is that they have occurred in Poland—the only noncapitalist country represented in this volume. Of course, there are many important differences between the politics, economics, and housing systems of socialist Poland and those of the capitalist West (and between individual nations in both blocs, too), but the impact of economic austerity on housing provision has been universal and has often taken rather similar general forms in very different societies. As this book shows, it has resulted in changes in housing markets and policies that are leading to the reemergence of large-scale housing problems—a prospect that would have seemed inconceivable to most observers a decade ago.

For 30 years after 1945, economic growth, rising real incomes, and the accession to power of welfare-oriented political parties in the advanced capitalist countries laid the basis for the most sustained improvement in popular access to good housing ever experienced. Although the means by which this access was achieved varied a good deal from country to country, by the 1970s some broadly common patterns had emerged. There was a massive growth of state involvement in housing provision—not only by means of subsidies but also by the extensive regulation of the conditions of production and consumption of housing. Moreover, there was a major change over time in the nature of this involvement. In the early postwar years, when the private housing market scarcely functioned at

all in many countries, governments intervened directly—for example, to determine and finance building programs, supply or guarantee finance, and control
housing costs. However, as economies grew and private markets recovered, most
governments moved away from direct subsidies and controls toward more indirect
forms of support for private market provision. In some cases this was for ideological reasons; more frequently the major objective was to reduce state expenditure (although this was not necessarily achieved).

This shift in the nature of state involvement varied in extent and timing from
country to country. For example, in the United States there was a rapid reversion
after 1945 to a housing market, underpinned massively by the federal government
but dominated by private enterprise. In Western Europe it took far longer to
establish this situation and, even today, the state plays a far larger role in many
European countries than in the United States (or Canada and Australia) in, for
example, the direct support of social housing (that is, housing provided by
nonprofit agencies targeted at low- and moderate-income households). Nevertheless, by the 1970s most advanced Western countries had housing arrangements
that were dominated by the private housing market, specifically by owner occupation. Private rented housing was apparently in irreversible decline; it had
been supplanted by owner occupation as the majority source of housing and
progressively confined to serving limited, upper-income submarkets as well as
providing last-resort accommodation to those whose incomes or other attributes
barred them from access to other tenures. Social rented housing, even in the
relatively few countries where it had become a significant source of accommodation for more than a small minority of poor households, was increasingly
seen as essentially lower-income housing—although this process of "residual-
ization" was uneven, being more apparent in some countries than others, and
in some parts of the stock (for example, high-density, high-rise projects) than
in others.

A resurgence of the private housing market (albeit in forms that often differed
considerably from those in the West) was even experienced in many of the
advanced socialist countries. Apart from their continuing tradition of rural owner
occupation, there was a rapid development in the urban areas of forms of cooperative housing. These have gradually become more and more like owner
occupation with now, in some countries, a free market in the buying and selling
of cooperative units. At the same time access to state housing has been increasingly restricted to lower-income households and some "key workers."

While the increasing dominance of the private market probably did little to
reduce inequalities in housing provision, this was masked by the general rise in
real incomes that occurred and that meant almost all households (whatever their
income level) gained access to improving housing conditions. Especially in the
1960s and early 1970s there were very rapid reductions in levels of housing
inadequacy and stress. In most countries the proportion of income spent on
housing rose, but the quality of the housing consumed also rose along with
households' ability to pay. Of course, there were some groups and some areas

that did not share in this general improvement. However, by the mid–1970s there would have been widespread agreement with the conclusions of a major review of housing policy by the British government, published in 1977. These were that the remaining housing problems were confined to a few localities— such as some of the inner cities—and to a few groups—such as single-parent families, the handicapped, and some of the elderly. These problems could, it was claimed, be solved by relatively modest adjustments in existing housing markets and policies. There was absolutely no need for any more radical changes in the existing housing arrangements that had proved so successful for the great majority of the population.

Even as these confident assertions were being made, however, the plunge into recession was accelerating, economic growth collapsed, real incomes stagnated and even began to fall, and unemployment rapidly reached levels that had not been seen since the 1930s. Government after government responded by abandoning or severely curtailing many social programs; most adopted deflationary economic policies in the belief that these were the only alternative to disaster. In many countries, housing bore the full force of these developments. Collapsing consumer demand (made worse by rocketing interest rates) devastated housing production. In some countries, for example the Netherlands and Denmark, private housing markets virtually collapsed. In other countries, although production declined, the recession had its greatest effect on other parts of the system. For example, in the United States, the established system of mortgage finance was destroyed. In most countries there were severe cuts in direct housing subsidies for the production of low- and moderate-income housing and reductions in rent subsidies too. Middle-income home owners, who mostly benefited from indirect (tax) subsidies, used their political clout to ensure that these mostly remained inviolate—but even they suffered from sharp increases in mortgage interest rates and a crisis of affordability.

The turbulence of the past few years has served to highlight the fact that housing markets and policies are *socially constructed*; they are molded by specific, historically determined features of each society. The structures of housing provision that arose in the postwar era were predicated on continuing economic growth, full employment, and the maintenance of welfarist policies. The collapse of the Keynesian welfare state presages a major reorientation of housing markets and policies that is now under way in all the advanced capitalist countries represented in this collection. The pressures for change are equally evident in many state socialist societies.

In this introductory chapter it is not possible to do more than summarize some of the changes in housing markets and policies that are widespread today. They include the following:

1. The growth of housing stress, which is evidenced, for example, by increasing housing cost/income ratios (resulting in sharp increases in mortgage foreclosures and rent arrears), by the reversal of previous trends concerning quality improvements and occupancy levels, and by the growth of households

unable to gain access to "conventional" housing solutions—indicated by increases in homelessness, and squatting, for example.

2. Certain demographic developments that, although they are affected to a degree by factors such as the growth of incomes, do, in themselves, have an important impact on housing needs, both qualitatively and quantitatively. These developments include the growth in the elderly population and the increasing number of single-parent and other small households. Overall, the growth in households and the changes in their composition result in an emerging pattern of demand that is very different to that which was dominant in earlier years and to which housing policies and markets were attuned.

3. Housing problems have spread to a wider range of areas and social groups than in the 1970s, especially to locations whose employment base has collapsed and to those groups, such as skilled manual workers, who have been among the people most severely affected by deindustrialization and by the "rationalization" of remaining industry.

4. There has been a further acceleration in the shift by governments away from directly subsidized housing supply toward reliance on individual subsidies (direct or indirect) and support for the private market. As previously mentioned, this does not necessarily result in reductions in aggregate state support for housing, but, generally, the intention is to alter the division of housing costs between the state and the individual so that the "social wage" in housing is reduced. This is most apparent in respect to subsidies for low/moderate–income rental housing, but the formidable resistance to cuts in assistance to owner-occupied housing is now being eroded in some countries.

5. At the same time as governments move yet further toward reliance on private housing markets (partly as a matter of political conviction and partly in the hope of reducing public expenditure), changes are occurring in this market that make it likely that more not less subsidization will be required if it is to play an expanded role in housing provision. In short, there is a growing contradiction between housing policy and housing market developments. Principal problems that the private market faces include the severe reduction in the capacity of key sectors of the population (especially first-time buyers) to afford new housing (built to the standards that have been established in recent years) and the breakdown of special protected circuits of housing finance that enabled cheap credit to flow into the housing market for so many years. In the 1970s owner occupation was boosted by the fact that many home buyers paid negative real interest rates for their loans. In the 1980s borrowers have paid real interest rates that are higher than they have been at any other time in living memory and a return to low or negative rates seems unlikely. The full effects of this factor are yet to be experienced, but in several countries the postwar expansion of owner occupation has already petered out.

Housing suppliers and consumers are adjusting to these problems in many different ways. For those at the very bottom of the market the situation is often desperate. Homelessness now threatens many of these people. If this ultimate disaster is avoided, increasing numbers of households find themselves paying scarcely bearable proportions of their incomes for shelter, economizing on housing costs by doubling up or by overcrowding, or accepting poorer quality and cheaper accommodation than hitherto (often more expensive in value for money terms). But the changes that are occurring do not simply affect the poor, for large sections of the population now find that they can no longer afford the standard of housing consumption established as the norm during the earlier years of prosperity. Among the innovations in housing markets and policies that are a response to this situation are the following:

- Efforts to reduce the cost of housing by, for example, reductions in technical and design standards, increasing density of development, deregulation, the use of new techniques such as manufactured housing, and a revival of self–building
- Measures to cushion the impact of rising housing payments by, for example, new forms of mortgage instrument and new subsidy systems
- The development of "new forms of tenure" such as shared equity ownership, socialized forms of owner occupation, various forms of cooperative and tenant-managed housing, homesteading, and "sweat equity" projects
- New initiatives to improve or maintain the quality of existing housing, such as policy changes that emphasize minimal repair work rather than major renovation, and schemes that are based on new forms of public/private partnership

Many of these developments are still on a small scale, although others—such as the changes in mortgage finance—are already having a major impact. Many of them are represented, by governments and by the private market, as positive developments. However, these claims will require careful scrutiny. For example, the growth of forms of cooperative and tenant-managed housing *may* result in greater consumer satisfaction than previous, bureaucratically controlled forms of provision, but it may also be seen as one consequence of a wider process of state disengagement from its housing responsibilities. Likewise, the trend that exists in many countries, toward devolving certain housing responsibilities from central to local government, is advocated as a way of ensuring that housing provision is more sensitively adjusted to the locally varying needs of the consumer. However, such changes have often been accompanied by deep cuts in centrally provided finance and many localities have found themselves with increased responsibilities but reduced resources to meet these responsibilities.

The breakup, under the impact of recession and austerity policies, of established structures of housing provision presents housing researchers with some new and challenging tasks. First, it is necessary to survey the changes that are occurring—no small task. Second, and more importantly, these changes must then be analyzed: why are they occurring; what are their consequences for consumers, governments, and private-sector agencies; and are they of major or only minor significance? Here there is likely to be much controversy, a point clearly illustrated by two of the contributions to this volume (by Hanna and

Lindamood, and Edwards et al.) that take a far more sanguine view of the effects, respectively, of high housing cost/income ratios and of increased sharing of accommodation than would many analysts, including this writer.

This collection provides one of the first attempts to come to grips with such questions and controversies in a cross-national context. Of course, no single volume can provide an authoritative survey of the full range of national variation in the restructuring of housing provision that is currently occurring. Nor can it fully cover even the limited range of new trends and developments that have been referred to in this chapter. However, the chapters that follow do begin to reveal some of the major dimensions of change, illustrating certain broad, cross-national similarities in the responses to austerity, as well as the distinctive nature of the detailed responses in each nation. There is not space here to explore these national variations, let alone the possible reasons for them, but among some of the most striking common features of the current situation revealed by these chapters are the following:

1. The severe obstacles that now appear to stand in the way of a further expansion of owner occupation and the growth of difficulties for existing owner occupiers (see especially the chapters by Fleming and Nellis, Hulchanski and Drover, and Roistacher).

2. The trend toward increasing reliance on the private housing market and toward the privatization of aspects of housing provision that were previously the responsibility of, or controlled by, government (see especially the chapters by Misztal and Misztal, Hulchanski and Drover, Hamnett, Houlihan, Roistacher, Maclennan and O'Sullivan, Ambrose and Barlow, Brindley and Stoker, and Forrest and Murie).

3. Reductions and other changes in direct subsidies for lower-income housing, accompanied by pressure for the maintenance or even an increase in assistance for home owners. This pressure is notably more successful in some countries than in others, but, overall, there is a growing disparity in the treatment of those already in the owner-occupied housing market and those who are in other tenures or who are attempting to become home owners (see especially the chapters by Fleming and Nellis, Misztal and Misztal, Hulchanski and Drover, Roistacher, Maclennan and O'Sullivan, and Oxley).

4. As a consequence of the above-mentioned developments, evidence that there is a widening gap between upper- and lower-income households in relation to housing provision (see the chapters by Fleming and Nellis, Misztal and Misztal, Hulchanski and Drover, Oxley, and Forrest and Murie).

Above all, it is this *polarization* in housing conditions and opportunities that seems the most important and universal consequence of the changes now occurring in housing provision. This development is hardly new. It characterized the development of unregulated and unsubsidized capitalist housing markets in the nineteenth century. In the contemporary era it has accompanied the growth of urban centers in many Third World societies, and it was never wholly absent from the housing systems of the developed countries in the recent period—even from those that took the most radical steps to eliminate housing inequality. However, after decades during which at least the grosser inequalities were eased and when all households benefited from a rising general level of housing consumption, the prospects for decent and affordable mass housing for many of those now entering the housing market are more crucially dependent than they have been since 1945 on their prospects for secure and well-paid employment. It is grimly ironic that the latter prospects are now less certain than at any time since this date. If secure employment and adequate wages can only be guaranteed for a much smaller proportion of the population than in the recent past—as seems likely—then the polarization of housing markets currently occurring is likely to be an enduring feature of housing in an era of austerity.

PART I

THE PRIVATIZATION OF HOUSING

2

Fiscal Reorientation, Centralization, and the Privatization of Council Housing

RAY FORREST AND ALAN MURIE

Abstract. This chapter examines the pattern of public expenditure on housing in Britain over the last six years. It demonstrates significant change in both the direction and nature of housing subsidies and assistance. Whereas considerable cuts have been made in capital investment on public housing, major increases have occurred in tax relief on mortgage interest and means-tested benefits channeled through the social security system. Revenue from the privatization of council housing has disguised the real extent of reduction in public-sector capital investment and has been a major factor in overall public expenditure planning. The main conclusions are that state housing expenditure has been reoriented rather than reduced, directed at consumption rather than production, and has involved a strengthening of central government control and an erosion of local autonomy and discretion.

INTRODUCTION

British housing policy since the mid–1970s and especially since the election of the Thatcher government in 1979 has been dominated by two factors: the need to reduce public expenditure and more pervasive support for the further growth of home ownership. Notions of fiscal crisis and fiscal austerity have permeated the policy debates. Ministers have frequently referred to ''what the country can afford'' as the background to public policy and public expenditure decisions (Murie 1985). Home ownership would transfer social and financial responsibilities from the state to the individual. Both ideological and fiscal objectives would be neatly achieved in one package. The depressed British economy could no longer afford the scale of public provision of the past. Collectivism would give way to privatized, individual solutions in housing, education, health, and transport. Subsidies would be drastically reduced and more narrowly concentrated on those in real need, leaving the majority to compete in a competitive free market.

Judged against the monetarist, free-market rhetoric of the New Right, what has been achieved falls far short of expectations and aspirations. The key institutions of the welfare state, such as National Health Service and state education, may be facing financial stringency but they remain largely intact. If inroads have been made it has been in the contraction of the state housing sector through privatization and reduced investment. It is in the housing sector where we should find the greatest contraction of the state in both its fiscal and regulatory roles. This chapter explores these assumptions and argues that what has occurred can be more accurately described as a reorientation in state housing expenditure and greater central control. While there have been significant changes in the pattern of public expenditure, it would be misleading to attribute changes in housing policy as logical and inevitable outcomes of fiscal constraint.

FISCAL REORIENTATION AND THE ATTACK ON COUNCIL HOUSING

The present government's stated policy priorities for housing are: to increase the level of home ownership; to encourage the repair and improvement of the existing stock; and to concentrate public resources within the housing program on capital provision for those in greatest housing need (HM Treasury 1985). For the Thatcher government one of the key policies designed to achieve these objectives has been the privatization of council housing. The further extension of home ownership, most notably through the sale of public-sector dwellings, has formed part of a broader restructuring of the welfare state (Forrest and Murie 1985a). With one-third of all British households in the public sector in 1979 there was seen to be opportunity for a significant transformation of the tenure structure. This has involved not only boosting levels of home ownership through encouraging tenant purchase but also reducing the role of council housing (housing provided by local government authorities) to a residual service for those in special and exceptional need. In 1986 the Conservative government achieved these objectives to only a limited extent. The council housing sector accounts for a significantly smaller proportion of households in both absolute and relative terms (for the United Kingdom as a whole less than 29 percent in 1983 compared with over 32 percent in 1979). However, in spite of unprecedented encouragement to buy, over one-quarter of households remains as tenants. Perhaps of greater importance, and contrary to the philosophy of the New Right, these changes have not meant a disengagement of government from the housing sphere. A plethora of special policies as well as continuation of existing measures to assist home ownership signify a shift in the nature, direction, and methods of state intervention in housing rather than a simple withdrawal or abandonment of the tradition of state intervention in housing through the general provision of council housing.

In simple terms, public expenditure on housing has experienced a series of cuts. The Labour government made major cuts in housing expenditure in 1976 and since the election of the Conservative government in 1979 further major cuts have been implemented. The severity of the cuts has relegated the housing program from a major to a minor one. As set out in the annual Public Expenditure Survey Committee White Papers, spending has fallen in real terms from £6.6 billion in 1979/80 to £3.0 billion in 1983/84 and a planned £2.4 billion in 1988/89 (at 1983/84 prices). This represents a reduction of 64 percent. Housing's share of total public spending has fallen from 7.6 percent in 1978–79 to an anticipated 3.7 percent in 1988/89. No other welfare program has been cut so substantially. The housing program has borne the lion's share of public expenditure cutbacks. In 1980 the House of Commons Environment Committee noted that housing cutbacks planned for the period up to 1983/84 accounted for 75 percent or more of all public spending reductions (Environment Committee 1980). O'Higgins (1983, 167–68) noted that "housing is not only the welfare programme suffering the largest cuts, it is also the only programme where cuts have been overachieved: by 1981/82 the estimated outturn cut was one-and-a-half times the size the government had planned in 1980."

The result, in terms of investment and subsidy, can be briefly summarized. Public-sector dwelling starts and completions have fallen dramatically. Council house building has declined to its lowest peacetime level since 1925; the availability of council housing to rent has declined for the first time in peacetime since 1919; exchequer (treasury) subsidies benefiting council tenants in general have been drastically cut and council rents have risen substantially. In 1978/79 average unrebated local authority rents were £5.90 per week and this represented 6.6 percent of average weekly earnings for adult males working full time. In 1982/83 rents were £13.58, representing 8.8 percent of earnings. Provisional figures for 1985/86 put average rents at £15.66 (8.1 percent of earnings). The reduction in general assistance subsidy for council housing and in housing capital expenditure generally has been achieved partly by switching housing subsidy expenditure into the social security budget. As rents have risen, so the costs of means-tested assistance with housing costs have increased. Because of changes in the administration of these benefits it is difficult to provide an accurate measure of increase. However, the best estimate shows almost a tripling of cash cost between 1979/80 and 1985/86 during which period housing capital expenditure (in cash terms) remained static. By 1985/86 housing benefit costs stood at £3056 million and this figure exceeded the total housing expenditure program. This represents a rapid growth in individual, means-tested assistance with housing consumption costs. The change is partly associated with the impact of unemployment and recession and partly with the characteristics of those living in council housing. Over recent years the sector has catered to an increasing proportion of supplementary benefit recipients (Forrest and Murie 1983). The growth of means-tested subsidy amounts to a significant *switch* in method of subsidy and does not involve as substantial a *reduction* in subsidy as appears from looking at housing expenditure alone.

Crucial to all these assessments, however, is the inclusion or exclusion of items as public expenditure for housing. There are two significant categories of public expenditure on housing that do not appear in the housing expenditure program. First, items counted as public spending but incorporated in other programs, the most important item being housing benefits, which appear in the social security program; and second, "tax expenditure" items, which are not defined as public spending at all, the most important of which include tax foregone as a result of mortgage interest relief, exemptions from capital gains tax of capital gains made on sale of main residence, and discounts to purchasers of council housing.

It is relevant to bear in mind that the structure of tax relief and other "subsidies" to home owners has not been reviewed. The cost of mortgage interest relief increased by almost five times in real terms between 1963/64 and 1983/84. In 1983/84, official estimates put the cost of mortgage interest tax relief at £2,750 million. This almost equaled the cost of the total housing program (£2,760 million) and compares with total capital expenditure (net of capital receipts) of £1,650 million (HM Treasury 1985). For 1985/86 the estimated cost of mortgage interest tax relief is, at £4,750 million, well in excess of the total housing program (£2,742 million) (HM Treasury 1986). The value of exemption from capital gains tax in each of these years is tentatively estimated at a further £2,500 million. Discounts for council house sales under the Right to Buy involved a new set of subsidies (with a new set of inequities). In 1983/84 the value of these discounts was £940 million (House of Commons Debates 1985). The limit on mortgages qualifying for tax relief has been raised at a cost of some £60 million in revenue foregone. Expressed in these ways, it would seem that either there has been little systematic application of notions of what the country can afford, or the view is that the country can afford substantial support for home owners but not for housing investment or other housing subsidies. There is, of course, considerable debate as to whether these items should be counted as subsidies to home ownership and hence as public spending, even though they are essentially income foregone rather than moneys paid out (see, for example, Ermisch 1984). Such debates, however, often proceed as if the exercise were merely technical, resting on accounting conventions. Balance sheets may not be politically constructed but they certainly have political implications and effects.

If the items referred to above are included in the public expenditure calculus then the impact of public expenditure and taxation decisions affecting housing is somewhat different from the official picture. As Tables 2.1 and 2.2 show, in 1985/86, for example, while expected outturn expenditure on the housing program is £2.7 billion, £3.2 billion will be spent on housing benefit. In addition, mortgage interest tax relief will cost some £4.7 billion. Capital gains tax exemption for 1985/86 is estimated at £2.5 billion. Public spending on mortgage tax relief was about one-third of the level of spending on the housing program in 1979/80, but in 1985/86 it has exceeded it. High interest rates have contributed to this, but tax relief continues to rise as house prices increase. Over the same period spending on housing benefit has also grown to a level where it exceeds the housing program. Discount on sales of council houses in England and Wales between 1979/80 and 1984/85 amounted to £4.7 billion.

Tables 2.2 and 2.3 illustrate the switch in housing expenditure when mortgage interest tax relief and housing benefit are added to the "conventional" picture of housing expenditure.

Even if we confine our analysis to include only housing benefit and mortgage interest tax relief, the total of the "other" housing expenditure after falling slightly in *cash terms* between 1980/81 and 1982/83 rose sharply in 1983/84 and has continued to rise since. What we have seen is a major transfer of resources from those programs conventionally included in the housing program (mainly subsidies to public-sector housing and new capital investment) toward other expenditure (housing benefit and support to home owners), rather than a simple cut in spending. In the government's own terms this must count as a major failure in public expenditure policy; but on the other hand the transfer—from support of the public sector to support of the private sector, from investment to subsidy, and from the subsidization of the production of public housing to the subsidization of individual consumption—reflects the priorities of the government.

In addition, within the official housing program not all expenditure is on council housing. In the period of reduced expenditure since 1979, a striking feature is that both the voluntary sector (housing associations) and home owners have obtained an increased share of this expenditure. In 1979/80 the housing association sector accounted for some 15 percent of net spending; by 1982/83 this had risen to 48 percent and it is expected that it will remain near that level in the foreseeable future. New dwellings completed by local authorities in England fell from 70,000 in 1979/80 to 27,000 in 1984/85; in the same period completions by new towns fell from 7,000 to 1,600 and those of housing associations fell from 16,700 to 12,800.

For home owners the most significant development has been the sixfold increase in improvement grant expenditure between 1979/80 and 1983/84. In 1983/84, improvement and thermal insulation grants, most of which are paid to home owners, accounted for some 28 percent of local authority gross capital expenditure. The 1986 public expenditure White Paper shows gross capital expenditure support to the private sector as £413 million in 1980/81 rising to £1345 million in 1983/84 and falling back to £840 million in 1985/86.

FISCAL OPPORTUNISM

The picture of fluctuations in *gross* capital expenditure understates what has been achieved. The results of the Right to Buy for council tenants and other measures have been to produce an enormous increase in the level of capital receipts, especially for local authorities. These rose fourfold between 1979/80 and 1982/83. As a result the level of *net expenditure* by local authorities has been reduced much more significantly than has gross expenditure. In real terms, new net capital expenditure by local authorities in 1982/83 was only about 25 percent of its 1979/80 level and in 1985/86 is planned to approach 20 percent. Although gross spending increased during 1983/85, the continuing high level of

Table 2.1
An Alternative Housing Program (£ Million Cash)

	1979/80 outturn	1980/81 outturn	1981/82 outturn	1982/83 outturn	1983/84 outturn	1984/85 outturn	1985/86 estimated outturn	1986/87 plans	1987/88 plans	1988/89 plans
Public Sector[1] Housing Expenditure										
Gross Capital Expenditure	3,152	2,933	2,563	3,301	3,981	3,914	3,283	3,253	3,210	3,110
Net Capital Expenditure (ie Gross Expenditure less value of capital receipts from the housing programme)	2,680	2,330	1,517	1,424	2,026	2,131	1,632	1,652	1,730	1,770
Total Current Expenditure	1,842	2,123	1,601	1,228	1,076	1,073	1,110	1,100	1,100	1,100
Total Housing Expenditure (capital and revenue)	4,522	4,452	3,118	2,652	3,102	3,204	2,742	2,752	2,830	2,880
'Other' Housing Expenditure										
Housing Benefit	932[2]	1,039[2]	1,395[2]	1,663[2]	2,624	2,954	3,214	3,277	3,320	3,420
Tax Relief on Mortgage Interest[5]	1,639	2,188	2,292	2,456	2,767[3]	3,500	4,750			
Total 'Other' Expenditure	2,571	3,227	3,687	4,119	5,391	6,454	7,964			

[1]Local authorities, new towns, Housing Corporation, and home loan scheme.
[2]Estimated figures. Payments of housing costs to supplementary benefit applicants not included in housing benefit for 1979–83.
[3]Excludes £55 million (mortgage interest relief at source).
Source: Annual Public Expenditure Survey Committee White Papers 1979/80 to 1986/87 and *Hansard* 49 (November 11, 1983).

Table 2.2
An Alternative Housing Program (Percentage Shares)

	1979/80	1980/81	1981/82	1982/83	1983/84	1984/85	1985/86
Total Housing Programme (£m)[1]	7,093	7,679	6,805	6,771	8,493	9,658	10,706
Public Sector Housing Expenditure							
Net Capital Expenditure	38	30	22	21	24	22	15
Current Expenditure	26	28	24	18	13	11	10
Total Capital and Revenue	64	58	46	39	37	33	26
'Other' Housing Expenditure							
Housing Benefit	13	14	20	25	31	31	30
Tax Relief on Mortgage Interest	23	28	34	36	33	36	44
Total 'Other' Expenditure	36	42	54	61	63	67	74

[1]As in Table 2.1.

Source: HM Treasury 1986.

Table 2.3
An Index of Housing Activity, 1979/80 to 1988/89 (1979/80 = 100)

Public Sector Housing Expenditure	1980-81	1981-82	1982-83	1983-84	1984-85	1985-86	1986-87	1987-88	1988-89
Gross Capital Expenditure	93	81	105	126	124	104	103	102	99
Net Capital Expenditure	87	60	53	76	80	61	62	66	66
Current Expenditure	115	87	67	58	58	60	60	60	60
Total Housing Expenditure	98	69	59	69	71	61	61	63	64
'Other' Housing Expenditure									
Housing Benefit	111	150	178	282	317	345	352	356	367
Tax Relief on Mortgage Interest	133	140	150	169	214	290			
Total 'Other' Expenditure	126	143	160	210	251	310			

Source: HM Treasury 1986.

capital receipts reduced the rate of increase of net spending, which even in 1983/84 reached only 40 percent of its 1979/80 level.

The government has used the level of capital receipts to permit the reduction of net new investment on a dramatic scale. In 1982/83 net capital expenditure by local authorities (£729 million) barely exceeded the net level of funding of housing associations by the Housing Corporation (£680 million). This raises major issues in relation to the use of capital assets. First, the real value of assets disposed of is far higher as a result of discounts. Second, the disposal of assets will lead in the medium or long term to additional and greater expenditure (if any attempt is made to replace lost relets or meet demand)—for example, on the acquisition of sites to replace those previously sold or the construction or acquisition of new housing. Finally, whatever view is taken of these longer-term arguments, and of the view that proceeds (however discounted) should be used for *additional investment*, the prospect of *declining receipts* poses a real threat to the maintenance of even the reduced housing program that capital receipts have facilitated.

Capital receipts associated with the housing program have been more substantial than those from any other program despite the publicity that some sales (such as British Telecom) have received. Sales of local authority dwellings have represented the most significant act of privatization or sale of assets carried out in the period since 1979 (for a more general assessment see Le Grand and Robinson 1984; Shackleton, 1984; Whitfield, 1983; Thompson, 1984). In 1979/80 total receipts from sales of other public assets were £370 million; in 1980/81/, £405 million; in 1981/82, £494 million; in 1982/83, £488 million; and in 1983/84, £1142 million. Total sales and repayments from the housing program for these years were £448 million, £568 million, £976 million, £1739 million, and £1789 million, respectively. The actual market value of council houses sold over this period exceeds £11 billion and discount exceeded £4.6 billion.

Table 2.4 details the composition of housing capital receipts since 1978/79. The volume of receipts has risen dramatically since 1979/80 with increasing levels of council house sales, and initial receipts from the sale of dwellings have supplanted repayments of loans as the principal source of receipts.

Council house sales in the period 1979/84 were more than double those in the previous 40 years combined and have exceeded those completed in the whole history of council housing. Neither sales nor capital receipts are a totally new phenomenon. The main difference in recent times, however, is in the relationship of the volume of capital receipts to capital expenditure. The local authority housing capital program has become substantially self-financing and the call of housing on the public-sector borrowing requirement has been considerably reduced because of the volume of capital receipts.

A number of arguments could be advanced over whether capital receipts "should" be reinvested in housing. Without entering into such a debate at length it is apparent that the housing sector's demands on "nonhousing" funds have been more substantially cut than is compatible with the level of gross capital

Table 2.4
Sources of Local Authority Housing Capital Receipts (£ Million Cash)

	1978-79 £m	%	1979-80 £m	%	1980-81 £m	%	1981-82 £m	%	1982-83 £m	%	1983-84 £m	%	1984-85 £m	%
Sales of land and other assets	24	5	38	8	96	17	99	10	135	8	103	6	105	7
Initial receipts from sales of dwellings	138	28	122	27	186	33	532	55	1,017	58	970	54	830	57
Repayments of sums outstanding on sales of dwellings	40	8	43	10	53	9	89	9	282	16	445	25	315	22
Repayments of loans by private persons	293	58	241	54	216	38	240	25	287	17	246	14	185	13
Repayment of loans by Housing Associations	7	1	4	1	16	3	15	2	18	1	25	1	30	2
Total	501	100	448	100	568	100	976	100	1,739	100	1,789	100	1,465	100

Source: Cmnd 9143 II and 9428 II and *Hansard* 49 (November 23, 1983), cols. 212–13.

expenditure. Without housing capital receipts in recent years either the housing program would have been even more severely cut or housing would have come into sharper conflict with other expenditure programs in resource demands.

At present it seems likely that capital receipts from the sale of council houses will diminish unless there are new measures to stimulate them. Interest in purchase by tenants has shown a steady decline despite more generous incentives. Many tenants who remain in the public sector may be too old or too young to consider buying, may be occupying an unattractive dwelling, or may simply be too poor, unemployed, or insecurely employed. Emergent government policy suggests a shift from incentives for individuals to purchase toward a greater emphasis on the wholesale transfer of local authority estates to private or quasi-public organizations. While the accumulated backlog of receipts could serve as a cushion for some years, any significant reduction in the longer term will require substantial new investment or more dramatic cutbacks.

In all of these changes, the government's attitude to council housing occupies a prominent position. Not only has its historical development represented a major and very visible ideological irritation for the Conservative party but its management and allocation has been one of the major areas in which locally elected councils could exert influence on the local social and economic structure. With the extension of home ownership high on the political agenda (with its symbolic value as the extension of citizenship rights) the disposal of council houses has been in the forefront of a broader ideological crusade. These ideological considerations have, however, progressively taken second place to more pressing fiscal imperatives. Council housing, unlike the National Health Service, has always been a minority provision for the working classes. Moreover, unlike cuts in education and health, disinvestment in council housing has less immediate consequences. Representing, as it has, the soft underbelly of the welfare state, it has been caught in a pincer movement between ideological commitments to individualism and to monetarism. The consequences of these commitments have increasingly fallen on local government expenditure given the failure of central government's macroeconomic strategies.

INCREASING CENTRAL CONTROL OF LOCAL PROVISION

In Britain, the responsibility for planning and meeting local housing needs has rested with local government. It is local government that has been blamed for failure to house the homeless or to build the right houses in the right places at the right time. While central government has provided the framework for local policy, it has always been able to argue that it is local decisions and local councils that should be reviewed when local shortcomings are apparent. In this way local government in housing has provided a convenient buffer for central government between itself and political action in relation to housing; but the Right to Buy has involved more direct central government intervention to secure the sale of local authority houses and contribute to the changing levels and priorities in central government's expenditure plans. This direct intervention has involved central government in taking more responsibility for housing and housing circumstances.

Central government from the outset took an active part in implementing the Right to Buy. The political and financial importance of this legislation meant that the task was not completed with the passage of legislation. The expectation of local obstruction, the desire to appeal over the heads of local administrations, and the desire to publicize the Right to Buy involved the central department with a substantial continuing role. Initially the government appears to have been satisfied to concentrate on publicity. In 1980/81, £655,000 was spent on advertisements on television and in national newspapers telling and reminding public-sector tenants of their new rights including the Right to Buy. In 1981/82, £239,000 was spent on publicizing the Right to Buy.

In this same initial period considerable press coverage was given to local housing authorities that expressed an intention not to implement the act. The minister of housing was at the same time making it clear that the government would use its powers of intervention. He was reported as saying these powers would be used to ensure that tenants in areas controlled by the Labour party were not denied the right to buy (House of Commons 1980).

Although the Department of the Environment has not been concerned to monitor the Right to Buy in terms of social or financial impact, it has from the outset obtained sales figures in the statistical returns made to it by local authorities. In addition, the department has obtained impressions on progress or delay through letters of complaint from or on behalf of tenants, from press reports, or from informal discussions between the department and the authorities. Where the secretary of state received information suggesting that significant delays were occurring or likely to occur he normally made a formal approach to the local authority concerned on the question of current and future progress. In such formal approaches the secretary of state usually sought overall statistical information on the number of Right to Buy applications received, the numbers at various stages in the sales process, and estimates of future progress. Where the information given in reply to such approaches indicated to the secretary of state the possibility that tenants were having difficulty in exercising their right to buy, further information and assurances were sought. In typical cases this involved meetings between the central department and the local authority. Following such further correspondence or meetings the secretary of state either stated that he would take no further action in light of assurances, undertakings, or indications of future progress (but usually requiring monthly progress statistics); or, where satisfactory assurances had not been forthcoming, gave a formal warning that he was contemplating using his powers of intervention under the act and requesting, within a specified time, further information on future progress. Where such formal warning was given and the information supplied still appeared unsatisfactory, local councillors were invited to a meeting with a minister. After that stage the formal warning could be withdrawn but monthly progress information is still required. This formal scrutiny and pressure has been widely used. Indeed in December 1983 the government was in contact with about 200 local authorities, most of which were Labour-controlled, about aspects of their performance in implementing the Right to Buy. This represented a much more active and interventionist stance than had generally applied in the housing area in the past.

The extreme example of intervention arose when the secretary of state was not satisfied by the progress and undertakings offered by Norwich City Council in respect of the implementation of the Right to Buy. Norwich was not refusing to implement the law but argued other priorities and issues of staff and costs in response to complaints about progress. The secretary of state used his powers under the Housing Act of 1980 to send in his representative to take over the administration of the Right to Buy. Such intervention was resisted in the courts by Norwich but the secretary of state's action was supported by the judiciary (Forrest and Murie 1985b).

The Housing and Building Control Act of 1984 was not introduced because of the Norwich intervention. Nevertheless there are aspects of the new legislation that represent a response to the kind of circumstances that led to the conflict and litigation involving Norwich. Some parts of the act can be seen as steps to close loopholes in the original legislation. For example, the new act provided a power for the secretary of state to give directions on covenants and conditions included in grants or conveyances, and to serve a notice requiring the landlord to produce documents or supply information. At the same time the legislation of 1984 required the landlord to meet a more stringent timetable in acknowledging the Right to Buy.

These sections of the 1984 legislation provide the central government with a more varied armory of mechanisms for intervention. In the event of future conflicts the long-drawn-out, public, and heavy-handed procedure culminating in the introduction of a "commissioner" could be avoided. Instead the secretary of state could carry out legal processes on behalf of individuals—and be seen to be acting on behalf of the powerless individual rather than basking in the arrogant exercise of power on behalf of a centralized bureaucracy. The consequence seems likely to be an even greater shift of real power to the center.

The Right to Buy has been a major element in pursuing the *ideology* of individualism and property ownership and in reducing the intrusiveness of the state. Ironically, in implementing this policy the central government has, in fact, become more rather than less involved. This has come about in two ways. First, the responsibility of central government for specific local patterns of housing tenure and opportunity has been greatly increased. While the central government in other areas, notably housing benefits, has sought to identify local administrations with responsibility for service delivery, the opposite has happened in relation to tenure mobility and housing choice. Second, the central government has increasingly become involved in the details of day-to-day policy implementation. This is apparent in the extent of monitoring and in the increasing detail of scrutiny. Whereas the Department of the Environment had little practical knowledge or experience of issues in conveyancing it has become involved in a detailed way and the Housing and Building Control Act provides powers to intervene over this and other areas.

These developments relate to a favorite theme of the New Right: that of the overburdened state. This notion derives from two main contentions. First, government at central and local levels has increased its role to a degree where its failings and lack of competence have become apparent. Second, the libertarian strand of the New Right's critique of the growth of government would point to the intrusiveness of state control and regulation of people's everyday lives. The growth of government has involved increasing failures to deliver what was intended and has been marked by an overextended bureaucracy that proves inefficient, unresponsive, and ineffective. It is argued that the development of local government and of various quasi-nongovernment organizations is evidence of this. Historically the central government has found it more effective to use other organizations than to try to do everything itself. Whether the central government uses such agencies (including local government) or becomes more involved in local service delivery and day-to-day policy implementation itself (for fiscal or any other reasons), the problems of an overextended bureaucracy become apparent. The Right to Buy represents a response to this situation. It is presented as part of the process of reducing the role of the state and transferring control and ownership to individual citizens. However, in order to deregulate or demunicipalize services the central government has become more enmeshed in local housing provision. Legislation, publicity, scrutiny, and subsidy have all been necessary elements in demunicipalization. The establishment of a Norwich Office of the Department of Environment sounds more like a further extension of the state than a disengagement. The questions pursued by that office and the contents of the legislative step that followed—the Housing and Building Control Act of 1984—involved more and more detail rather than withdrawal. The most obvious conclusion is that greater intervention was needed to secure disengagement.

As in other areas of state involvement the consequence, if not the intention, of recent policy development has been to strengthen the central levels of government at the expense of the local levels. Arguably, therefore, the state is not so much "rolled back" as withdrawn into a centralist shell less open to democratic demands and public scrutiny. As the central government becomes more obviously directly responsible for local circumstances and living conditions so it becomes the target for criticism and complaint. It becomes more directly and obviously responsible and is less able to shelter behind other organizations. Thus, in achieving one set of objectives, the central government could be diminishing the mechanisms that strengthen and legitimate its role. By changing the established structure of responsibility the central government risks upsetting these mechanisms. The increased concentration of power through legislation and other policy action has political implications *beyond* those of the individual policies themselves. Problems of legitimacy are more likely to arise when the failure to deliver services effectively is unavoidably the responsibility of central government and the failure cannot easily be attributed to other organizations.

EMERGING ISSUES

The policy of privatization through council house sales did not emerge because of some financial calculation. Rather it was presented as a means of extending home ownership, redistributing wealth, and reducing the power and control of the state. However, as the policy has emerged since 1979 it has increasingly contributed to the relief of fiscal problems. Large capital receipts have helped the government meet its spending plans without raising taxation. Without such receipts either spending programs would have had to be cut further or policies on taxation and borrowing revised. But the appeal and apparent success of the policy raises important issues about the future development of privatization and the emergence of a crisis in housing supply and condition.

Dilemmas in relation to the future of privatization are already emerging. The sale of council houses to sitting tenants has a declining appeal as tenants in the best position to buy and in the best properties complete their purchases. But what of the very large (by international standards) remaining state housing sector? And how can the level of capital receipts generated by this asset be maintained? The emerging solution appears to involve alternative forms of privatization.

The Housing and Planning Bill of 1986 is designed to facilitate the sale of estates or portfolios of properties to privately financed housing trusts and approved landlord bodies and to generate capital receipts. Unlike sales to sitting tenants, however, such sales obviously do not also meet the tenure or other housing aspirations of households. A large number of council tenants may have expressed a desire for home ownership. There is little evidence, however, that any wish to become private tenants.

After six years of obsessive concern with privatization and the extension of home ownership there is considerable evidence of a coming housing crisis in the United Kingdom. An official government report estimated the need for expenditure of £19 billion on the existing council stock (Department of the Environment 1985). New building is still at minimal levels. Damning criticisms of current housing policy have been made in recent well-publicized reports by the Church of England (1985) and an Inquiry chaired by the Duke of Edinburgh (National Federation of Housing Associations, 1985), hardly traditional critics of a Conservative government.

In housing opportunities and conditions as in other areas, the gap between rich and poor has widened over the past six years. Some groups have experienced a deterioration in their living conditions and life chances (Central Statistical Office 1985). Yet in 1983 the combined cost of mortgage tax relief, central and local government subsidies, benefits, and improvements grants amounted to over £10 billion, around two-thirds higher than in 1979. Political and legislative energies and fiscal resources have been directed at the emasculation of local government and local housing provision with greater central control and allocation of subsidy. As the figures referred to earlier illustrate, despite the rhetoric of austerity, the reality has been profligacy in subsidizing consumption for the relatively privileged at the expense of much-needed new investment in housing production for lower-income groups.

REFERENCES

Central Statistical Office
1985   *Social Trends* 15. London: HMSO.
Church of England
1985   *Faith in the City*. London: Church House Publishing.
Department of the Environment
1985   *An Inquiry into the Condition of the Local Authority Stock in England*. London: HMSO.
Environment Committee
1980   *Enquiry into the Implications of the Government's Expenditure Plans 1980–81 to 1983–84 for the Housing Policies of the Department of the Environment*, HC 714. London: HMSO.
Ermisch, J.
1984   *Housing Finance: Who Gains*? London: Policy Studies Institute.
Forrest, R., and A. Murie
1983   "Residualisation and Council Housing: Aspects of the Changing Social Relations of Housing Tenure." *Journal of Social Policy* 12, no. 4, 453–68.
1985a   "Restructuring the Welfare State: Privatisation and Public Housing in the UK." In *Housing Needs and Policy Approaches & Trends in Thirteen Countries*, edited by W. van Vliet—, E. Huttman, and S. Fava. Durham, N.C.: Duke University Press.
1985b   *An Unreasonable Act? Central-Local Government Conflict and the Housing Act 1980*, School for Advanced Urban Studies, No. 1, University of Bristol.
HM Treasury
1985   *The Government's Expenditure Plans 1985–86 to 1987–88*, Cmnd 9428. London: HMSO.
1986   *The Government's Expenditure Plans 1986–87 to 1988–89*, Cmnd 9702. London: HMSO.
House of Commons
1980   House of Commons *Parliamentary Debates*, 16.04.80 cols 1983–4.
Le Grand, J. and R. Robinson (eds.)
1984   *Privatisation and the Welfare State*. London: Allen and Unwin.
Murie, A.
1985   "What the Country Can Afford? Housing under the Conservatives in 1979–83." In *Implementing Government Policy Initiatives: The Thatcher Administration 1979–1983*, edited by P. Jackson. London: Royal Institute of Public Administration.
National Federation of Housing Associations
1985   *Inquiry into British Housing (chaired by HRH the Duke of Edinburgh) Report*. London: National Federations of Housing Associations.

O'Higgins, M.
1983   "Rolling Back the Welfare State: The Rhetoric and Reality of Public Expenditure and Social Policy under the Conservative Government." In *The Year Book of Social Policy in Britain 1982*, edited by C. Jones and J. Stevenson. London: Routledge and Kegan Paul.
Shackleton, J.
1984   "Privatization: The Case Examined." *National Westminster Bank Quarterly Review*, May, 59–73.
Thompson, G.
1984   "Rolling Back the State? Economic Intervention 1975–82." In *State and Society in Contemporary Britain*, edited by G. Mclennan, D. Held, and S. Hall. Cambridge: Polity Press.
Whitfield, D.
1983   *Making it Public*. London: Pluto Press.

3

The Privatization of Housing Renewal: Dilemmas and Contradictions in British Urban Policy

TIM BRINDLEY AND GERRY STOKER

Abstract. In recent years, the number of substandard older houses in Britain has been increasing, especially in the owner-occupied sector. During its first few years of office, the Thatcher government increased public spending on renovation grants for private owners. But in 1985 the government proposed an alternative strategy to privatize housing renewal, calling for a greater contribution from individual owners, private house builders, and building societies. The prospects for achieving this are examined and it is shown that the policies proposed fail to resolve serious dilemmas. Privatization implies deepening contradictions between political, environmental, and social objectives.

INTRODUCTION

This chapter is concerned with the recent development of policies to privatize the renewal of the older housing stock in Britain. About one-third of Britain's stock of some 20 million dwellings was built before 1919, mostly in the form of two-story terraced houses. This older stock, which still forms much of the inner areas of the major cities, has been the focus of renewal policies throughout the postwar period. Although it is mostly privately owned, originally by landlords but today with two-thirds or more in owner occupation, the state has been heavily involved in the renewal of this housing. Renewal programs have been planned and managed by local authorities and the government has invested substantially in redevelopment and grant aid for individual owners.

Since 1979 the Conservative government led by Margaret Thatcher has challenged the established consensus over the extent and forms of state intervention. Drawing on the political philosophy of the New Right, it has sought to reduce the role of the public sector and to increase that of the private sector in a wide range of policy fields. By the mid–1980s this principle, known as privatization, was being applied to housing renewal. This ran directly counter to strong demands from professional and lobby groups for a major increase in government action and expenditure.

The chapter deals first with the background to housing renewal policies and their recent history. Evidence points to the failure of policies based on gradual renewal in the 1970s to prevent the continuing decline of much of the older housing stock to the point where all the main professional groups consider that housing renewal is in crisis. The second section examines the response of the Thatcher government to this perceived crisis. Up to 1983 there was a large increase in state spending on some aspects of renewal, but since then the government has been developing policies more consistent with its general philosophy. In the third section we consider the prospects for privatization. The potential response of three groups is explored: individual house owners, house-building and development companies, and building societies. While there is evidence that all three groups have responded to particular opportunities for investing in renewal, the dilemmas and contradictions of the privatization strategy have resulted in unprecedented political conflict in this policy area. We conclude that while privatization may be successful in meeting one set of political objectives, it will leave many social and environmental problems in its wake.

THE CRISIS IN HOUSING RENEWAL

The role of government in improving the condition of the housing stock has a long history in Britain, beginning with public health legislation in the mid-nineteenth century. After World War I, the state became centrally involved in the provision of subsidized rented housing and in the 1930s embarked on a major program of slum clearance and redevelopment. This program was resumed on a large scale in the 1950s, continuing at the rate of some 60,000 dwellings per year until the mid–1970s. The program was carried out by municipal government, each local authority undertaking the tasks of identifying the slums, drawing up clearance programs, purchasing large areas of housing by compulsion, demolishing the houses, and rehousing the residents in council-owned houses and flats (apartments). The result was a substantial replacement of older privately rented housing by newly built council housing.

Private owners, both landlords and owner occupiers, also had a role in the renewal of the stock. The government subsidized them with renovation grants, which met 50 percent of the cost of installing basic amenities (standard grants) or full repairs and improvements (improvement grants). The postwar ambition of redeveloping most of the older housing stock was moderated in the 1960s, as economic difficulties forced expenditure restraint. Public support for slum clearance also waned, as it was criticized for breaking up local communities and for replacing traditional family houses with unpopular types of flats and maisonettes. The emphasis on repairs and improvements by private owners therefore was increased and received a major stimulus in a Housing Act of 1969. The combination of additional government funding, unconditional grants, the growth of owner occupation, and a boom in land and property values led to a rapid increase in house improvements in the early 1970s. Demand for renovation grants peaked at 361,000 in 1973 (Gibson and Langstaff 1982, 68).

The obvious popularity of housing improvement, together with the rising costs and growing unpopularity of slum clearance, gave rise to a new approach to the problem in the 1974 Housing Act. This was the principle of gradual renewal, a continuous process of repair, improvement, and piecemeal replacement of older houses, intended to maintain the stock in a sound condition while avoiding the disruption and high costs of large-scale clearance (Department of the Environment 1975). Although it was a radical departure from the policies of the 1960s, gradual renewal had widespread support. It was promoted by both major political parties, at least at the national government level, and endorsed by the main professional bodies involved. Slum clearance programs were run down and gradual renewal came to be the consensus approach of the 1970s.

Gradual renewal was conceived under a Conservative government, and partly intended to reduce government expenditure, but it presupposed a major role for the public sector. The 1974 Housing Act emphasized the need for local authorities to prepare renewal strategies, to designate Housing Action Areas (HAAs) for intensive renewal activity, to form action teams, and to use more of their general housing resources for renewal. Both local authorities and publicly funded housing associations were expected to provide rented housing by buying and improving older houses, and by small-scale new building. To a degree this emphasis on the role of the public sector reflected the fact that a Labour government implemented the policy during the 1970s, but the concept of gradual renewal always implied public-sector planning and management and a substantial public-sector resource input.

Toward the end of the 1970s policy analysts and professional institutes were claiming that this formula had failed in significant respects, to the extent that housing renewal was facing a "crisis." Research reports published in the late 1970s criticized the performance of gradual renewal, mainly in terms of the low numbers of houses being improved (Paris and Blackaby 1979; Royal Town Planning Institute 1979). The problem was seen to be essentially one of resources. On the one hand, public-sector investment was inadequate, mainly the result of central government expenditure restraint but also a product of poor management of resources by some local authorities and lack of commitment to the policy by others. On the other hand, private-sector investment was inadequate because renewal areas did not generally have the confidence of the funding institutions (particularly building societies), it was not profitable for private house builders to redevelop them, and private owners were generally unable or unwilling to invest.

The result was low levels of house improvement in the declared renewal areas, a large and constant number of dwellings classed as "unfit for human habitation," and seriously rising numbers in need of major repairs. In spite of a rapid fall in the number of houses lacking basic amenities, the professional consensus in the early 1980s, confirmed by the government's own national house condition surveys, was that much of Britain's housing stock was deteriorating and likely to get worse. The 1981 survey showed that more than one in four private-sector homes was unsatisfactory, with over 3 million properties needing repairs costing more than £2,500 (Department of the Environment 1982). An added factor was the realization that one key element of gradual renewal, demolition and replacement of the worst houses, had almost ceased, with the number of demolitions in England and Wales down to 10,000 in 1984 and still falling (Department of the Environment 1985).

THE RESPONSE OF THE THATCHER GOVERNMENT

During the early years of the Thatcher government, evidence of the growing crisis in housing renewal accumulated. Professional institutes and lobby groups produced further reports pointing to the "expanding core of bad housing," and calling for more action and expenditure by the government within the existing policy framework (Association of Metropolitan Authorities 1981; Royal Town Planning Institute 1981; Institution of Environmental Health Officers 1983; Institute of Housing 1984). Two major national investigations of housing and the inner cities, one chaired by the Duke of Edinburgh and the other produced for the Church of England, also highlighted this problem and called on the government to act (National Federation of Housing Associations 1985; Archbishop of Canterbury's Commission 1985).

In the face of this chorus of support for a reinvigorated program of gradual renewal, the government at first appeared to accept its critics' case. Initially, in its first Housing Act of 1980, it offered more grant aid for basic repairs to older property. Shortly after this, restrictions on grant expenditure were briefly lifted, in 1982 and 1983, and grant levels were raised to 90 percent of eligible costs. These measures stimulated a boom in grant take-up, especially for repairs, similar to that of the early 1970s. Funding for external block repair schemes, known as "enveloping," was also increased. But it never seemed likely that expenditure would be sustained at this high level and tight spending restrictions were reimposed after the 1983 General Election (Gibson and Perry 1984).

Shortly after this, the government embarked on a full review of its housing renewal policies. The review had to confront two serious dilemmas that resulted from seemingly incompatible objectives. The principal aims of renewal policies, to maintain the housing stock and ensure minimum standards for low-income groups, appeared to be compromised by other policy commitments. The first dilemma stemmed from the fact that it had inherited a policy—gradual renewal—that depended on major public-sector input. Influential critics of this policy claimed it had failed to halt the decay of the worst housing stock because the public-sector input had been too low. The Thatcher government, however, was deeply committed to the view that the state should do less, not more, and that public expenditure should be reduced. The second dilemma arose from the government's overriding belief in owner occupation, a cornerstone of its strategy for "popular capitalism," and its desire to extend owner occupation as far down the income scale as possible. The same critics also pointed out that most of the worst houses were now in the hands of poor owner occupiers, who were never likely to be able to afford to repair them, let alone replace them. Insofar as each of these dilemmas posed a fundamental test of the government's political ideology, it was not obvious how they could be resolved, if at all.

To understand the government's policy intentions in housing renewal, it is necessary to relate these to its underlying philosophy. For the Thatcher government, cuts in state expenditure and a regime of "fiscal austerity" have not simply been a short-term expedient, they have constituted part of a coherent political strategy, usually described as privatization. In broad terms, privatization refers to "a set of polices which aim to limit the role of the public sector, and increase the role of the private sector, while improving the performance of the remaining public sector" (Young 1985, 2). Since 1979, this has formed a key element in the government's approach to a whole range of policy fields. It has involved the sale of public-sector assets, the ending of state monopolies, the contracting out of services in public institutions, and the creation of new opportunities for private service provision and investment. At the same time, the public sector has been made to adopt a range of private-sector management practices and to charge market prices for many of its services.

A full account of British housing policy since 1979 will be found in other chapters in this volume. The main forms of privatization have been the compulsory sale of council houses and the sale of council-owned land for private development. Privatization has led to substantial increases in council rents, the virtual ending of local authority house building, and a corresponding relaxation of control over private house building. It also defined the terms in which the government was searching for a coherent response to the "crisis" in housing renewal.

That response began to take shape with the publication in May 1985 of a Green Paper, *Home Improvement: A New Approach* (Department of the Environment 1985). This contained proposals for future policy and legislation that would bring about a major shift of responsibility from the public to the private sector, amounting to the effective privatization of housing renewal. Two broad changes were proposed: first, a marked reduction in government support for repairs and improvements by individual house owners; and second, an increase in the role of the private corporate sector, principally house builders and financial institutions.

Government support for individual house repairs and improvements was to be reduced in several ways. The maximum standard of improvements qualifying for grant aid was to be reduced, thereby cutting the value of individual grants. For the first time, grants would be means-tested against the owner's income and savings, and not just related to the age and condition of the property. Improvements above the grant-aided standard might then be eligible for new, discretionary loans advanced against equity in the property itself. As a result of these changes, commentators expected that government expenditure on housing renewal would fall to about one-quarter of its 1983/84 peak, and grant aid for individual dwellings could fall by two-thirds (Jacobs 1985). The government's response to the dilemma posed by owner occupiers was therefore to propose concentrating its support on the poorest, and to limit the scope of grant aid to basic standards.

Proposals for increasing the role of the private corporate sector in housing renewal represented the government's response to the dilemma of inadequate resources. As in other areas of privatization, the aim was to supplement and where possible substitute government funding with private-sector resources. The proposals included asking the building industry to publicize the need for timely repairs and to improve the quality and reliability of its service to home owners undertaking repairs and improvements. The financial institutions, and in particular the building societies, were asked to continue and extend the provision of loans for renovation work. More importantly, there was a strong hint that, while renovation would normally be expected to be the most cost-effective solution, the rate of clearance should increase. Local authorities would remain responsible for identifying housing that required clearance, and owners would retain their existing rights to object; but redevelopment would have to draw extensively on private-sector funding. Local authorities would be given "a statutory duty to seek the involvement of the private sector in redevelopment schemes . . . and empowered to offer pump-priming finance to developers" (Department of the Environment 1985). Owners whose properties were cleared would be entitled to market value compensation and additional financial help toward house purchase, probably in the form of an interest-free loan.

Thus by 1985 the Thatcher government had produced a response to the widely proclaimed crisis in housing renewal that appeared consistent with its overall political philosophy. Privatization was to be achieved by restricting government support to low minimum standards and the poorest households, by calling on property owners to contribute more of their own resources, and by exhorting the private corporate sector to combine profitable investment with a more responsible attitude to renewal. These policies were almost the exact opposite of those advocated by the critics of housing renewal in the professions and housing lobby groups, who favored a return to greater state intervention and more public expenditure on improvement and redevelopment (a fuller discussion of changing professional influences will be found in Chapter 14).

THE PROSPECTS FOR PRIVATIZATION

For privatization to succeed, it has to stimulate new private investment to replace the withdrawal of state funding. In this section we examine whether the two main agents of the privatized housing renewal strategy—individual house owners and corporate-sector institutions—are likely to increase their investment and in what particular aspects of renewal. There is a variety of evidence against which to judge the new policies. Government surveys and other research studies have investigated the older housing stock, its ownership, and its position in the housing market. The attitudes of the corporate sector can also be seen from recent studies and investment trends. The indications are that a substantial increase in the involvement of private corporate bodies can be expected but that individual house owners are in a weaker market situation.

Individual House Owners

Research by the government itself has shown that most of the substandard older housing stock is now owned by relatively poor owner occupiers. The correlation between poor-condition housing and low income increased between the major surveys of 1976 and 1981 (Department of the Environment 1982). Two major groups of owners are elderly whites and ethnic minority families, especially Asians. In addition to the constraints of low income, many of these owners have little motivation to carry out repairs and improvements. Often they are unaware of the need for major repairs, unwilling to accept the disruption of building work and uncertain about grants and other assistance.

The proposals in the 1985 Green Paper to target lower levels of grants on the poorest owners appear to respond to these conditions. However, the policies actually suggested have severe limitations. First, the chosen method of targeting—means-testing against the owner's income and savings—is generally known to act as a disincentive. No means-tested benefit is fully taken up, and it is normally those in the greatest need who fail to come forward (Townsend 1975). Second, the choice of a low level of grant aid with the option of an equity-sharing loan for further improvements is not well-matched to market conditions. Research in inner-city areas has shown that older terraced houses do not increase in value as rapidly as the general housing market, even when improved (Karn et al. 1985). Experience suggests that grant and loan ceilings based on average costs will often fall short of the actual costs of repairs and improvements, so that additional loans will be required. Many properties will therefore lack sufficient equity to sustain full improvements, making any investment by their owners very poor value for money.

The contradiction in this aspect of the privatization strategy lies in the assumption that a less-subsidized market will stimulate more private investment. The evidence is that the worst housing, increasingly occupied by the poorest owners, exists in the weakest and most marginal of markets. A reduction in grant aid is therefore likely to undermine that market still further, rather than to reinvigorate it. In other fields, it is claimed that privatization tends to impose social costs on the most disadvantaged in society, "to enlarge inequalities in the distribution of resources . . . and widen social divisions" (Walker 1984, 34). This appears equally true of housing renewal, from the viewpoint of existing owners.

The second and potentially most radical element of the new strategy is the intended role of the private corporate sector. The Green Paper proposals, which at first appear quite modest, have to be understood in the context of trends over the past few years. The government has been able to draw on an increasing interest shown by the private corporate sector in housing renewal during the early 1980s, stimulated partly by changing patterns of market demand but also partly by aspects of privatization itself. The two most significant developments have been the growing role of private house builders in renewal, and the increasing interest shown in this field by the building societies.

Private House Builders and Developers

From the late 1970s, private house builders were encouraged to build on inner-city sites as a contribution to general urban renewal policies. This has occurred on a small scale in several cities, most notably in London's Docklands where a Development Corporation took over in 1980 and spent heavily on site preparation. Generally, however, builders have been cautious. They see more profit in developing green-field sites, and judge the market for new houses in the inner cities to be very limited.

The same considerations apply to a second area of renewal activity by house builders: the conversion of former industrial premises for residential use. A small market for luxury flats has been created, again mainly in London's Docklands, but in the provincial cities few parts of the inner areas are judged to have the same potential.

Under the new strategy for housing renewal, there is some prospect of an increased contribution from private house builders. Many of the initiatives described have depended on limited and locally specific government subsidies, in the form of site reclamation and preparation, reduced land costs, or direct financial aid (for example, Urban Development Grants). These limited subsidies are planned to continue, and the Green Paper proposed additional help for developers involved in housing improvement.

General market conditions in the inner-city areas, however, continue to look relatively unattractive to private developers. The Property Advisory Group, writing in 1980, identified three types of locations: those where the private sector will develop unaided, those where a public expenditure stimulus might attract involvement, and those where the private sector will not undertake any schemes. Advocates of privatization are optimistic about changing some of the less-favorable market perceptions. Possibly the government also feels it can cajole private companies to accept a lower rate of return on some investments in order to meet community responsibilities. Other companies might undertake particular schemes to benefit their public image, and builders and developers might consider more risky or less-profitable schemes in periods of economic downturn.

Yet the overwhelming message from the property development industry is that there are very severe limits on what can be expected from it. The Property Advisory Group has warned the government that it "cannot change fundamentally the attitude of the private sector towards investment in areas which are either unattractive or where there is little prospect of them becoming attractive'' (Department of the Environment 1980, para. 7.28). This emphasizes the need for continual and extensive public expenditure if urban renewal is to be achieved in areas of low private-sector demand.

Where private house builders are involved in housing renewal, it has to be asked who benefits from the new housing provided. Evidence on the income levels of existing residents of substandard housing, and inner-city residents in general, suggests that few can afford a new or thoroughly modernized house. In London's Docklands, admittedly a unique local housing market, buyers in the renewal areas have been similar to buyers of new property in the suburbs (Greater London Council 1984). Private house builders have not yet been involved in clearance and redevelopment schemes, but if they were it is unlikely that displaced residents would be able to afford new housing. This aspect of the privatization of renewal therefore poses the contradiction that those most in need of improved living conditions are the least likely to benefit from the particular forms of renewal that will result.

Building Societies

While the interest of house builders in housing renewal seems likely to remain limited, that of the building societies is potentially much greater. Building societies exist for the sole purpose of lending money, raised almost exclusively in the personal savings market, for house purchase. They finance about 80 percent of all house purchases, and about half of all owner-occupied dwellings are currently mortgaged to them.

Building societies share much of the same outlook as private developers and builders. Although they are constituted as mutual and nonprofit-making institutions, they act in most respects like other commercial enterprises (Boddy 1980). Building societies have ''all the usual trappings of modern big business: plush office blocks, boards of directors, professional managers and slick television advertising'' (Barnes 1984, 3). Although they are strongly committed to the promotion of owner occupation, they have been cautious in advancing loans on older property in the inner cities. In the early stages of gradual renewal they were accused of undermining local authorities' renewal efforts by ''redlining'' certain areas where they refused to lend at all. From the late 1970s, building societies gradually came to support renewal policies and to seek a wider role in this sector of the housing market.

Two main factors account for the growing interest of building societies in housing renewal. First, the market for older, terraced houses in the inner-city areas has changed as a growing demand for owner occupation has brought more and more of them into this tenure. The building societies contributed to this trend by lending more freely on older property. During the 1970s, the proportion of total building society mortgages lent on pre–1919 dwellings rose from 17 percent to 28 percent (Building Societies' Association 1983, 6). With more than one-quarter of all loans going to older property, the building societies have become deeply committed to the inner-city renewal areas.

The second factor is the growth of practical cooperation between building societies and local authorities. This stemmed largely from a measure adopted by the Labour government in 1975 to help more people become owner occupiers in the inner cities. Building societies agreed to set aside a share of their mortgage funds for applicants referred to them by a local authority. Although the scheme itself had mixed results, it had two indirect consequences: first, it helped to encourage societies to lend more freely on older property and, second, it opened the way to other forms of cooperation between societies and local authorities, which subsequently become far more important than the scheme itself. Cooperation was extended to many aspects of housing renewal, both improvement and new building. It included special allocations of funds, for example, for lending on house improvements in HAAs or on low-cost housing schemes; regular liaison meetings; and the secondment of staff to agency service teams, advising house owners on improvements. Societies also supported improvement for sale and shared ownership schemes in renewal areas.

Some societies went further and set up house building companies to provide new and improved houses for sale and to rent. The societies were not empowered to develop land themselves, nor could they establish subsidiaries. They therefore had to create independent bodies to do this, to which they were linked by common directorships and their commitment to fund development by the new body. The pioneer, as in other aspects of housing renewal, was the Abbey National Building Society, which founded the Abbey Housing Association Limited in 1980. Other societies have followed suit, concentrating on markets that are less-well-serviced by the major house builders, such as low-cost housing for first-time buyers and apartments for the elderly. By the end of 1985 over 3,000 dwellings had been completed.

Significant as the rapid growth of building society activities was, it had only a marginal impact on the housing renewal process. By the mid–1980s the societies felt they had gone as far as they could within the limitations of their statutes. They mounted a concerted campaign for legislative reform, arguing that their 100-year-old constitution was no longer appropriate to their present-day role (Building Societies' Association 1984). They believed that they needed to be able to compete more effectively in the personal savings market, by offering a wider range of financial services. They also expressed a desire to play a larger part in housing provision generally, particularly in renewal, and they pressed for powers to take "an initiative role in inner-city redevelopment" (Building Societies' Association 1983, 21). In practice, this meant the power to purchase existing dwellings and vacant sites and to undertake development. They would then carry out their own programs of house improvement, new building, and possibly clearance and redevelopment.

In making these proposals, it is clear that the societies were looking to their own interests. On the one hand, some of their former advantages in the savings market had been eroded, and they needed reforms to maintain their dominant position in mortgage lending (see also Chapter 6). On the other hand, in the area of housing renewal they had something to offer the government in exchange for reform. Housing was their natural field of operations and therefore the most plausible area for them to expand. At the same time, they were stepping into a rapidly widening gap between what was needed and what existing policy frameworks could provide. The government therefore readily accepted their main proposals and supported the principle of a wider role for the societies in "meeting general housing needs," arguing that "more flexible use of some building society resources would be a powerful private sector contribution to the development of the country's housing stock" (Treasury 1984, para. 3.14).

During the 1985/86 parliamentary session the legislative basis of the building societies was reformed, enabling them to take on the active role they had demanded. With this new legislative base, they looked set to become the principal agent in the privatization of housing renewal. For two main reasons, the position of the societies differs markedly from that of private house builders and developers, and from other financial institutions. First, building societies live in fear of government intervention and control over their activities, simply because of their enormous power and resources in the housing market. They have long maintained a relatively privileged position in terms of the legal and fiscal framework in which they operate, and the threat of withdrawal of these advantages, in the name of competition or social justice, gives governments a significant informal influence over the societies (Boddy 1981). In particular, it is the status of the building societies as mutual institutions that makes them inherently vulnerable to government attempts to persuade them that they have wider social responsibilities. According to the head of one society, "we are in business not so much to maximize profits but rather to help our members in their housing and financial needs. As those housing needs change, so we should adapt to meet them as well" (Melville-Ross no date). Second, as building societies have invested more funds in some of the older housing areas under the policy of gradual renewal, so they have acquired a substantial stake in the future of such areas. In order to protect their existing assets, they may be drawn into further funding of rehabilitation or redevelopment, simply to maintain property values and prevent the bottom falling out of the low-income housing market. Some local authorities have already recognized the vulnerability of the societies in this respect and have begun to use it as a bargaining counter in negotiations with them.

Recent research has confirmed that the building societies have substantially increased their investment in older housing, particularly in the better-quality stock (Karn et al. 1985). In the process, they have also extended their lending to lower-income groups, helping more people to become owner occupiers. However, it is significant in the context of the privatization strategy that there remains a substantial minority of the older housing stock, generally that in the worst condition, where societies remain highly reluctant to lend. This is the same segment of the market identified earlier, where price rises do not match those in the wider market. Owner occupiers of this stock are typically financed by short-term bank loans or informal loans from relatives and friends. This suggests that, while the social contradictions of this aspect of privatization are less marked than those noted above, the underlying commercial interests of the building societies seem likely to exclude both the dwellings and the owners most urgently in need of assistance with housing renewal.

CONCLUSION

This chapter has examined attempts by the Thatcher government to privatize housing renewal. As in other policy fields, this involves reducing the role of the state and putting a greater responsibility onto private householders and the corporate sector, in a market context. We have argued that the privatization of housing renewal involves two key dilemmas for the government. These are how to reconcile the effective renewal of the housing stock and the maintenance of minimum housing standards with, first, the extension of owner occupation to lower-income groups and, second, the withdrawal of public-sector investment in renewal. The government's response has been to propose reduced levels of grant aid for individual owners, to call for more renewal activity by private house builders, and to seek a greater contribution from the building societies.

The evidence available suggests that this privatization strategy contains significant contradictions. The reduction in direct support for lower-income owner occupiers appears likely to weaken an already marginal market in substandard housing. Private house builders have shown some interest in profitable development in renewal areas, particularly where subsidies have been available, but they cannot sell new houses at prices that the poorest owners of older property can afford. The building societies are keen to expand their role in housing renewal and have increased their lending on older housing in recent years, but their commercial interests are likely to continue to steer them away from housing in the worst condition and the poorest owners.

The conclusion from this analysis is that privatization is based on the sacrifice of previously acknowledged public policy goals in the field of housing renewal. A significant proportion of the market in older housing—that is, both the property and its occupiers—is clearly excluded by privatization policies and conditions in this sector must be expected to deteriorate. Whether this is due to a blind faith in market processes or a cynical disregard for the consequences, the end result is likely to be the decline of the marginal housing stock to the point where it has to be demolished. In this situation, much of it would have been abandoned and the house builders and building societies would be free to move in, disperse the remaining residents, and redevelop the sites.

The privatization of housing renewal marks the end of a postwar history of consensus in this field and an absence of party political conflict and controversy. Instead, distinctive and conflicting party positions on housing renewal policy have developed, in which there appears to be a growing alliance between the Labour party and the housing professionals. Recent statements show that, if returned to power, Labour plans to undertake a massive program of public-sector investment in house building and renewal. While a role for the private sector is recognized, the Labour party believes that public-sector investment and management are essential to ensure a housing stock of a standard and condition suitable for the next century (Labour Party 1985).

The privatization of housing renewal raises critical issues for the planners, architects, and other professionals in this policy area. Their claims of a crisis of underinvestment in the housing stock have been greeted by a government response to the effect that any extra resources must come from the private sector. It would seem that these professionals have two choices. Either they attempt to make a privatized housing renewal work or they align themselves with political forces to the center and left of the party spectrum that would be prepared to consider a substantial increase in public-sector investment.

A final issue, which has not been properly addressed thus far, is the likely reaction of inner-urban area residents to the privatization of housing renewal. It is important to recognize that the social and political character of these neighborhoods has changed in some significant respects in the last two decades. The level of owner occupation has increased, as has the degree of community feeling and commitment, particularly where significant numbers of ethnic minorities are present (Stoker and Brindley 1985).

The potential strength of political organization and mobilization at the neighborhood level has also grown, a reflection of the area focus of a range of housing renewal and other policies, the provision of support resources from community workers and others, and a greater willingness within society at large to challenge authoritative decision makers. These factors mean that any housing renewal policy must seriously address the public acceptability of its prescriptions. If the policy threatens or seriously fails to satisfy the needs of inner-area residents the response is less likely to be the quiet acceptance of the slum clearance era and more likely to be similar to the protest and unrest that in part contributed to the end of that era. Advocates of the privatization of housing renewal tend to underplay such issues. The assumption is, for example, that the good public image of building societies will dissolve any resistance from residents. This seems grossly optimistic. Faced with living in rotting houses or threatened by private-sector-led and -financed slum clearance, the reaction of inner-city residents is likely to be hostile, vocal, and well-organized. In many respects the Conservative party has found its most potent political weapon in housing policy. Its championing of owner occupation is widely perceived to have contributed greatly to its electoral successes. Perhaps, though, in the privatization of housing renewal some of the contradictions and tensions inherent in its policy will emerge in a way that brings not political credit but long-term damage.

REFERENCES

Archbishop of Canterbury's Commission
1985 *Faith in the City*. The Report of the Archbishop of Canterbury's Commission on Urban Priority Areas. London: Church House.

Association of Metropolitan Authorities
1981 *Ruin or Renewal: Choices for our Ageing Housing*. London: AMA.
Barnes, Paul
1984 *Building Societies: The Myth of Mutuality*. London: Pluto.
Boddy, Martin
1980 *The Building Societies*. London: Macmillan.
1981 "The Public Implementation of Private Housing Policy: Relations between Government and Building Societies in the 1970s." In *Policy and Action*, edited by Sue Barratt and Colin Fudge. London: Methuen.
Building Societies' Association
1983 *Report of the Support Scheme Working Group*. London: BSA.
1984 *New Legislation for Building Societies*. London: BSA.
Department of the Environment
1975 *Housing Act 1974: Renewal Strategies*. Circular 13/75, London: HMSO.
1980 *Structure and Activity of the Development Industry*. Report of the Property Advisory Group, London: HMSO.
1982 *English House Condition Survey 1981: Part I: Report of the Physical Condition Survey*. London: HMSO.
1985 *Home Improvement: A New Approach*. Command 9513, London: HMSO.
Gibson, Michael S., and Michael J. Langstaff
1982 *An Introduction to Urban Renewal*. London: Hutchinson.
Gibson, Michael, and John Perry
1984 "Housing Renewal in Crisis." *The Planner* 70 (April), 8–13.
Greater London Council
1984 *London Docklands: Review of the First Two Years' Operation of the London Docklands Development Corporation*. London: GLC.
Institute of Housing
1984 "Housing Bill." *Housing* 20, no. 12, 5, 8.
Institution of Environmental Health Officers
1983 *The Future of the Housing Stock*. London: IEHO.
Jacobs, Anne
1985 "Home Repairs Set to Save Grant Millions." *Sunday Times*, 12 May, 5.
Karn, Valerie, Jim Kemeny, and Peter Williams
1985 *Home Ownership in the Inner City: Salvation or Despair?* Studies in Urban and Regional Policy 3. London: Gower.
Labour Party
1985 *Housing: Labour's New Deal*. NEC Consultative Paper. London: Labour Party.
Melville-Ross, Tim
n.d. "The Role of Building Societies in Housing."
National Federation of Housing Associations
1985 *Inquiry into British Housing*. Chairman, H.R.H. The Duke of Edinburgh. London: National Federation of Housing Associations.
Paris, Chris, and Bob Blackaby
1979 *Not Much Improvement*. London: Heinemann.
Royal Town Planning Institute
1979 *Housing Renewal Policy: Will it Work?* London: RTPI.
1981 *Renewal of Older Housing Areas: Into the Eighties*. London: RTPI.
Stoker, Gerry, and Tim Brindley

1985   "Asian Politics and Housing Renewal." *Policy and Politics* 13, no. 3, 281–303.
Townsend, Peter
1975   *Sociology and Social Policy*. London: Allen Lane.
Treasury, Her Majesty's
1984   *Building Societies: A New Framework*. Command 9316. London: HMSO.
Walker, Alan
1984   "The Political Economy of Privatisation." In *Privatisation and the Welfare State*, edited by J. Le Grand and R. Robinson. London: Allen and Unwin.
Young, Stephen
1985   "The Nature of Privatisation." Paper presented to the annual conference of the Political Studies Association, University of Manchester, 16–18 April. Unpublished.

PART II

NATIONAL PERSPECTIVES

4

Housing Subsidies in a Period of Restraint: The Canadian Experience

J. DAVID HULCHANSKI AND GLENN DROVER

Abstract. This chapter documents the shifting pattern of Canadian housing subsidies and their distributional impact during a period of restraint that began in the early 1970s. While subsidies on social housing were held to a minimum, private-sector subsidies increased dramatically. As a result, higher-income home owners as well as investors in private rental housing are found to have gained the greatest benefits from "restraint." In addition, households in the highest two income quintiles made substantial gains in home ownership rates whereas the households in the two lowest quintiles increasingly became tenants. A much greater polarization of households by tenure and income has resulted and Canada's rental sector is increasingly becoming a residual one, the domain of the bottom 40 or 50 percent of the income scale.

INTRODUCTION

From 1973 to 1984 Canada had three official recessions accompanied by policies of monetary and fiscal restraint (Canada, Department of Finance 1984a, 9). During that period (the Trudeau years), housing expenditures, in contrast to other social programs, fared rather well owing to the small size of government housing programs, the negative impact of high interest rates on housing starts, the political impact of affordability problems, and the increased use of tax expenditures. In theory, Canadian restraint measures were intended to be directed in such a way that those who were most in need would be helped by social housing programs. In reality, the social and private housing sectors were treated quite differently. Contrary to popular belief, subsidies on social housing were held to a minimum while private-sector assistance fluctuated dramatically depending upon market conditions. In addition, while much of private-sector support was provided in the form of relatively hidden tax expenditures, nonmarket social housing subsidies were provided up front through direct public expenditures. The net distributional effect of the changes increased the bias of Canada's complex set of housing subsidies toward home ownership and private rentals over various forms of social housing.

In general, the affordability of accommodation and profitability of the housing sector have been a major preoccupation of governments in most Organization for Economic Cooperation and Development (OECD) countries during the past decade (Burke et al. 1981; Howenstine 1983, 119ff; Stone 1983, 99ff). What has made the Canadian response distinct is not the recession, which has parallels in other countries, but the particular nature of the Canadian economy. Canada is among those few countries that have been classified as dominion capitalist (Ehrensaft 1981, 99ff). A defining characteristic of a dominion capitalist country is that while it enjoys an advanced standard of living similar to metropolitan nations such as the United States or West Germany, it is also economically truncated. Hence it is very vulnerable to major structural changes in the world economy and dependent on metropolitan countries to provide the initiative in overcoming recessionary tendencies. Some features that have circumscribed the economic truncation of Canada are export dependency on primary products, a small highly sheltered manufacturing sector, a plethora of foreign-based multi-nationals, and trade domination by the United States (Pesando 1983; Laxer 1973; Rotstein 1984, Canada, Department of Finance 1984b). In housing, as in other areas, economic truncation means that Canada not only is fiscally restrained by its southern neighbor but also restricted in the policy options that are considered politically acceptable. As in the United States, reliance on private-sector housing is greater than in most countries of Europe. Similarly, home ownership is ideo-logically espoused more than rental accommodation. Therefore, intervention in the housing market is more restricted than in most other OECD nations except the United States.

The response of the Trudeau government to the recessionary challenge was a mixture of restrictive monetary policies and compensating fiscal policies. The restrictive monetary policies were initiated in 1975 following the worldwide inflation that began to accelerate following the increases in oil prices by Orga-nization of Petroleum Exporting Countries (OPEC) nations (1973) and wheat prices in the United States (1972). They have only begun to ease off during the past few years. Normally Canada has had a high interest rate policy to assure the inflow of capital from the United States. With two exceptions (1973 and 1975), high interest rates were maintained during the recession (C. D. Howe Institute 1983). As a consequence, the unemployment rate also tended to be higher than in most OECD countries and Canadian mortgage prices were high relative to those in the United States.

Prior to the 1973–84 period of restraint, monetary policies were offset, to some degree, by fiscal initiatives. Since 1973, that practice has continued with one major difference. Because of restraint, high interest rates and a tight money supply have been associated with a loss in government revenue and increased tax expenditures. Hence, there was a rapid increase in the government debt. The increase was particularly dramatic in the past four years (Canada, Department of Finance 1985a). Social housing expenditures were controlled during the period but, significantly, restraint in direct expenditures was offset by tax expenditures for private-sector housing. One reason for the difference in treatment was the necessity to offset the rising problem of affordability for the middle classes in the context of recessionary pressures. Still another was the degree of freedom allowed by the relatively low level of overall public expenditure in the Canadian housing market. Throughout the recessionary period, direct housing expenditures—that is, the annual budget of the Canada Mortgage and Housing Corporation (CMHC)—accounted for less than 1 percent of gross national expenditures (GNE) and only 2–5 percent of total government expenditures. As Figure 4.1 indicates, the peak in direct housing expenditures occurred in 1975, the year in which the program initiated in response to the economic instability of 1973/74 began to be implemented. After 1975, however, government restraint measures came into play, limiting the size of direct housing expenditures relative to the rest of the budget. Overall social expenditures of government were not primarily responsible for growth in the deficit during the restraint period (Statistics Canada 1984). Comparative data show that from 1973 to 1984 Canada spent less than all the countries of continental northern Europe except Switzerland. Expenditures exceeded only those of the United States and Britain (OECD 1984).

The modesty of the Canadian welfare state is important to keep in perspective as we turn to an examination of housing subsidies. Unlike social welfare developments in Europe, which already had been initiated prior to World War II, Canadian welfare measures were not consolidated until the 1960s. The wartime apparatus that gave the Canadian state extensive involvement in most aspects of the economic sphere was systematically dismantled after 1945 to be replaced by private enterprise. Rent control, price and supply controls, and social programs were transferred from the federal government to provincial jurisdictions or ended. Wartime Housing, a major state developer and landlord during the war, was replaced by the Canada Mortgage and Housing Corporation, a mortgage bank primarily for financial institutions. The large stock of public housing during and immediately after the war was sold off (Wade 1986). The period from 1945 to 1963 saw few changes.

The 1964 amendments to the National Housing Act (NHA) introduced, for the first time, an effective public housing construction program and a nonprofit housing program for the elderly. Between 1949, when public housing was first introduced, and the 1964 NHA, only 12,140 public housing units had been built. In contrast, about 40,000 private-sector rental units were subsidized as of 1964. The entire emphasis of Canada's National Housing Act was on increasing access to mortgages for individual home ownership and on subsidizing private-sector rental starts. By the mid–1960s, this attempt to leave housing totally within the private sector had failed. However, the social housing programs introduced in 1964 were carefully designed to supplement, not replace, private-sector housing activities and subsidies. The new nonmarket housing programs were designed

Figure 4.1
CMHC Expenditures, 1973–84 (As Percentage of Government Expenditures and GNE)

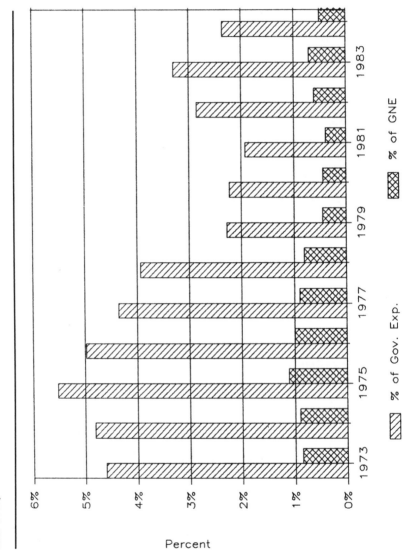

Source: CMHC, *Annual Report* and *Canadian Housing Statistics*, various years.

to be very narrowly targeted and relatively small in scale so as not to compete with the private sector. As a result, the federal and provincial governments began jointly financing nonmarket housing for certain categories of "worthy poor," generally single-parent families on welfare and the elderly. About 170,000 public housing units and about 19,000 senior citizen housing units were built under the 1964 NHA (Dennis and Fish 1972; Rose 1980).

The election of a majority Liberal government in 1968 and a minority government in 1972 combined with economic prosperity and growing demands for social reform to create major new government initiatives in the 1970s. The 1973 NHA (approved just before the 1974 recession) introduced public, private, and cooperative nonprofit housing programs, a rural and native housing program, and a public land banking program for assisted housing. These expanded the potential scope of Canada's nonmarket housing programs. The targeted group was expanded to include low- and moderate-income households so as to achieve a broader social mix within housing projects. The cooperative housing program was a major innovation for Canada, allowing the residents jointly to co-own and manage their housing on a nonprofit, nonequity basis. Funding for these programs, however, was never very substantial and they have continually been under attack from the housing industry lobby. About 180,000 nonprofit and cooperative housing units have been built since 1973. The total size of Canada's nonmarket housing sector is, nonetheless, still very small. The public housing and nonprofit housing programs have resulted in about 380,000 new or rehabilitated units, representing only about 4 percent of Canada's housing stock (CMHC, *Canadian Housing Statistics*, various years).

HOUSING SUBSIDIES 1973 TO 1984: FAVORING PROFITABILITY

The years of restraint from 1973 to 1984 were essentially a period of conflict over the spoils of the newly created welfare state. More specifically they were a struggle over state expenditures to promote private capital accumulation and federal social initiatives. Prior to 1963, the postwar compromise between capital and labor, extracted at a high cost in Europe, required little more of the Canadian government than a few transfer programs. From 1963 to 1973, the expansion of federal social programs was a principal factor in the rapid growth of state expenditures. After 1973, pressures to support private capital accumulation again took the ascendancy (Drover and Moscovitch 1981). Wage controls, cutbacks in public expenditures, changes in unemployment insurance, the erosion of health insurance, the expansion of the prison system, the promotion of private sector housing, and the stimulation of tax expenditures were all fostered to right the imbalances of the previous decade. Housing was also singled out as a cause for concern.

The years following 1973 were volatile owing to the highly unfavorable macroeconomic conditions noted above combined with rapid increases in the cost of housing and the failure of the private rental supply sector. Hence there were dramatic swings in housing expenditures and rapid turnover in the establishment and abandonment of housing subsidies. Virtually all the activity has focused on the private housing market because of pressure from developers to stimulate housing production through tax expenditures. The nonprofit and cooperative housing programs, which had been poised for takeoff after the 1973 NHA revisions, depended extensively on direct public expenditures. They increased initially, as a result of the new legislation, but social housing expenditures, contrary to earlier expectations, continued to comprise a very small portion of Canada's housing subsidies.

In response to political pressure and economic necessity, the government introduced a range of subsidies to meet rapid changes in the housing market. Social housing subsidies (nonprofit and cooperative) usually involved direct subsidies and loans. The entrepreneurial programs were more variable. In addition to direct subsidies and loans, home ownership and private rental housing were subsidized by tax expenditures, such as the Registered Home Ownership Savings Plan (RHOSP) and the Multiple Unit Residential Building (MURB) program. RHOSP was continued throughout the period of restraint while the much more expensive MURB program was turned on and off. The MURB program allowed wealthy individuals to shelter income from other sources by investing in apartment projects. The initial attempt by restraint-minded finance ministers to discontinue MURBs brought protest from the investment and development lobbies. Direct subsidy programs, such as the Assisted Home Ownership Program (AHOP) and the Assisted Rental Program (ARP), accounted for a smaller portion of these expenditures. Both direct and indirect approaches to stimulating private-sector housing investments also spawned additional subsidy initiatives, particularly in the dramatic downturn of economic activity after 1981 (Hulchanski and Grieve 1984). In general, subsidies were modified in response to three policy initiatives during the 1973–84 period. We call them Keynesianism (1973 to 1978), Keynesianism in retreat (1978 to 1981), and Keynesianism in disguise (1981 to 1984).

THE KEYNESIAN RESPONSE: 1973 TO 1978

The period from 1973 to 1978 was a period of dramatic expansion in government housing subsidies. It was a response to the political pressures caused by rapid increases in the cost of housing and to the economic pressures caused by a significant fall in housing starts. Housing starts, both ownership and apartment, dropped dramatically in 1973, at the beginning of the recession, and did not pick up until 1975 when several programs aimed at stimulating housing investment came on stream (Figure 4.2). Job maintenance and job creation became important considerations when the unemployment rate began to rise in 1974 and continued to rise each year until leveling off in 1978. In response to the rising inflation rate, wage and price controls were introduced in 1975. The

Figure 4.2
Housing Starts in Canada (By Type of Unit, 1970 to 1984)

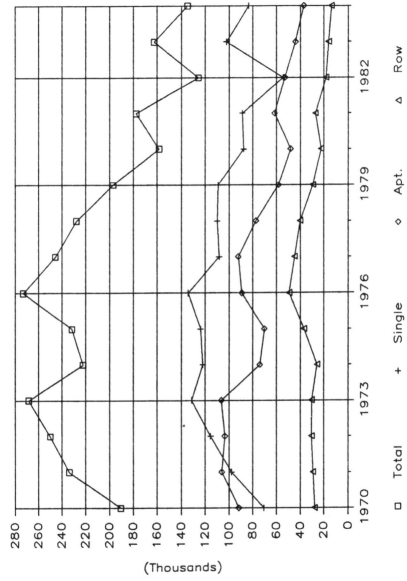

Source: CMHC, *Canadian Housing Statistics*, various years.

housing sector was dramatically affected by these initial years of economic instability. The rules of the housing investment game, which worked so well during the prosperous 1960s and early 1970s, no longer applied. Canada's largest development corporations, responsible for the 1960s apartment construction boom, had all made the same investment decision by the mid–1970s: to abandon the residential sector. It was no longer as profitable and the risks were much greater. The impact of this decision was mainly felt in the rental sector. The single-family housing sector continued to be dominated by smaller builders.

The federal response to this situation was to have the government spend its way out on the assumption that the problem was only temporary. Though restraint measures were introduced in most key sectors with the imposition of national wage and price controls, and social expenditures were contained, the federal government could not allow housing starts to fall even further (Canada, Department of Finance 1974). The middle class was increasingly vocal about house prices and tenants about rising rents and the residential construction firms were increasingly vocal about their survival. A quick response, therefore, was necessary for reasons of legitimation and accumulation. As a result, an unprecedented range of federal housing activity was initiated, expanding existing programs and introducing several new home ownership and rental supply programs. Virtually all the new expenditures were directed to the private housing market. On the other hand, the government had no intention of expanding its role in social housing. It was seeking a temporary "quick fix" for the slump in private housing investment.

For the ownership sector, AHOP was expanded and RHOSP was introduced "in order to assist young people in accumulating the capital required for a down payment on a house" and as a means of providing "an important new source of mortgage funds to finance the construction of the new housing we require" (Canada, Department of Finance 1974, 18). For the private rental sector the ARP was initiated and the MURB tax provision introduced, creating a tax shelter for wealthy investors by permitting capital allowances on new rental projects to be written off against other income. In addition, because of tenant concerns over rising rents and as part of wage and price controls, all provinces adopted rent controls by 1976. No new social housing programs were introduced and funding levels for the 1973 NHA's nonprofit and cooperative housing programs remained very low. The changing macroeconomic conditions brought about by the 1973 recession focused federal housing activity solely on the private housing market.

The action by the federal government did have its impact on housing expenditures and housing starts. Housing expenditures increased sharply. As Table 4.1 indicates, total CMHC expenditures, which include all the federal government's direct housing subsidies and loans, increased from $1 billion in 1973 to $1.85 billion in 1975. CMHC expenditures remained close to the $2.0 billion level until 1978. *Not* included in CMHC's budget are the housing subsidies provided through the tax system. RHOSP and MURB, for example, cost the federal government an average of $60 million and $110 million annually during

Table 4.1
CMHC Social Housing and Market Housing Expenditures, 1973–84 (Millions of Canadian Dollars)

	Total CMHC Expenditures	Total Social Housing	Social Housing as a % of Total CMHC Expenditures	Total Market Housing	Market Housing as a % of Total CMHC Expenditures
1973	$ 1,062.6	$ 477.8	45.0%	$ 175.8	16.5%
1974	1,339.9	498.9	37.2%	484.2	36.1%
1975	1,846.0	937.5	50.8%	526.2	28.5%
1976	1,907.9	930.1	48.7%	351.1	18.4%
1977	1,889.8	678.4	35.9%	511.3	27.1%
1978	1,879.3	696.8	37.1%	276.2	14.7%
1979	1,190.3	458.2	38.5%	113.7	9.6%
1980	1,323.6	476.8	36.0%	82.1	6.2%
1981	1,333.2	557.9	41.8%	101.1	7.6%
1982	2,214.4	747.7	33.8%	885.8	40.0%
1983	2,767.8	920.8	33.3%	1,029.4	37.2%
1984	2,140.1	1,107.3	51.7%	178.2	8.3%
Total	$ 20,894.9	$ 8,488.2	40.6%	$ 4,715.1	22.6%
Annual Average	$1,741.2	$ 707.4	40.6%	$ 392.9	22.6%

Source: CMHC 1982, 1984.

this period (Dowler 1983). Unlike the United States, Canada does not publish annual tax expenditure accounts. The only reliable estimates are from 1979 when estimates were published for the first time. In response to growing public concern over corporate tax breaks, some tax expenditure information was published in 1985 (Canada, Department of Finance 1985b). Data for the housing sector, however, were incomplete.

It is important to note that these annual federal housing expenditure levels do not reflect total new spending commitments. Many housing programs were structured in such a way so as to pass the costs onto future budgets. The stream of subsidies was dispensed over a number of years and federal accounting methods did not provide an estimate of the total being committed in each year. ARP, for example, subsidized 122,600 units between 1975 and 1978 but cost CMHC only $31.7 million in those four years. From 1979 to 1984, however, another $184.2 million in ARP subsidies were paid out by CMHC (CMHC 1984). This type of subsidy will continue for many years. Furthermore, rental investors were permitted to stack the ARP subsidy with the MURB tax incentive. The MURB subsidy is also dispersed over a number of years, with only a small portion of the cost of the program delivered in the year the project was built.

The Keynesian response did have an impact on housing starts. As Figure 4.2 indicates, both single-family and apartment starts increased in 1976, though they began to fall thereafter. There would have been no increase and the fall would have been much more dramatic if the government had not intervened. Most purchasers of new single-family houses received one or more forms of subsidies. Virtually all the rental starts after 1974 were subsidized. Only a minority of these subsidized starts were in the nonmarket social housing sector. The majority of the rental subsidies were investment incentives to private developers. This helped maintain the fiction that there was indeed a viable private rental sector. This rental sector, however, was no longer responding to supply and demand signals in the marketplace. It was responding to the very lucrative government subsidy programs. The government was, in effect, bribing private rental investors. If the bribe offered was substantial enough, rental investment would take place. Once ARP ended in 1978, apartment starts slumped to the lowest levels in 20 years in spite of tremendous demand and even though a major private rental tax subsidy program continued to exist (MURBs). Vacancy rates across the country were at their lowest levels in the postwar period. With a growing federal deficit and the growing realization among policy makers that the slump was not a temporary aberration, the Keynesian response was abandoned and restraint, or at least the appearance of restraint, was introduced.

KEYNESIANISM IN RETREAT: 1978 TO 1981

The second period represents an attempt by the federal government to further restrain its spending. The need for restraint in the growth of government expenditures was discussed in the March 1977 budget and became a major theme thereafter. In terms of total housing expenditures, however, the restraint was limited and largely cosmetic. The reason for this was the relatively small size of housing expenditures. Though direct housing expenditures and the indirect housing-related tax expenditures had increased significantly since 1973, housing still comprised one of the relatively small categories of government spending. Because of this and because of the continuing need to play a role in both legitimation and accumulation with respect to housing, the impact of federal restraint on housing was both small and temporary.

By examining CMHC's budget, it would appear that significant cuts were made in housing programs because in 1979 the total budget fell to $1.2 billion from $1.9 billion the year before, a 37 percent decrease in just one year. A number of programs were indeed cut, but they accounted for only a part of the decline in CMHC's budget. In 1978, as part of its restraint program, the federal government also decided to minimize its direct mortgage lending activity. Prior to that, the social housing programs, as well as some of the market housing programs, had been receiving full or partial mortgages directly from CMHC.

After 1978, a new formula required these programs to obtain their mortgages from private lenders, thereby permitting the government's role in direct lending to decline while increasing the role of the private sector—a major objective of restraint.

This shift from government to private lending accounted for a great deal of the "decline" in CMHC expenditures between 1979 and 1981 (see Table 4.1), but the decline was partly illusory. It allowed for the appearance that federal spending as well as the government's role in the housing sector were being cut in response to restraint measures when in fact it simply passed on even greater costs to future budgets. Because the government borrows money at a better interest rate than is obtainable by social housing agencies in the private mortgage market, the subsidies provided to social housing had to be increased to cover the difference. These additional subsidies, however, did not benefit low- and moderate-income groups since they were used to pay the additional costs involved in using private mortgage lenders. Financial institutions became the primary beneficiary of this budgetary maneuver.

Another way in which the impact of restraint on housing was more illusion than fact relates to the proportionate increase of housing-related tax expenditures. RHOSP was maintained and MURB, though discontinued for a year, was also reintroduced in 1980 to "reduce shortages of rental accommodation and provide a needed stimulus for the construction industry" (Canada, Department of Finance 1980, 104). Because of the continuing failure of the private rental sector to supply units on a nonsubsidized basis, the government gave in to the tremendous pressure from the housing industry and the tax shelter investment industry and reintroduced the lucrative MURB tax incentives. By maintaining RHOSP and MURB, future middle-class home owners and wealthy individuals in the 50 percent tax bracket retained their respective housing investment subsidies in spite of restraint. Since these did not show up in the federal budget they were easier to retain than the direct spending programs. The federal government thereby benefited politically by maintaining these programs and it assisted private accumulation in both the troubled ownership and rental sectors. RHOSP helped address the high cost of becoming a home owner and MURB addressed the lack of profitability in the private rental sector.

The housing measures introduced during this second period were totally in keeping with the growing neoconservative approach to government budgets that was emerging under the Liberal government at the time. Measures were taken to reduce the growth in the size of direct expenditures and to increase the reliance on the private sector wherever possible. This political agenda, combined with the unstable macroeconomic conditions, had its impact on the housing policy-making process within CMHC. By the late 1970s, the national office of CMHC became a virtual lobby organization for the housing industry. The perennial struggle within the CMHC bureaucracy between the social housing people and the market-oriented people was won by advocates of the private market. CMHC's research activity and policy advocacy shifted to the promotion of measures aimed at promoting and assisting the "efficient" private housing supply sector and at attacking nonprofit and cooperative housing programs as being "inefficient and poorly targeted."

By 1980, both CMHC and the housing industry lobby began advocating the replacement of social housing programs with a national shelter allowance scheme (Hulchanski 1983; Clayton Research Associates 1984; Steele 1985). Shelter allowances were favored because they provided low-income households a monthly check to help them obtain housing from the private sector, rather than rely on government social housing supply programs. The private commodity nature of the rental stock would thereby be maintained. The debate was no longer one of whether or not there would be large-scale housing subsidy programs. The debate had become one of whether the housing subsidies would be provided on a market or nonmarket basis.

By the early 1980s, the housing debate in Canada, which was generally phrased in terms of improving efficiency of government subsidies by targeting programs only at the "truly needy," became a surface manifestation of a much deeper clash, best characterized as the "market-welfare" and "social-welfare" housing options. Owing to the inability of the private housing sector to supply moderate-cost housing without substantial subsidies to investors, the fundamental policy issue was whether public funds should be used to maintain the private housing supply sector, the commodity form of housing, or whether the government should improve and expand its nonmarket social housing supply programs. The series of ad hoc programs during the 1973–78 period were largely based on the assumption that the problem was temporary and that the "market-welfare" programs would be temporary. When some of the key programs were withdrawn in 1978, however, housing supply slipped into further decline and prices in the existing stock dramatically increased. After a few years, it was more than apparent that something had to be done, and pressure was placed on the government by the early 1980s to introduce new subsidy programs.

KEYNESIANISM IN DISGUISE: 1982 TO 1984

The attempt to minimize housing expenditures did not last very long. Mortgage interest rates began to rise dramatically, moving from 11 percent in late 1979, to a peak of 21 percent in August and September of 1981, and leveling off in the 12–13 percent range during 1983 (CMHC 1983, 65). A housing crisis of major proportions was created by the addition of these highest ever mortgage interest rates to the already troubled housing sector. In addition to the low vacancy rates, the lack of unsubsidized private rental construction, and the high cost of single-family housing, many home owners were facing foreclosure when they renewed their mortgages. All the ownership subsidy programs of the previous eight years were aimed at inducing moderate-income tenants to become home owners. The normal mortgage at that time was for a five-year period. The five years came due when interest rates were at their highest in the early 1980s. Many simply could not afford to carry the new, much higher monthly cost of the mortgage.

The mortgage crisis became a political crisis for the government at a time when the ruling Liberals were already highly unpopular. Middle-class home owners began forming organizations to resist foreclosure and to lobby for reductions in interest rates. The housing industry also became a very active lobby, owing to the impact of interest rates on housing starts. In spite of its restraint program, new housing initiatives were announced in both the November 1981 and the June 1982 federal budgets. In a period when Keynesian fiscal policy was supposed to have been discarded, the federal government went on a spending spree in order to create jobs (Canada, Department of Finance, 1982). A new program, the Canada Home Ownership Stimulation Plan (CHOSP), gave $3,000 grants to all purchasers of new housing and to first-time home buyers who purchased an existing house. Spending on the Canada Home Renovation Plan was doubled as were the number of units subsidized by the Canada Mortgage Renewal Plan which was expanded to include a larger number of households. Funding for 2,500 more social housing units was also provided. This was the first time since the 1973 introduction of the social housing programs that the federal budget made a special additional allocation to nonmarket housing.

The problem was deeper than housing. In a fashion similar to the previous 30 years, the government used spending on the housing sector in a countercyclical fashion even though the economic circumstances were totally different from the high-growth period of the 1950s and 1960s. A Keynesian policy was being implemented in a non-Keynesian period. None of the new housing programs represented an attempt to stabilize or improve the operation of the housing market. In fact they resulted in the opposite. Nor were they designed to help the housing situation of low- and moderate-income Canadians. They were simply an immediate response to an immediate economic and political crisis. Middle-class home owners and real estate investors were the primary beneficiaries. Some 250,000 home owners received the $3,000 CHOSP grants and rental investors received Canada Rental Supply Plan (CRSP) subsidies for construction of 33,000 rental units in addition to the on-going MURB tax incentive, which was subsidizing about 20,000 rental units per year. In comparison, there was only an additional allocation of 2,500 social housing units.

IMPACT: POLARIZATION BY TENURE AND REGRESSIVE DISTRIBUTION OF SUBSIDIES

One impact of housing subsidies during a period of restraint was the polarization of households by tenure. This trend has become common to most advanced Western nations (Hamnett 1984; Harloe 1985; Paris 1984). In addition, the system of housing subsidies and incentives has been one of the more regressive categories of social expenditure in Canada in terms of assistance to lower-income individuals, a trend Canada shares with the United States (Dolbeare 1985).

Table 4.2
Average Dollar Benefits per Tax Filer from Federal Housing Tax Expenditures, 1979

Total Income Group	Average $ Benefit from Housing Tax Expenditures
Under $ 5,000	$ 32
5,000 − 10,000	171
10,000 − 15,000	314
15,000 − 20,000	619
20,000 − 25,000	964
25,000 − 30,000	1,312
30,000 − 50,000	1,994
50,000 −100,000	3,670
$100,000 & over	6,753

Source: Canada, Department of Finance 1981.

Expenditures on social housing programs, in particular, have been one of the smaller spending items in the system of direct and indirect housing subsidies. Larger benefits to middle- and high-income Canadians have been extended through housing-related tax expenditures. The $125 million annual cost of RHOSP, for example, has been available only to those who could afford to defer expenditures of $1,000 a year. The MURB program, in similar fashion, led to over $1.5 billion in foregone revenue in eight of the past eleven years. MURB, like RHOSP, benefited higher income groups.

Table 4.2 provides a summary of who benefited from housing-related tax expenditures. For every $100 spent directly, $30 to $50 was spent indirectly by way of tax expenditures. Tax expenditures in general, and housing tax expenditures in particular, mainly benefited the higher-income households (see Table 4.2). The greater one's income, the greater the housing tax expenditure benefits received (Canada, Department of Finance, 1981). Moreover, it is not only the regressive nature of housing tax expenditures that is at issue, but also their size relative to direct housing expenditures. Housing tax expenditures are two to three times greater than direct spending programs on housing. In most other budgetary categories, the relationship between the two types of spending is just the op-posite—tax expenditures are less, between 30 and 50 percent according to the Auditor General, than the direct expenditures. This means that in housing, for every $100 in direct total expenditures, some $200 to $300 are spent in tax expenditures.

Table 4.3
Changes in Home Ownership Rates Within and Between Income Quintiles, 1967, 1973, 1977, 1981

	% of Households Owning Their Unit				Change 1967–1981
	1967	1973	1977	1981	
Lowest Quintile	62.0	50.0	47.4	43.0	−19.0
Second Quintile	55.5	53.6	53.3	52.4	− 3.1
Middle Quintile	58.6	57.5	63.2	62.7	+ 4.1
Fourth Quintile	64.2	69.8	73.2	75.0	+10.8
Highest Quintile	73.4	81.2	82.3	83.5	+10.1
Total	62.7	62.4	63.9	63.3	+ 0.6

Source: Statistics Canada 1983.

Another indicator of the distributional impact of housing subsidy programs was obtained by examining trends in the distribution of home ownership among income groups. Table 4.3 demonstrates that there were gains among the top two quintiles and declines in the bottom two. The percent of households owning their own units remained virtually the same during the period. What was dramatic was the change in *who* were home owners. During a period in which a great deal of direct and indirect subsidies were provided to the ownership sector and to first-time home buyers, households in the highest two income quintiles made substantial gains in home ownership rates (up by 10 percent each) whereas the households in the two lowest quintiles increasingly became tenants. The middle quintile household remained about the same. Since 1973, however, the home ownership rate of the second quintile also declined, from 53.3 to 52.4 percent. In short, fewer households in the lower 60 percent of the income range were home owners in 1981 than they were back in 1967. The temporary programs introduced since that time have not been able to outpace the tide of rising house prices and mortgage interest rates. This trend, of course, was not due solely to the regressive nature of housing program subsidies. Macroeconomic trends, as we have seen, continued to work against lower-income households. The 1967 data are included to allow for comparison after the onslaught of recession in the mid–1970s.

The increasing rates of home ownership among the upper income groups also indicate an equally significant and very troubling trend for the rental housing sector. The rental sector was becoming an increasingly residual one, containing virtually all lower-income Canadians and very few higher-income Canadians. This had not always been the case. Table 4.4 indicates that as recently as 1967 the tenant population was divided almost equally between each of the income quintiles. The only exception was the highest quintile. By 1982, however, the number of higher-income tenants (in the fourth and fifth quintiles) declined while the number of lower-income tenants (in the first and second quintiles) increased, both significantly. This means that those households able to take advantage of the home ownership option did so, leaving virtually all those who had no choice in the rental sector. In general, then, the private-sector programs were supply incentives without providing direct benefits to lower-income households. By contrast, about 80 percent of the residents in nonprofit and cooperative housing projects were low- and moderate-income households. Nevertheless, through the period of restraint, the private-sector subsidies were much larger than the non-profit and cooperative subsidies. MURB tax benefits were especially costly.

CONCLUSION

More analysis needs to be done on the effectiveness of these past programs. The federal government, in the period since 1973, appeared to have taken the easy way out by assuming that housing problems were temporary and that minor, temporary programs would help improve the situation. This was much easier

Table 4.4
Renter Households by Income Quintile, Canada, 1967, 1973, 1977, 1981

Income Quintile	1967	1973	1977	1981	Change 1967–1981
Lowest Quintile	20.4	26.6	29.1	31.1	+10.7
Second Quintile	23.9	24.7	25.9	26.0	+ 2.1
Middle Quintile	22.2	22.6	20.4	20.3	− 1.9
Fourth Quintile	19.2	16.1	14.8	13.6	− 5.6
Highest Quintile	14.3	10.0	9.8	9.0	− 5.3
Total	100.0	100.0	100.0	100.0	

Source: Statistics Canada 1983.

than attempting to develop a longer-term policy framework. It also appears that these programs did not really address the affordability problem. Only the small-scale nonprofit and cooperative housing programs contributed to increasing the stock of affordable housing. The units subsidized by ARP, MURB, CRSP, AHOP, and CHOSP were subject to inflation in the speculative real estate markets.

As for the immediate future, there appears to be a relatively clean slate. Most of the housing programs introduced by federal budgets since 1973 had been discontinued by mid–1984. The election of a Conservative government in September 1984 overturned the liberal legacy of Trudeau and resulted in the elimination of housing programs and significant budget cuts. In the government's November 1984 "economic statement," spending on social housing and housing rehabilitation programs was cut significantly and the last phase of the private rental supply program (CRSP) was cut entirely (Canada, Department of Finance 1984c). In its May 1985 Budget the Conservative government eliminated one home ownership tax expenditure program, the Registered Home Owner Savings Plan. However, the budget provided individuals with an exemption from capital gains taxes to a lifetime maximum of $500,000. This was in addition to the already existing exemption of capital gains taxes on the sale of the primary residence. Though the intent was to stimulate new job creation, no distinction was made between capital gains accumulated from past investments versus new investments. One result may be that long-term owners of the existing rental stock will cash in on their buildings and for wealthy individuals to begin buying second and third houses as speculative investments. The new capital-gain exemption, therefore, is likely to have serious ramifications on the affordability of both rental and ownership housing in Canada.

A period of rather severe restraint in government housing expenditures began in 1984. This restraint is not only due to the market housing orientation of the new government, but also, and probably mainly, to the relatively low and stable mortgage interest rates. Whether, however, the new government pursues the same line of policy as its Liberal predecessors remains to be seen. A sharp drop in housing starts or an increase in interest rates causing housing costs and rents to jump suddenly will likely force the new government to behave very much like its predecessor. The economic and political costs of doing otherwise are very high. The alternative—planning and implementing a comprehensive national housing policy and a set of coordinated national programs based on the lessons of the past—is not yet on the new government's agenda. Many of the key variables—interest rates, unemployment levels, changes in real income—are largely determined in the United States. Canada first needs to confront the much larger problem of its dependency status before more independent housing policy initiatives can be undertaken. For the foreseeable future, it appears that the inequities of the current housing expenditure system will continue, that Canadians will continue to be even further polarized by tenure based on their income, and that Canada's rental sector will increasingly become a residual one, the domain of the bottom 40 or 50 percent of the income scale.

REFERENCES

Burke, P., C. Casey, and G. Doepner
1981 *Housing Affordability Problems and Housing Need in Canada and The United States: A Comparative Study*. Washington, D.C. and Ottawa, Canada: HUD and CMHC.
Canada, Department of Finance
1974 *Budget Speech*. Ottawa: Department of Finance, May.
1980 *Budget Speech*. Ottawa: Department of Finance, October.
1981 *Analysis of Federal Tax Expenditures for Individuals*. Ottawa: Department of Finance.
1982 *Budget Papers*. Ottawa: Department of Finance, June.
1984a *Economic Review, April 1984*. Ottawa: Department of Finance.
1984b *A New Direction for Canada: An Agenda for Economic Renewal*. Ottawa: Department of Finance.
1984c *Economic and Fiscal Statement*. Ottawa: Department of Finance, November 8.
1985a *Canada's Economic Prospects, 1985–1990: The Challenge of Economic Renewal*. Ottawa: Department of Finance, May 23.
1985b *Account of the Cost of Selective Tax Measures*. Ottawa: Department of Finance, August.
Canada Mortgage and Housing Corporation
1982 *Canadian Housing Statistics*. Ottawa: CMHC.
1983 *Canadian Housing Statistics*. Ottawa: CMHC.
1984 *Annual Report*. Ottawa: CMHC.
C. D. Howe Institute
1983 *Interest Rates and Recovery: Report of a Symposium*. Montreal: C. D. Howe Institute.
Clayton Research Associates
1984 *A Longer Term Rental Housing Strategy for Canada: A Report Prepared for the Housing and Urban Development Association of Canada*. Toronto: Housing and Urban Development Association of Canada.
Dennis, M., and S. Fish
1972 *Programs in Search of a Policy: Low Income Housing in Canada*. Toronto: Hakkert.
Dolbeare, C. N.
1985 *Federal Housing Assistance: Who Needs It? Who Gets It?* Washington, D.C.: The National League of Cities.
Dowler, R.
1983 *Housing Related Tax Expenditures: An Overview and An Evaluation*. Toronto: University of Toronto, Centre for Urban and Community Studies, Major Report 22.
Drover, G., and A. Moscovitch
1981 "Inequality and Social Welfare." In *Inequality: Essays in The Political Economy of Social Welfare*, by Allan Moscovitch and Glenn Drover. Toronto: University of Toronto Press.
Ehrensaft, P., and W. Armstrong
1981 "The Foundation of Dominion Capitalism: Economic Truncation and Class Struc-

ture.'' In *Inequality: Essays on the Political Economy of Social Welfare*, by Allan
Moscovitch and Glenn Drover. Toronto: University of Toronto Press.

Hamnett, C.

1984   "Housing the Two Nations: Socio-Tenurial Polarization in England and Wales,
1961–81.'' *Urban Studies* 43, 389–405.

Harloe, M.

1985   *Private Rented Housing in the United States and Europe*. London: Croom Helm.

Howenstine, E. J.

1983   *Attacking Housing Costs: Foreign Policies and Strategies*. New Brunswick, N.J.:
Rutgers University, Center for Urban Policy.

Hulchanski, J. D.

1983   *Shelter Allowances and Canadian Housing Policy*. Toronto: University of Toronto,
Centre for Urban and Community Studies. Research Paper 147.

Hulchanski, J. D. and B. Grieve

1984   *Housing Issues and Canadian Federal Budgets 1968 to 1984*. Vancouver: UBC
Planning Papers, School of Community and Regional Planning, University of
British Columbia. CPI #12.

Laxer, R.

1973   *Canada Ltd.: The Political Economy of Dependency*. Toronto: McClelland and
Stewart.

OECD

1984   *Observer*. No. 126, January, p. 5. Paris.

Paris, C.

1984   "Private Rental Housing in Australia.'' *Environment and Planning A* 16, 1079–
1098.

Pesando, J.

1983   "Real Interest Rates in Canada in 1983.'' In *Interest Rates and Recovery*, by C.
D. Howe Institute. Report of a Symposium. Montreal.

Rose, A.

1980   *Canadian Housing Policies (1935–1980)*. Toronto: Butterworths.

Rotstein, A.

1984   *Rebuilding From Within*. Toronto: Canadian Institute for Economic Policy.

Statistics Canada

1983   *Household Facilities by Income and Other Characteristics*. Ottawa: Supply and
Services Canada. Catalogue 13–567.

1984   *National Income and Expenditure Accounts*. 1969–83. Ottawa: Supply and Services Canada. Catalogue 13–201.

Steele, M.

1985   *Housing Allowances: An Assessments of the Proposal for a National Program for
Canada*. Toronto: Canadian Home Builders Association.

Stone, M. E.

1983   "Housing and the Economic Crisis: An Analysis and Emergency Program.'' In
America's Housing Crisis, edited by Chester Hartman. New York: Routledge and
Kegan Paul.

Wade, C.

1986   "Wartime Housing Limited, 1941–1947: Canadian Housing Policy at the Cross-
roads.'' *Urban History Review* 15, no. 1, 41–59.

5

Housing Policy in the United Kingdom: Efficient or Equitable?

DUNCAN MACLENNAN AND ANTHONY J. O'SULLIVAN

Abstract. This chapter focuses on the tenure structure of housing policy in the United Kingdom and its development, particularly since 1979. The basic structure of policy is shown to be unfair in its distributive impacts, and inefficient in relation to policy objectives. Expenditure trends over the period 1975–85 are shown to have strengthened these conclusions rather than weakened them.

INTRODUCTION

Housing is a complex commodity that satisfies a range of household wants or demands. Housing is also an expensive commodity. In most advanced market economies current payments for housing absorb between 15 and 25 percent of average household income. Reflecting the importance of housing to households, and the drain on household resources housing generates, postwar governments of all political persuasions have articulated their primary objective to be a "decent home for all families at a price within their means" (Department of the Environment 1977, 7).

Housing policy for the most part can be conceived of as an attempt to alter the price of acquiring housing services. This has two dimensions. It is an attempt to alter the relative price of housing vis-à-vis nonhousing commodities, but it also impacts on the relative price of housing situated in different tenures. Much of the implementation of housing policy involves dwelling-tied price subsidization, the economic rationale of which has been severely criticized as a general basis for subsidies although it may be justified in certain "second-best" circumstances (Robinson 1981). As questionable have been the equity effects of policy (O'Sullivan 1984). In the United Kingdom it is clear that differing policy priorities prevailing at different times have resulted in different rates and forms of intervention. This process has produced a diverse structure of government intervention that is inefficient and inequitable.

The range of instruments employed in policy implementation is extensive:

different systems of administered prices in public and social rental sectors, tax expenditures, income supports, and direct investment measures. Policy diversity, in relation to both objectives and implementation, is also enhanced by the involvement of both central and local government, plus important "quasi-autonomous nongovernmental organizations" (or quangos) in key sectors of policy. As a result, policy is designed and effected in a piecemeal fashion. For operational purposes it is organized along the main tenure groupings, which are not only influenced by differing policy instruments but have a different controlling mix of central-local sovereignty. For instance, owner-occupation policy instruments are largely controlled by the central government. Financial policy for public housing embodies a continuing tension between central government financing and local government resources and service delivery. Housing associations are largely centrally financed but directly controlled largely through the Housing Corporation. Private rented housing is subject to rent controls, tenure security provisions, and tax arrangements controlled by the central government. In the United Kingdom, the question, "Whose Housing Policy?" has become paramount as central and local views on the adequacy of policy diverge.

In the next section we consider the financial and organizational characteristics of the main tenure sectors, and the ways in which policy measures in these tenures interact. It is indicated that housing policy is inequitable. Moreover, we show policy to be inefficient. This is true with regard to both efficiency in production (the technical relationships between policy inputs and outputs) and the efficacy of housing policy. Further, we will question the desirability of some housing policy objectives themselves. The third section focuses on the changing resource commitments to policy; and the fourth section on the major impacts of this changing commitment. In the last section we offer some conclusions.

TENURE POLICIES AND INTERTENURE IMPLICATIONS

The Private Rental Sector

Currently 8 percent of British households reside in the private rental sector, although this proportion may rise to more than 50 percent in poorer, central-city areas. This contrasts with a figure in excess of 90 percent in 1915. The decline in the general importance of this tenure is strongly related to housing policy in this sector vis-à-vis that in other tenures. Private renting has become unattractive to suppliers, but no less so to consumers. Rent controls of varying degrees of restrictiveness have existed since 1915. Together with the limited tax provisions facing landlords (investment in residential property does not qualify for sinking fund or depreciation tax allowances) these controls have made investment in private rental dwelling stock particularly unattractive. Through time there has been a marked decline in the supply of rental units and in the quality of residual units.

It is important to recognize, however, that postwar demand has been shifting away from the private rented sector for reasons unrelated to the consequences of rent control. Since 1963 demand for owner occupation rather than private renting has been boosted by the considerable tax expenditures available to owner occupiers (discussed later) and by favorable property rating practices (Hughes 1982). In addition, at least until the 1980s demand for public over private renting has been induced by the existence of more favorable price-quality configurations in local authority (LA) dwelling stock. Currently, the bulk of the sector consists of older, low-quality, and low-amenity dwelling stock and, in effect, caters primarily for households without resources to enter owner occupation and without the "needs" characteristics to be admitted to higher-quality public housing. The position in London is somewhat different in that the higher proportion of middle-income and mobile young households has been housed by landlords' avoidance of the Rent Acts. In 1985, for instance, only one-third of new rentals in London were controlled.

Rent control remains an important element of current housing policy. It achieves short-term policy objectives with no requisite exchequer (treasury) commitment, except on policing and administration. However, in the longer term, rent controls, undermaintenance of private rented stock, and the prospect of a better deal if they can relocate in other tenures has and will continue to induce households to do so. Moreover, during the postwar period, the preponderance of low-income households living in poor housing conditions in this tenure sector, facing capital market impediments to becoming owner occupiers, has generated sustained pressure for public investment. In the 1950s and 1960s this was partially reflected in slum clearance with public rehousing and in the 1970s by a growing commitment to rehabilitation. Over the longer term rent control and subsidy policy have increased the burden on LA housing investment.

Housing Associations

The Housing Association (HA) sector is also small, although there are more than 2,000 associations. However, associations have a particular significance in older housing rehabilitation and special needs provision. Funded by the central government through the Housing Corporation, HAs have, particularly since 1974, become a major impetus to diversifying rental tenures and since 1980 have absorbed around 25 percent of public capital spending on housing. The growth of this sector throughout the 1970s reflected a switch in emphasis in housing policy from demolition and public rebuilding to inner-area rehabilitation. The program has had a variable geographic expression and impact (Maclennan 1985), but has largely been directed toward large cities and, within them, toward inner areas containing low-income residents in depreciated properties, both owned and rented. Despite a massive degree of subsidy (at around 90 percent of capital costs) the rehabilitation program has come to form an increasingly important share of public capital spending on housing. We return to this issue in the sections on "Fiscal Commitment" and "Housing Cuts."

The Owner-Occupier Sector

Owner occupation has grown rapidly in the postwar period, housing 26 percent of households in 1947, 56 percent by 1979, and 62 percent by 1983 (Treasury 1984b). Growth of the sector has been encouraged by all postwar governments, through the housing finance and more generally the overall tax system. Governments have in effect legitimized reducing the relative cost of owner-occupied housing vis-à-vis that of housing in other tenures, on the basis of responding to a "natural" preference on the part of households for home ownership; the last major governmental review of housing policy, for example (Department of the Environment 1977), spoke typically of home ownership as satisfying "deep seated social aspirations." It has also been argued, somewhat unconvincingly given the lack of perception of disrepair by owners revealed in the English House Condition Survey, that ownership leads to better long-term maintenance. Of course, since 1980 the "advantages" of the property-owning democracy have been much stressed by government.

To be sure, the growth of owner occupation has been supported by growing real incomes, and by social and demographic change. Rapid tenure shift has been facilitated by high levels of new household formation. The latter has also been influenced by emergent demographic and social trends. For instance, more single-person or split households have formed, and wives' earnings have undoubtedly become a critical element of initial home ownership (Holmans 1983). However, interacting with income and demographic pressures on demand for owner occupation have been factors that stem from housing policy itself. This is central to the issue of optimal tenure structure. A failure to recognize these policy influences biases judgment in favor of further private-sector (ownership) expansion.

The most important factor involves relative subsidization. The subsidization of LA tenants is dealt with later. Here we must note that considerable confusion characterizes much debate concerning owner-occupier subsidization. Mortgage interest tax relief is frequently argued to be a subsidy to owner occupiers. Arguably, however, owner-occupier housing is an investment good; a physically productive asset. This asset both generates an (imputed) income and sustains considerable capital appreciation. In the United Kingdom other physical assets similarly attract tax relief on interest paid in respect of loan finance raised for their purchase. But income flowing from the employment of such capital assets in productive activities is subject to tax, as is any real capital gain made on asset resale. It is these taxation principles that are abrogated in the treatment of owner-occupier housing. And, formally, these tax expenditures are in per capita terms greater than subsidy defined by mortgage interest tax relief, which is now running close to £5,000 million annually in the United Kingdom. Moreover, comparing the relative treatment of households in similar income groups, owner occupiers receive larger formal subsidies than other tenure groups in all but the lowest income decile, and the size of this differential increases as income increases (Robinson 1981; Hughes 1979).

In broad terms, a given sum of uncollected tax revenue adds to the Public Sector Borrowing Requirement (PSBR) as much as an equivalent sum of direct expenditure. Privatization of housing provision via extension of owner occupation has been, and is still, extensively subsidized. It creates large claims upon the PSBR and shifts budget scrutiny from public expenditure (tax expenditures not being formally recognized as public spending in the United Kingdom framework of national income accounting conventions although they are now noted in the Annual White Paper on public spending).

In addition, inflation (in conjunction with the structure of the United Kingdom tax system) has accentuated the growth of owner-occupier housing by concentrating household investments into dwelling stock. Inflation has been pro-ownership biased (Dougherty and Van Order 1982). It increases nominal income tax obligations, which can be reduced by raising mortgage commitments. The nontaxation of housing-imputed income acts in a similar fashion. Again, and particularly where the rate of house price appreciation exceeds returns on other assets, nontaxation of capital gains on housing biases asset choices toward owned housing. At the same time, with fixed nominal mortgage debt, real debt falls in inflationary periods. Estimates suggest that the impact of inflation was such as to have made the real cost of owned housing capital negative in the 1970s (Atkinson and King 1980). A marked effect of macroeconomic policy since the 1970s has been that since 1980 policies to restrict inflation have increased real interest rates, initially slowed income growth, and increased unemployment. All of these forces acted against ownership growth from 1980 to 1985.

In spite of inducements, however, some of the expansion into owner occupation in the United Kingdom has not occurred as the result of preference fulfillment—whether independently formed or fiscally induced—but rather as a result of policy in other tenures thwarting the fulfillment of preferences. Between 15 and 20 percent of first-time buyers were, in large cities, unwilling purchasers in the late 1970s. That is, they had failed to find suitable-quality private rentals or they had been offered an inferior rent/quality alternative in the public rental sector (Dawson et al. 1982; Karn 1980).

Other policy initiatives in the owner-occupier sector have been directed to the extension of this form of privatization of housing provision. At the cheaper end of the owner-occupied market, local authorities have played a significant role in lending for house purchase, and in allocating improvement grants. The former strategy was largely curtailed after 1979, although the building societies provided replacement funds; the latter program, though peaking in 1983, has had a major role since 1980. In the 1970s, the sale of council housing was also left largely to the discretion of local authorities. However, policies to encourage the selling of council stock, as a policy instrument designed to encourage privatization and at the same time generate capital receipts, underwent a significant transformation in 1980. The advent of Right to Buy legislation in the 1980 Housing Act, involving large fiscal inducements coupled with transference of right to purchase, aimed at a large-scale removal of public-sector housing stock into the owner-occupied sector. The impacts of this legislation became rapidly evident, and almost 1 million dwellings have been sold to date. Absolute and proportionate reductions in the size of the public housing sector have ensued and with dwelling sales consisting particularly of the best-quality stock (Forrest and Murie 1982). In 1980/81 the average discount was 39 percent on assessed values, which probably already understated market values by 10–15 percent. This massive capital subsidy, unrelated to tenant income, again does not appear as an item of public expenditure on housing. The discount, in strict economic terms, has no rationale and must be viewed as yet another major ad hoc distortion of the subsidy system.

Housing policy toward the owner-occupier sector clearly sustains considerable horizontal and vertical inequities in the relative assistance for defraying housing costs that households receive. Clearly such policy represents a highly cost-inefficient route to achieving the primary policy objective. Indeed, it is not evident that owner-occupier housing policy is capable of achieving this objective. More-over, apart from being regressive and inefficient, policy toward the owner-occupier sector has had a questionable macroeconomic impact. That is, national investment and savings patterns may have been shifted toward the housing sector as a consequence of policy. A recent OECD Study (Wood 1986) gests tax-induced distortions in relative asset values cause significant shifts in investment patterns. Offsetting reductions in government expenditure have led to a balanced budget multiplier effect depressing aggregate demand. Further, with productivity levels in the construction industry being lower than in the rest of the economy (National Economic Development Office 1977) this may have had a detrimental effect on the longer-run growth rate of national output. Wood's empirical analysis, covering the period 1973–83, indicates owner-occupier housing policy in the United Kingdom has probably had such impacts. This is inconsistent with macroeconomic policy and stated desires to encourage industrial investment and small firm formation. More generally government policy formulation should take account of the fact that without real income growth, increasing levels of owner occupation can erode nonresidential demand and investment in the economy.

The Public Housing Sector

British public housing is primarily local public housing. Although only one person in four lives in council housing in Britain, there are marked interregional and intraurban variations in the significance of this sector. The "North" of Britain has some 40–55 percent of households in council housing with the "South" falling in the 20–30 percent range. Moreover, high concentrations of such housing typify urban centers, and around half of the residents in cities with populations exceeding 500,000 live in council housing.

Until 1980 the sector had a long and complex history of expansion with initial levels of municipal construction recorded in 1919. Dwellings were, and still are, constructed according to local investment decisions, being financed by 60-year loans. Central government retains control over the total volume of investment, by setting total housing expenditure limits, and influences the investment mix by differential subsidy and building standards. Capital investment in housing gives rise to a stream of income from tenants over time, as well as involving a stream of interest and capital repayments on loans for building and management costs. These streams are formally separated into an annual Housing Revenue Account (HRA). As well as rental income, this account records, on the income side, finance from the central government to subsidize LA housing activity, and permitted contributions to the account from locally collected rates. The HRA is not inflation indexed; historic cost is the critical accounting criterion. With regard to rental income, LAs are not required to relate the rent charged on a dwelling to its cost of construction, and in fact rent and cost pooling gives an authority complete freedom as to what rent structure their stock has. Typically these structures are very flat; similar types of dwelling regardless of when they were built, or where in the jurisdiction of the authority they are located, command the same rent at any given time. More generally rent and quality variations are not closely related.

In general, owing to subsidy and historic cost influence, council rents fall below market rents. Since 1972, rent rebates, related to household income, have been available. By 1979, one-third of tenants received rebates. A household renting an LA dwelling receives a subsidy that is defined by the difference between the gross rent that would be required to generate a net real return on the current value of the dwelling equal to the net real return on owner-occupied housing and the actual rent the dwelling commands. If one assumes competitive conditions prevail in the construction industry, the former is equivalent to the rent that would be payable on housing of a given capital value if it were available in an unregulated private sector. On average, the subsidy received by a household with a given income renting LA housing has been less than that enjoyed by owner-occupier households characterized by an equivalent income, except for the very poorest households (Robinson 1981). Current directions in housing policy (see the section on ''Housing Cuts'') may be exacerbating this.

The direct contribution of central government to local authorities' HRAs rose as a consequence of inflation from between 20 percent of HRA income in 1970 to 43 percent by 1979, and comprised payments relating to a diverse set of specific subsidies introduced between 1920 and 1970 by various housing acts. After 1977, the central government required LAs to produce Housing Plans, or Housing Investment Programs, outlining how much each intended to spend on land purchase, new building, modernization, rehabilitation, and mortgage lending. Thus the central government could assess overall housing capital spending

intentions and, then, in reconciling these with its own plans for housing expenditure, ration out spending entitlements across capital expenditure headings
and authorities.

At the same time, the Labour government proposed the introduction of a single
Housing Support Grant (HSG) for HRA purposes. The grant was introduced in
Scotland in 1979/80, and in the rest of the United Kingdom in the following
year. HSG was proposed as a means of rationalizing the existing framework of
public housing subsidies to LAs. With the abolition of these subsidies, it was
decided that HSG should equal the difference between an authority's assessed
HRA ''expenditure needs'' and their ''basic means,'' or capacity to meet such
needs from local HRA income sources (rents and local rates). However, the
central government retained the right to decide what constitutes both ''expenditure needs'' and ''basic income'' (as well as the proportionate contributions to
such income to be made from rent and local rates), and in addition can alter the
aggregate sum of HSG available. Now HSG supports only 7 percent of HRA
costs and it is geographically limited to around 20 percent of authorities.

Through the Housing Plan system and with the introduction of HSG the degree
of central control over public housing has tightened markedly. There is a cross
link between capital and current spending in the Scottish context through rate
fund contributions to the HRA, as deductions of capital spending entitlement,
on a pro rata basis, are made for any excess in rate fund contribution made to
the HRA over the centrally stipulated level. Thus the central government can
ensure that reductions in HSG are borne by tenants as increased rents rather than
by local ratepayers. It is through the HSG/Housing Plan system that post–1979
cuts in public housing expenditure have been predominantly channeled.

Public housing was initially intended to provide an adequate and qualitatively
relatively uniform standard of housing for a wide spectrum of income groups.
Over time, however, the locations, environments, house types, and subsidy
arrangements that were initially found to be attractive or favorable to households
began to acquire as much quality variation as prevails within the private housing
system. More or less attractive areas of council stock have emerged and as
housing aspirations and real incomes have grown tenants have become increasingly preoccupied with locational and amenity issues.

There is no close association of housing age and quality. In many urban
authorities older public housing commands high preference rankings whereas
ten-year-old estates may lie vacant and deteriorating. Further, this variation in
housing quality is rarely encapsulated in the relatively flat rent structures set by
LAs. As a result, in low-quality areas, tenants may be paying close to, or in
excess of, likely market rent levels, whereas in higher-quality estates rents may
lie well below market rents. This quality variation and its allocative effects may
be unacceptable per se in a public housing system, but they become even less
tolerable when the distributional consequences are recognized. That is, either
allocation systems and/or the dynamics of public-sector entry, mobility, and exit

have tended to sort low- and high-income households apart into good- and bad-quality housing.

This seems to imply that increased rental revenues could be raised from the public sector without particular damage to low-income groups if rents were restructured. However, one must evaluate such a change in the policy context of Right to Buy legislation. Although a restructuring of rent profiles to more accurately reflect quality variation in the housing stock would be an improvement in terms of both equity and efficiency considerations ceteris paribus, more generally the result would be to increase the rate of transfer of the best-quality stock to the private sector. Thus over time the average quality of public-sector stock could decline and the quality of housing careers for low-income households remaining in the sector would be severely curtailed. The force of this conclusion is increased by the continuing constriction on local authority new building activity. Thus we have a situation where the patent rationality and desirability of a reform of one aspect of housing policy is severely undermined by the way in which it would interact with other policy elements. At the heart of the problem lies the absence of any link between pricing and investment strategy for public-sector housing.

FISCAL COMMITMENT TO HOUSING POLICY

Having outlined the tenure structure of housing policy in the United Kingdom, it is appropriate to establish expenditure trends. Since 1975 there have been marked reversals in expenditure commitments, not just to individual programs but also to the overall housing budget.

Public real resource commitments to housing policy in the United Kingdom expanded in most years from 1960 to 1975, with minor falls in some periods for cyclical (1969) or ideological (1971) reasons. Between 1970 and 1975, real (1979 prices) policy expenditure grew from over £4.5 billion to in excess of £7 billion and almost doubled its share of public expenditure from 2.6 percent to 5 percent. However, from 1975 to 1979 the absolute level was reduced from £7 billion to £5.3 billion, and the share of public spending fell back to 3.5 percent. These reductions did not reflect a fundamental shift in government belief about its role in the housing sector, but were being viewed as unfortunate but temporary stringencies imposed as a result of macroeconomic difficulty. At the same time there were attempts to restrain rises in current housing costs in order to preempt inflationary wage demands. Restrained growth of, or cuts in, public spending produced particularly marked cutbacks in housing and environmental expenditures, capital suffered in relation to current and transfer spending, and local spending was more restrained than for central governments. Specific housing-sector cutbacks over this period are indicated in the first column of Table 5.1. In 1978/79 spending on capital, for example, lay at 53 percent of its 1974 level. Improvement by LAs and lending to housing associations expanded in real terms.

Table 5.1

Real Housing / Total Policy Expenditures in the United Kingdom as a Percentage of Earlier Real Expenditures: Expenditure Acknowledged as Such by Central Government

Capital Expenditure

	1978/9 as a % of 74/5	1983/4 as a % of 74/5
All public capital	60	54
All housing capital	53	23
All local authority Housing capital of which	58	21
1. Land purchase	32	11
2. New Construction	85	29
3. Improvement	95	112
4. Improvement grants	42	193
5. Lending for purchase	21	3
6. Loans/grants to housing assocs.	96	43
New towns and Scottish Special Housing Assoc.	75	2
Sales/repayments	191	434
Housing Corporation	208	206

Current Expenditure

	1978/9 as a % of 74/5	1983/4 as a % of 74/5
All public current	109	125[1]
All local authority Current	107	119[1]
Current housing	115	50
Central subsidies to local authorities[2]	120	21
Rate fund contributions to local authorities	87	128
Central govt. subsidy to New Towns/ housing associations	167	141
Total "general" subsidies	116	44

[1]Estimated outturns.

[2]From 1980/81 specific subsidies were replaced by Housing Support Grant (HSG).

Source: Treasury 1980, 1982, 1984a.

Table 5.2
Acknowledged Housing Expenditures in Nonhousing Programs

		1978/9 as a % of 74/5	1983/4 as a % of 74/5	1983/4 as a % of 80/1
(a)	Rent rebates:			
	From central govt.	103 }	641[1] }	504[1]
	From local authorities	126		
(b)	Rent allowances	143	1,117[1]	868[1]
(c)	Total income related subsidies	113	699[1]	552[1]

[1]From November 1982 for some and April 1983 for all cases, this includes assistance with rent through housing benefit formerly met through supplementary benefit.

Source: Treasury 1980, 1982, 1984a.

However, cuts in individual improvement grants and reductions in LA lending for house purchase hampered progress at the cheaper end of the housing market. Reflecting macroeconomic concerns, all current account headings expanded save for "Rate Fund Contributions" to HRA. "General" and "Income Related" subsidies expanded at approximately the same rate.

Since 1978/79 there has been a further sustained reduction of housing program expenditure. The figures in Tables 5.1 and 5.2 indicate the reducing scale and structure of policy. There has been a further marked reduction in overall housing capital expenditure, which in 1983/84 stood at 23 percent of its 1974/75 level. LA spending on new dwellings was curtailed to 29 percent of its 1974/75 level by 1983/84, compared with 85 percent in 1978/79. Clearly the "Housing Investment Program" system has been used to reduce capital commitments. In addition, HSG ("Central Subsidies to Local Authorities") has been used to reduce overall current account spending. However, reflecting rising LA rents and unemployment, income-related subsidies have expanded quite markedly, as shown in Table 5.2

Rehabilitation expenditure has experienced mixed fortunes. Non-HRA (that is, private-sector) improvement expenditure (193 percent of its 1974/75 level in 1983/84) overshadows the more modest expansion of LA improvement expenditure over the same period (112 percent). There has been considerable contraction of LA involvement in housing association capital expenditure. Housing Corporation capital expenditure, however, remained in real terms roughly at the same level in 1983/84 as in 1978/79.

Expenditure under the housing program has been reduced since 1980/81 by between 12 and 15 percent a year. By 1984 real total housing program expenditure was only one-third of its 1975 real level. Regarding the sectoral pattern of contractions, LA general subsidies (HSG) and LA capital spending have borne the brunt of program contraction. Since 1984 further contractions, of much smaller magnitudes, have been experienced.

Program reductions in the post–1979 period reflect a general desire to reduce the scale of public spending and an intention to increase privatization of housing; and public housing is now seen as a potentially major source of revenue. Hence HSG has been reduced, rents raised by over 20 percent per annum since 1980 in the public sector, and in 1980 a no-profit restriction on HRA removed. Notably since 1983 rents in England have increased at approximately the rate of inflation either because there is so little HSG left to reduce or because government has recognized the major impact of rent rises on the cost of living index. Since 1980 around one-quarter of authorities have raised surpluses, albeit small, upon their HRAs. That is, council housing in some areas is becoming a generator of revenue.

In the 1970s, restraining public-sector rent rises and expanding housing subsidy was deemed conducive to controlling inflation. Present policy to control inflation implies that rents must be raised and general subsidies reduced.

Privatization of housing provision has been verbally encouraged by government, but it has not provided an operational context in which such provision can progress efficiently or fairly in light of the accepted primary objective of housing policy. Discounted council house sales have extended owner occupation, but only through the transfer of dwellings between tenures. Tax expenditures, ceteris paribus, increase aggregate demand for new and existing owner-occupier dwellings. Demand has been further enhanced by trends in relative subsidization as real public-sector rents have risen sharply. Improvement grants have generated demand for builder activity. These are the major ways in which privatization has been encouraged, but through such policies it is often the relatively more affluent households who have most benefited. No major policy initiatives have developed to address traditional market imperfections that may prevent households achieving "a decent home at a price within their means," nor has positive policy been initiated to rectify the problems faced in the low-income private rental sector. Pricing and investment strategy in the public sector have become more rather than less at variance since 1979. Moreover, since 1979, the overall thrust of macroeconomic policy to reduce inflation and to raise real interest rates, in conjunction with reduced income growth and rising unemployment, has produced a macroeconomic context that has reduced private demand and proved extremely disruptive to private-sector supply activity. In the context of the housing sector, real public cuts and private slump form a particularly worrying policy context for the expanding household numbers of the 1980s.

HOUSING CUTS: IMPACTS AND ALTERNATIVES

The Housing Association Movement

Public capital resourcing for housing association activity is not likely to expand in real terms beyond its 1984 level. This has important implications for rehabilitation expenditure. Until 1980 program growth was predominantly limited by the capacity to plan and program projects. Since 1980 acquisitions for improvement have run well ahead of rehabilitations, and even without further purchase schemes it will now require five years to improve already acquired stock. In addition, individual associations have begun to pressure the Housing Corporation to adopt more explicit and "fairer" allocation of the total budget, which is now the effective constraint on improvement. In response the Housing Corporation can make several adjustments. Rehabilitation standards may fall and there may be greater attempts to channel private capital into rehabilitation. If there were some positive policy in this sector to raise private involvement, public expenditure commitments could be reduced without prejudicing inner-city areas currently being rejuvenated. At the same time the pressure for association investment in special needs housing is growing and associations are likely to acquire a new role in modernizing rundown council stock (see also Chapter 3).

The Public Housing Sector

With capital cuts and council sales LA stock has been contracting since 1980 in absolute and proportionate terms. This reduction of rental opportunities is of concern in some areas, not only for households experiencing substandard accommodation with a preference for council renting, but in terms of wider social considerations; "trends associated with marriage and divorce, single parenthood and the elderly, all suggest the need for a more, rather than less flexible tenure structure" (Forrest and Murie 1982). Low levels of private construction since 1980, combined with population/household growth trends, exacerbate the emerging situation. Regarding existing public housing, the adequacy of the present capital expenditure level is doubtful. Large tracts of public housing in British cities will continue to be undermaintained. Such housing is not likely to be sold, or to attract joint public/private ventures. Regarding non-HRA improvement expenditure, in many inner-city areas the improvement grant activity has played a major role in arresting decline although there are still 1 million unfit units occupied by poor and old households. This support for the private sector, together with home loan activity, has been instrumental in attracting urban private improvement and new building. Many of these developments are now at a stage where sudden reductions in expenditure may erode renovation potential. By 1986 the cutback in LA home loan schemes had had little effect on inner-city owner-occupied markets, as building societies have moved lending downmarket.

Clearly LA receipts from sales of dwelling stock (see Table 5.1) could have been an important role in financing local capital spending plans. The maximum discount of 50 percent was extended to 60 percent in 1984 as the rate of sales decreased. Although receipts depend on the level of discount, and are likely to fall as the best stock is transferred to ownership, they could represent an important revenue source. Currently, after outstanding debt on a dwelling is paid LAs are allowed to retain 40 percent of receipts in England and Wales; in Scotland they are returned at the discretion of the central government. However, LAs are obliged to grant mortgages for purchase, and the full mortgage amount is counted against current-year capital spending. Net capital inflow thus depends on private financing of purchase. Moreover, carryover of receipts across fiscal years is not allowed, and this places unreasonable burdens on expenditure planning. A more effective system of carryover and reduced discounts could considerably ease capital constraints on local housing authorities. Since 1983, revealing that the Treasury was surely antihousing rather than solely antiborrowing, English councils have been restricted to spending only 20 percent of their receipts in a single year. Thus as the council stock deteriorates, £5,000 million of forced saving lies unused in their bank accounts and unemployment rises above 3.5 million.

Regarding current expenditure, HSG has been reduced to minimal levels. HRA cost structure is such that reducing cost levels is very difficult. HRAs can achieve surplus or balance only by marked increases in rental income. The overall incidence and effects of reducing HSG have varied across LAs. By 1983 a large number of authorities received no HSG. Generally they are the larger urban authorities. But smaller LAs, with low costs and rents, can be required to raise rents substantially (even where HSG is close to zero) to a regional average if they are not to lose resources from the general block grant (Gibson 1981). The overall effects of rent rises depend on local adjustment. LAs may restructure rent profiles, thus loading rent rises onto higher-quality stock. But the response to this has been increased demands for the right to buy. Thus the public expenditure savings of reduced HSG are largely offset by new tax expenditures arising in the owned sector and sales discounts. A further difficulty in raising rents is that already-difficult-to-let housing may become impossible to let and as a result incorrect rent levels/structures will raise vacancy levels, with ongoing debt commitments and no rent income in the public sector.

Private-Sector Responses

Problems emerging from the reduction in the role of and resources for the public housing sector would not be as great if housing resources could be efficiently transferred to the private sector. Falling levels of new private investment have accompanied public cuts. The construction sector has been ravaged by macroeconomic policy and by 1982 had reached prewar levels of collapse. Subsequently output recovered slightly, but there has been no rapid or sustained expansion. Falling levels of new private investment would not be so worrying if demand for housing were static and falling. But demographic/social trends indicate household numbers will rise rapidly to the end of the 1980s. Thus in crude terms, without a major surge in private-sector housing investment, there is the possibility of housing shortages emerging more akin to the 1950s than the 1970s.

No systematic positive measures have been introduced to encourage privatization of housing provision efficiently or equitably. Although tax expenditures remain buoyant, contributing to continued growth in demand for owner occupation, there has been little attempt to improve financing, surveying, and bidding arrangements in the market; that is, traditional areas of imperfect competition will persist.

The implications of housing-sector trends are that shortages will reemerge in all sectors. Further, in the private-owned sector these shortages will be reflected in a further real house price boom unless real national income falls markedly. Such price rises will increase tax expenditures. Public-sector waiting lists will grow. Ultimately the areas and groups that inevitably suffer in periods of housing shortage—such as inner-city areas and the low paid—will be the major losers.

CONCLUSIONS: IS POLICY EFFICIENT OR FAIR?

To evaluate policy, it is necessary to go beyond the delimitations of national income accounting conventions and beyond a concern with trends in aggregate expenditure. Within the cutting exercises that have occurred in the post–1975 period there has been a radical restructuring of housing policies and a major redistribution of public expenditure. Cuts in Housing Support Grant have reappeared in the social security program as Housing Benefit and over the longer term are replaced by owner-occupier tax expenditures. Within the housing program there has been a major expenditure shift away from capital expenditure and within this aggregate away from new buildings into rehabilitation. More generally, there has been a trend toward the replacement of local with central sovereignty on issues of housing provision. HSG has been used to coerce local housing authorities to replace policies based on local perceptions with those based on central government wishes. Authorities no longer in receipt of HSG can no longer be subject to coercion in this fashion. But other instruments can be devised, and capital allocations have also been used to impose central policy positions.

The replacement of some price subsidization with income subsidies in the public sector is not of itself inefficient, but it must be evaluated within the context of post–1980 Right to Buy provisions of policy, the refusal of central government to integrate public-sector pricing, and investment strategies and continued price subsidization of other tenure sectors. Vertical inequities in owner-occupier-sector assistance have been established since the late 1970s, as have horizontal inequities in such assistance vis-à-vis assistance to households in other tenures. Housing policy since 1975 has been increasing the degree of such inequities. By 1984/85 when gross provision for all recognized housing public expenditure was £4.1 billion, tax expenditures to owner occupiers were in excess of £5.5 billion (Treasury 1984b).

The Thatcher administration has placed consistent stress on the need for efficiency in public expenditure. However, in the housing area the motivating force appears to have been a simple and overriding desire to reduce the size of public-sector involvement in direct housing provision. For privatization to prove beneficial, there would need to be a rational market policy of withdrawal from public provision. There has been no attempt to increase competition except in owner-occupier capital markets, and even here there has been no full deregulation; building societies still enjoy substantial tax and cartelization privileges. Moreover, macroeconomic policy, as noted, has left the construction sector in no shape to contribute to a privatization process.

At heart, the privatization process has involved continuance of owner-occupier price subsidization together with Right to Buy legislation involving distributionally indiscriminate discounting procedures. It is not obvious that this is the best way to respond to households' "deep-seated aspirations." What is obvious is that such a policy is not an efficient route to ensuring "a decent home to all families at a price within their means." Housing policy in the United Kingdom has a markedly pro-ownership and antirental slant. Antipathy toward the public sector and indifference to the private rental sector continue to characterize housing policy in spite of the income profiles associated with these tenures (Robinson et al. 1985). Meanwhile, the bulk of available resources continues to be directed to those who do not require assistance.

To summarize, the housing sector has in the past absorbed in an inefficient and inequitable fashion a great deal of national resources; but the path to greater efficiency and equity does not lie in constructing negative controls on public investment, leaving the private rental sector to wither, and disguising private sector subsidization. The transition to a private housing market requires a gradual, planned, and fair shift of resources. Central government in the United Kingdom does not have positive or constructive policy for the private sector. Espousals of rationalization of housing provision through privatization have been used as red herrings to detract attention from the preference of government to extricate itself from involvement in an inefficient and inequitable system of direct provision rather than attempt to provide it more efficiently and fairly. As a result, the inefficiencies and inequities that characterized United Kingdom housing policy in the pre–1979 period have been exacerbated. There is nothing to suggest that this process will not continue.

REFERENCES

Atkinson, A., and M. King
1980   "Housing Policy, Taxation and Reform." *Midland Bank Review* Spring, 7–16.
Dawson, D., C. Jones, D. Maclennan, and G. Wood
1982   *The Cheaper End of the Owner Occupied Housing Market.* Edinburgh: Scottish Office.
Department of the Environment
1977   *Housing Policy: A Consultative Document.* London: HMSO.
Dougherty, A., and R. Van Order
1982   "Inflation, Housing Costs and the Consumer Price Index." *American Economic Review* 72, 154–64.
Forrest, R., and A. Murie.

1982   "The Great Divide." *Roof.* 7, 19–21.

Gibson, J.

1981   "The New Housing Subsidy System and its Interaction with the Block Grant." Unpublished.

Holmans, A.

1983   "Demography and Housing in Britain: Recent Developments and Aspects for Research." Unpublished.

Hughes, G.

1979   "Housing Income and Subsidies." *Fiscal Studies* 1, 20–38.

1982   "The Incidence of Domestic Rates and Alternative Local Taxes." *Fiscal Studies* 4, 23–38.

Karn, V.

1980   *Low Income Owner Occupation In Britain and the United States.* Washington, D.C.: Urban Institute.

Maclennan, D.

1985   "Urban Housing Rehabilitation: An Encouraging British Example." *Policy and Politics* 13, 413–29.

National Economic Development Office

1977   *Construction In the Early 1980s.* London: HMSO

O'Sullivan, A. J.

1984   "Misconceptions in the Current Housing Subsidy Debate." *Policy and Politics* 12, 119–44.

Robinson, R.

1981   "Housing Finance and Choice of Tenure." In *Agenda for Britain*, Vol. 1, edited by C. Cohen. London: Philip Allen, 210–33.

Robinson, R., A. J. O'Sullivan, and J. LeGrand

1985   "Inequality and Housing." *Urban Studies* 22, 249–56.

Treasury

1980   *The Government's Expenditure Plans 1980/81 to 1983/84.* Cmnd. 7841. London: HMSO.

1982   *The Government's Expenditure Plans 1982/83 to 1984/85.* Cmnd. 8494-I and II. London: HMSO.

1984a   *The Government's Expenditure Plans 1984/85 to 1986/87.* Cmnd. 9143-I and II. London: HMSO.

1984b   *The Next Ten Years: Public Expenditure and Taxation into the 1990s.* Cmnd. 9189. London: HMSO.

Wood, G.

1986.   "The Taxation of Housing in OECD Countries: An Overview." Unpublished.

PART III

COMPARATIVE STUDIES

6

The Rise of Competitive Mortgage Markets in the United States and Britain

ELIZABETH A. ROISTACHER

Abstract. In the United States and Britain, depository institutions that specialize in mortgage lending have in the past operated in a market protected by government- and industry-imposed regulation. These protections resulted in inequitable transfers among mortgagors and depositors and caused disruptions in the functioning of mortgage markets. Since 1980, the sheltered market structure afforded housing finance institutions has eroded as a consequence of changes in both economic and regulatory environments, and mortgage markets are becoming increasingly competitive. The high interest rate environment that coincided with and helped foster the end of sheltered mortgage markets posed problems for lenders and borrowers. The problems have been more severe in the United States than in Britain, where change has been slower and less necessary. It would appear, however, that these are short-term adjustment problems, that for the most part mortgage markets will function more efficiently than in the past, and that there are only limited needs to assist home owners in this new environment. Instead, it would be more appropriate for housing policy to redirect itself toward ending the inequities and inefficiencies that exist in the differential treatment of renters and owners.

INTRODUCTION

Economic policy and the economic climate of the 1980s have reshaped housing policies and housing finance systems in Britain and the United States. The Reagan and Thatcher governments established the reduction of inflation and promotion of economic growth as primary objectives and used as the tools to achieve these ends a combination of austerity in social spending (in particular, on housing), tight monetary policy, and tax reductions. Their political philosophies emphasize increased reliance on the private market through deregulation and "privatization" (notably the privatization of public housing in Britain). This chapter focuses on the economic and regulatory environments governing mortgage finance that have evolved in conjunction with, and to some extent as a result of, these general macroeconomic policies, their effects on housing finance and home ownership, and implications for housing policy.

Prior to the 1980s, depository institutions in both countries specializing in housing finance operated in an environment of restricted competition as a result of special protections by government, many of which date back to the 1930s. The creation of protected markets has been justified by policy makers as a means of promoting home ownership, in addition to promoting stability of the financial sector and the safety of depositors' funds. In the past, protected institutions found this sheltered environment to be conducive to stable and profitable operation.

Economists in Britain and the United States have argued that these special protections hindered the functioning of the mortgage market and had adverse redistributional consequences, benefiting institutions and existing home owners at the expense of prospective home owners and depositors (see Villani and Hendershott 1977, Carron 1983, and White 1986 on the United States; Whitehead 1983, and Gough and Taylor 1979 on Britain). In the 1970s mortgage markets in both nations suffered from periods of severe funds shortages. In the United States, thrift institutions (depository institutions that specialize in mortgage lending) suffered serious economic erosion from the combination of regulation and high inflation.

Both systems have recently been functioning in a more-competitive, less-protected environment, with the supply of mortgage funds and the mortgage lending rate set within general financial markets rather than in a sheltered marketplace. While these changes promise an end to many of the previous problems, the transitional period has been characterized by a number of new problems. In the first half of the 1980s, the cost of a mortgage and the risks borne by many borrowers were greatly increased. From the lenders' perspectives, mortgage arrears and delinquencies increased significantly. In the United States, many institutions faced insolvency and mandatory mergers.

Even if many of these problems prove to be those of a difficult adjustment to a more competitive environment during a time of high unemployment and interest rates, important questions remain about the long-run resolution of these changes: Will increasing concentration associated with deregulation offset some of the purported benefits of increased competition? What will happen to the supply and cost of mortgage loans? What, if anything, should governments do to promote home ownership if the costs and risks of borrowing are now higher?

The next two sections review in detail the U.S. and British systems, how they have changed, and the new problems that have developed. The final section summarizes the changes that have taken place and their benefits and costs. It also outlines some possible directions for housing policy in this new environment and places these in the context of broader housing policy.

THE U.S. THRIFT INDUSTRY

A Brief Look at the Industry and Its Pre–1980 Problems

The U.S. housing finance sector is composed of a broad range of participants. Thrift institutions, composed of savings and loan associations and savings banks, accounted for just under 50 percent of mortgage originations in 1985. Commercial banks accounted for some 20 to 25 percent of originations, and mortgage companies that originate mortgages for immediate sale to the secondary market accounted for a similar share (U.S. Department of HUD 1985).[1] Secondary markets, through which existing mortgages can be sold to a broad range of investors, are highly developed. The following discussion will focus primarily on the problems of the more than 3,000 thrift institutions subject to federal regulation.[2]

Thrift institutions specialize in home mortgage loans as a result of legal restrictions and regulation. In addition, a special tax incentive allows a "bad-debt write-off" in excess of actual losses for depository institutions that hold certain minimum proportions of "qualifying assets," in particular, home mortgages.[3] Thrifts raise the majority of their funds through retail deposits. In contrast to commercial banks, thrifts were prohibited from making commercial loans and short-term consumer loans, could not offer complete checking services, and were restricted with respect to raising funds in wholesale markets. The great majority of thrift institutions are mutual associations in which depositors are the passive "owners," generally leaving all decision making to management. A small but growing number of thrift institutions are stockholder-owned, operating explicitly to maximize earnings.

Until 1986 thrifts and commercial banks were subject to deposit-rate ceilings on passbook accounts, the dominant form of deposits at the beginning of the 1970s; other types of deposits earned somewhat more in exchange for fixed maturities and minimum balances. Thrifts were given a slight interest rate differential (from one-quarter to one-half of a point) above commerical bank deposit-rate ceilings to compensate for their legal inability to offer checking accounts and other services.

Deposit-rate ceilings eliminated price competition among institutions and induced them to turn to a variety of different forms of nonprice competition to attract depositors. These included offering gifts to new depositors, expansive branching, and lavish furnishings of offices (Carron 1982, 13). Restrictions on how thrifts could invest their surplus and the cushion created by tax benefits accommodated excessive outlays for such nonprice competition. Moreover, the mutual form of organization, together with deposit-rate ceilings that precluded higher earnings for depositors, encouraged managers to use surplus funds to compensate themselves through generous salaries and perquisites.

Prior to 1979 federally chartered institutions were permitted to offer only mortgage loans with a fixed interest rate for the duration of the loan. In some states, mortgage rates were subject to usury ceilings, but in general the rate on new mortgage loans was set by prevailing economic forces. The combination of fixed-rate mortgages and deposit-rate ceilings created serious problems during the 1970s, a period of interest rate volatility and unanticipated high rates of inflation.[4] Initially, deposit-rate ceilings caused "disintermediation" of funds as deposits were transferred to higher yielding forms of saving—in particular, money market mutual funds—offered by other financial intermediaries, reducing the supply of mortgage funds. Thrifts tried unsuccessfully to have rate limitations imposed on money market mutual funds to make them less attractive (Carron 1983, 73). Thrifts were not willing to do away with deposit-rate ceilings to attract funds, but their position did necessitate offering higher rates on nonpassbook accounts.

During the 1970s, while the ceiling on passbook accounts was raised only slightly, thrifts were authorized to raise rates significantly on other deposits and to offer money market certificates that provided higher yields to depositors with large accounts. By 1981 less than 20 percent of deposits remained in passbook accounts (Larkins 1982, 28). While thrifts were better able to retain or attract funds, the return on (long-term) fixed-rate assets fell farther and farther behind the rising cost of (short-term) funds, eroding the financial viability of the industry. As interest rates rose, the gap between the yield on new and existing mortgages widened substantially, resulting in a transfer of wealth to existing mortgagors initially paid solely by depositors with low-rate accounts and subsequently by the institutions as well through declines in net worth. By 1981 the thrift industry as a whole registered a loss (Mahoney and White 1985, 138).

Changes in the Thrift Industry Since 1980

Since 1979 federal regulators have allowed thrifts to offer variable or adjustable-rate mortgages (ARMs) that permit yields on assets to adjust to the short-term cost of funds. ARMs did not account for a significant share of originations until 1982 or 1983 as restrictions on the instruments were reduced and as interest rates climbed. According to Federal Home Loan Bank Board data, during 1984 ARMs reached a high of 70 percent of new commitments, but as interest rates fell through 1985 and early 1986 the fixed-rate mortgage regained its popularity, and the ARM share fell to 30 percent.

The erosion of the industry during the 1970s helped to induce the passage of the Depository Institutions Deregulation and Monetary Control Act of 1980, specifying a phase-out of deposit-rate ceilings by 1986 and permitting thrifts to offer checking-like services and to make limited investments in consumer loans, commercial paper, and corporate debt securities. State usury ceilings were preempted, increasing the earnings potential on otherwise constrained loans. (See Brewer et al. [1980] for a comprehensive review of the 1980 act.)

However, by 1982, high interest rates had dramatically accelerated the financial deterioration of the thrift industry, inducing the Congress to pass the (Garn-St. Germain) Depository Institutions Act (see Garcia et al., 1983). Its best-known provision authorized thrifts and commercial banks to offer money market deposit accounts, resulting in a strong net deposit inflow in 1983 after a long period of outflows. Garn-St. Germain also allowed special accounting treatment of institutions with inadequate net worth to allow them to continue to operate,[5] and permitted both interstate and interindustry mergers as a means of strengthening weak institutions. Such mergers had previously been prohibited by a variety of state and federal laws. The 1982 law also permitted federally chartered institutions to switch from mutual to stockholder ownership form, a potential spur to operating efficiency.

The ability of thrift institutions to diversify their assets was greatly expanded under Garn-St. Germain beyond what had been permitted by the 1980 legislation. While a thrift can now potentially invest as much as 55 percent in commercial loans and 30 percent in consumer loans, it is likely that many thrifts will not choose such high levels of nonmortgage lending both because it would render them ineligible for the bad debt write-off and because they lack expertise outside of mortgage lending.

There have been other weaknesses evidenced in the new regulatory and economic environments. The combination of capital influx as a result of the introduction of money market accounts and high nominal (not adjusted for inflation) and real interest rates (adjusted for inflation) produced what might be judged ex post as an excessive degree of risk-taking. For example, during the 1982–84 period adjustable-rate mortgages were offered with special early-year discounts to promote demand and to help borrowers "qualify" for the loan. After the initial year, borrowers could face substantial "payment shock" as the rate jumped because of an end to the first-year "discount" plus a second-year rate adjustment. Sharp increases in mortgage delinquency and foreclosure rates during 1984 and 1985 reflect the consequences of such lending strategies.[6]

Problems have been exacerbated by a number of other economic phenomena. High employment in the early 1980s increased the likelihood that households would be unable to meet mortgage payments, and declines in real house prices in some regions made it economically rational for some households to walk away from mortgages, even if they could afford to continue their payments.

In addition to higher risks associated with mortgage lending, expanded lending powers authorized in 1980 and 1982 contributed to financial difficulties for some lenders. Many nonresidential loans are not only inherently riskier than mortgage lending, but risks are further compounded in the short run by the lack of experience that thrifts have in these areas. Edwin Gray, chairman of the Federal Home Loan Bank Board, an agency that supervises most federally chartered thrifts, reported that by 1984 bad loans rather than the high cost of funds constituted the predominant problem of troubled institutions (those with low or negative net worth) (*Business Week* 1985).

Lower interest rates during 1985 and 1986 have helped to reduce institutional troubles associated with the high cost of funds. Indeed, the thrift industry returned to record levels of profitability by 1985, although some 10 percent of thrifts continued to have substantial problems (Nash 1985). However, as long as outstanding long-term commitments remain an important component of thrift portfolios, short-term rises in interest rates will continue to pose a threat to institutions. Although thrifts now have the opportunity to invest in adjustable-rate mortgages and other short-term assets, the recent shift back to fixed-rate mortgages could, in the face of unexpected increases in inflation, lead to a repeat of financial difficulties for the industry if these loans are held in portfolio rather than sold to the secondary market.

In addition to deregulatory and economic pressures, the system of federal deposit insurance has further encouraged excessive risk-taking (Kane 1983; Garcia et al. 1983). Premiums charged by federal deposit insurance agencies are uniform and do not take account of a particular institution's investments. In such a system, institutions with conservative lending practices effectively cross-subsidize less-cautious institutions, creating a so-called moral hazard: "Rational" institutions are induced to increase the risks they take because of protection from loss, thus driving up the overall level of risk taken by the industry. The general public, including institutions and their depositors, assume that the federal government will stand behind the insurance agencies should reserves be inadequate to meet losses. Because this is probably a realistic expectation, the structure of the system not only contributes to excessive risk-taking but also increases the likelihood that taxpayers will be put at risk.

One by-product of partial deregulation and increased competition has been an accelerating rate of mergers as weaker institutions are taken over by healthier ones.[7] Between 1980 and 1983 some 20 percent of savings and loan associations and 10 percent of savings banks were merged with other institutions. Most mergers have been voluntary, but in 1983 49 percent of mergers required special supervision or financial assistance by regulatory authorities (Mahoney and White 1985, 154).

It has been argued (Carron 1982, 47) that such mergers would not only help to phase out troubled institutions but would also increase the efficiency of the industry by eliminating institutions too small to capture economies of scale (lower unit costs for larger firms). While some research finds evidence of scale economies (McNulty 1982), a recent study of the banking industry (Rhoades 1985) finds that banks acquired through merger do not perform any better than non-acquired banks, a conclusion that corroborates a number of previous studies.

The increased rate of mergers raises the question of whether competition in the short run will lead to excessive concentration of economic power in the long run. It seems reasonable to conclude that excessive market power is not a major problem for mergers within the thrift industry; the commercial banking sector and the mortgage banking sector provide sufficient mortgage market competition, and depositors are hardly captives of the thrift industry.

If there are potential threats to competition, it is more likely to be the result of interindustry mergers as commercial banks acquire thrifts. Recent and prospective changes in state and federal laws foreshadow an end to prohibitions against interstate and interindustry mergers. Whether increased benefits from the elimination of such barriers will outweigh the costs from excessive concentration remains an open question. There is evidence that monopolization of the market as a result of protective state laws has kept deposit rates down and has driven up the cost of loans (White 1986, 24). White suggests that limits to scale economies in combination with an elimination of barriers to entry will produce a market structure that provides the benefits of competition without a tendency toward excessive concentration. However, very large financial institutions have yet to be included in empirical studies. Such institutions may be able to capture scale economies through advertising and may also benefit from economies of scope—that is, across activities—that smaller, less-diversified institutions have not been able to achieve. Thus, a certain amount of competition may generate short-run gains in the efficiency of the financial sector, but continued concentration could create an oligopolistic market. The paucity of adequate empirical data on the costs and benefits associated with large financial institutions leaves the determination of appropriate merger policy very much open to judgments—and sometimes biases—of policy makers.

The Impact on Home Ownership

The special treatment of thrift institutions had long been promoted on the grounds that it encouraged home ownership. While there is broad-based voter support for this goal, legislative support of housing in the United States was largely the result of lobbying by a diverse housing constituency including home builders, construction workers, real estate agents, and thrift institutions. Donald Hester (1977, 657) suggests that these diverse groups chose to support protection for the thrifts because they "view(ed) their fate as tied to that of savings institutions." In the past, housing policy in the United States has very much been determined by this special-interest lobby (see also Carron 1983).

More recently, thrifts have been seeking expansion of their powers into traditional commercial banking activities, a change that other participants in the housing lobby have viewed as a threat to their own interests. The general political concern with financial stability has made the concerns of these other housing interests less effective. Similarly, builders and construction workers found Washington unreceptive to their pleas for special legislation in 1982 to subsidize mortgages as high interest rates were weakening housing demand. Such subsidies, which had been instituted in the past as a stimulus to a depressed economy, were considered counterproductive in an environment in which high interest rates were a means of retarding inflation.

How well was housing served in the years in which the thrift industry was more highly regulated? Some home owners were fortunate recipients of low fixed-rate mortgages because lenders did not accurately anticipate inflation. However, many others were excluded from the housing market during periods of disintermediation. Funds shortages produced two sorts of problems. Where interest rates could legally adjust upward, new borrowers would have to pay more than in a less-restricted market. Where rates could not rise because of state usury ceilings, lenders could practice nonprice discrimination, a power likely to have worked to the detriment of minority and female borrowers and to the detriment of properties in less-desirable ("redlined") neighborhoods.

While the old system did pose certain problems for home ownership, the recent transitional period has presented new problems. Adjustable-rate mortgages shift some interest rate risk from lenders to borrowers. The complexities of adjustable-rate mortgages and the proliferation of instruments has made it increasingly difficult for consumers to compare instruments and understand the new risks they are taking on. Lenders have increased protection against rate increases and have tightened underwriting standards, partly voluntarily but also in response to tighter standards set by secondary agencies and mortgage insurers. Nevertheless, borrowers now have more options than before. On net, the system in the long run should be one that is better off for home owners except in periods of adverse macroeconomic circumstances: High interest rates can jeopardize a household with an adjustable-rate mortgage.

Even if the savings and loan industry is absorbed by the commercial banking sector, there is little threat to the size and competitiveness of the mortgage market. The continuing expansion of secondary markets, with private firms entering the field, suggests that the supply of mortgages should easily accommodate the demand for mortgages. While the mortgage market in the first half of the 1980s has been subject to adjustment problems, as the secondary market and insurers become better at assessing risks in a noninflationary housing market, the prospect that the mortgage market will function more efficiently in the future seems the most reasonable prediction, especially if there is some effort not only by market participants but also by regulatory agencies to improve financial standards. Federal regulators have already proposed more stringent requirements that should reduce risk-taking by thrift institutions (Nash 1986).

HOUSING FINANCE IN BRITAIN

The Building Society Industry Before 1980

The British building society industry provides an interesting comparison to the U.S. thrift industry. Building societies serve the same general function as thrifts: they specialize in home mortgages and raise funds primarily through retail deposits. As of the end of 1985 there were 167 societies, most of which are members of the Building Societies Association (BSA), the industry trade group that has tended to speak for the industry, set industry policy, and has served as a liaison with the government (BSA 1986a, 31).

Like most thrift institutions in the United States, these are also mutual associations owned by passive shareholder-depositors. Building societies accounted for some 75 to 90 percent of net mortgage lending in Britain throughout the 1970s, with the remainder of the market being shared by local governmental authorities, (commercial) banks, and a variety of other institutional lenders. There are as yet no well-established secondary mortgage markets in Britain, placing some constraint on the potential supply of mortgage finance.

In sharp contrast to U.S. lenders, building societies have offered variable-rate mortgage loans for the entirety of the postwar period. Existing borrowers and new borrowers, therefore, do not pay different rates. The variable-rate loan has allowed the building society industry to adapt relatively easily to variations in interest rates and inflation. However, the political acceptability of these loans hinged to a great degree on the industry's ability to moderate fluctuations during periods of high interest rates, an ability that has diminished in the face of increasing mortgage market competition in the 1980s.

Again, in contrast to the U.S. thrift industry, the building society industry has operated less through government regulation and more through a kind of self-regulation with a strong role of moral suasion on the part of government. While prudential requirements are set by government, the government does not regulate either mortgage or deposit rates, nor does it operate a deposit insurance scheme. Rather, in the past the BSA effectively "regulated" deposit and mortgage rates through its rate "recommendations." A high degree of institutional compliance and an absence of interindustry competition in savings and mortgage markets permitted the industry to operate as an effective cartel until the early 1980s (Gough and Taylor 1979; Whitehead 1981). Its relatively strong control over its cost of funds and its investment earnings have rendered the industry extremely sound financially.

The absence of interindustry competition was maintained through special tax treatment of building societies. Prior to 1980, building societies were able to attract savings at a below-market cost of funds primarily because of a composite tax arrangement with Inland Revenue. Under this arrangement, societies pay income tax on behalf of their depositors and pay interest to depositors net of tax; the rate of tax societies pay, however, is a weighted average, zero for nontaxpaying depositors and the basic rate for taxpaying depositors. The net result is that societies have had a lower cost of raising deposits compared to commercial banks, allowing societies to offer mortgage loans at a lower rate and/or to offer taxpaying depositors a higher post-tax rate of interest.[8] Societies, as mutual associations, have also paid a lower rate of corporation tax and profits tax on certain types of investment (Gough 1982, 99).

Because the BSA cartel power was used to keep the mortgage rate artificially low, the industry had the appearance of not exploiting its market power and, at least superficially, operating in the public interest. The government exempted the industry from antitrust legislation, the Restrictive Practices Act of 1976, on the grounds that the BSA "recommended the lowest possible mortgage interest consistent with what was regarded by the societies as prudent" (Gough and Taylor 1979, 20). A low mortgage rate is especially attractive politically when all mortgagors are affected by rate changes, as is the case in Britain.

The mortgage rates "recommended" by the BSA tended to be so low that an excess demand for funds and consequently mortgage rationing characterized the decades prior to 1980, especially during the 1970s (Boddy 1980, 59; U.K. Department of the Environment 1977, 105). The shortage of funds allowed banks, to the extent that they made mortgage loans, and a few small societies to charge higher rates on loans (Boleat 1982, 185).

In sum, until the 1980s the BSA was able to "regulate" mortgage rates, a role usually left either to the market or to government. Such private regulation, moreover, was probably less in the public interest in effect or intent and more to the benefit of the industry. By setting the mortgage rate below its market-clearing level and creating excess demand for mortgages, societies could select among potential borrowers according to what they themselves deemed to be risk-reducing criteria. Such a conservative lending strategy can also be discriminatory: for example, there is some evidence that societies have practiced "redlining" of older neighborhoods (Boddy 1980, 69).

Despite the pressures of inflation during the 1970s, the economic health of the British building society industry was not threatened because it was able to adjust both the deposit rate and the mortgage rate in response to market pressures. Yet, at the same time, it maintained some competitive edge over commercial banks in both the savings and mortgage markets. Although the government was not formally involved in the determination of interest rates, during the 1970s it used moral suasion and, on one occasion, a bridging grant (Boddy 1980, 19), to prevent the industry from having to raise deposit and mortgage rates too sharply. Thus, financial solvency was not an issue.

The building society industry has historically been characterized by a continuous pattern of mergers. In 1900 there were almost 2,800 societies. Between 1950 and 1980 the number of societies fell from 819 to 273, and by the end of 1985 only 167 societies remained (BSA 1986a, 31). These mergers, with rare exception, have been among healthy institutions. Although mergers involving smaller institutions have probably promoted economies of scale, Gough (1979) reports finding little evidence of additional economies as institutions have grown larger. Gough argues that most mergers are not based on efficiency gains but rather serve the interests of some building society managers whose salaries and other perquisites tend to increase with the size of the institution. Gough (1982, 118) also finds a pattern of excessive branching by societies. In Britain as in the United States, the mutual form of organization and the protected market structure have supported an inefficient housing finance sector that has operated more to maximize the welfare of managers than that of depositors or mortgagors.

The Changing Environment of the 1980s

In the early 1980s, substantial changes in the economy and in the regulation of commercial banks helped to reshape housing finance and weaken the protected position of the building society industry. On the savings side, the government itself became a major competitor to building societies through aggressive expansion of its National Savings program. National Savings, which had taken no more than 15 percent of net personal savings during the 1970s, increased its share to nearly 40 percent in 1981, putting upward pressure on the deposit rates offered by building societies and banks and on mortgage rates. By the end of 1981 the recommended mortgage rate returned to its record high of 15 percent, previously reached in November 1979.

In addition, building societies also had lost some of their competitive edge in attracting savings because of an erosion in the value of the composite tax rate as the proportion of taxpaying depositors has increased (Whitehead 1981, 40).[9] The higher mortgage rate, in combination with some other factors, induced the banks to expand dramatically their share of new mortgage commitments. First, a 1980 change in commercial banking regulations freed up the use of their funds (*Bank of England Quarterly Bulletin* 1982). Second, high interest rates had reduced loan demand from their traditional borrowers, the commercial sector. It has also been argued that the banks sought to attract new depositors by expanding their mortgage lending. In 1981 banks increased their share of the mortgage market to 24 percent and in 1982 their share rose to nearly 36 percent; during the 1970s they accounted for 5.5 percent of the market (BSA 1986a, 32).

The effect of the new competition from the banks was an end to mortgage shortages as the interest rate effectively rationed funds. The cartel power of the BSA has been sharply eroded, if not totally eliminated, as societies decided that they needed to be able to respond to the competitive market with a greater variety of savings instruments and more interest rate flexibility. In 1983 the BSA relaxed its "recommended rate" policy (*Bank of England Quarterly Bulletin* 1985, 83).

By 1984, fierce competition in the mortgage market appeared to slacken. As (nominal) interest rates began to fall, the banks retreated from their highly aggressive posture. For 1984, the banks' share of the mortgage market fell to 14 percent and mortgage shortages began to reappear (*Bank of England Quarterly Bulletin* 1985, 83). However, their share rose again in 1985 to 23 percent, probably enough to restore effective competition to the mortgage market. Banks have been attempting to expand the mortgage business through such incentives as a one-year discount for first-time buyers and payment of legal fees for borrowers who switch from another financial institution (BSA 1986a, 5). In early 1986 the BSA announced that "in the future [it would] have no role . . . in advising building societies on interest rate changes and announcing such changes on behalf of the industry" (BSA 1986b, 1).

British housing finance has entered a new era. The banks have settled into taking a larger share of the mortgage market than they did prior to the 1980s, and they have recently been incorporated into the composite tax arrangement (albeit at a time when its value has eroded substantially). American banks have also expanded into mortgage lending in Britain. The experience of the early 1980s appears to have awakened a sleepy industry that had in the past chosen to operate in a protected cocoon with a highly conservative lending strategy. The BSA has sought to expand its powers, including: offering conveyancing and other homebuyers' services, as well as banking services; making unsecured loans; and holding and developing land. In addition, the industry has lobbied to be able to expand some operations to other countries in the European Economic Community (see BSA 1983, for the original proposals). As of early 1986, Parliament was considering a bill to implement many of these proposals. Even if the industry does not achieve all it has sought, it is clear that societies will become increasingly diversified.

The Impact on the Mortgage Market and Home Ownership

While inflation in the 1970s and the new competition for building societies in savings and mortgage markets in the 1980s have not led to the serious financial disruptions that continue to shake the U.S. thrift industry, the changes in the economy and mortgage market in the 1980s have had some similar repurcussions for home owners.

As was the case in the United States, the changes in the mortgage market coincided with a period of higher interest rates and, in particular, with higher real interest rates. The real mortgage rate, negative in the second half of the 1970s, reached more than 6 percent in 1983 and 1984. The macroeconomic conditions of the early 1980s have, as in the United States, resulted in increasing mortgage delinquencies, although these are still low in comparison to the United States.[10] High real interest rates, the absence of real house price appreciation, and high unemployment are contributing factors (BSA 1985b). Delinquency problems may be exacerbated by an increase in loans to purchasers of council housing, who are probably more vulnerable to income and unemployment than the usual building society borrower. Building societies financed some 60 percent of council house sales in 1984, but these loans accounted for only 6 percent of all building society loans that year (BSA 1985a, 3).

The building society industry has probably been willing to expand lending to council house purchasers to indicate a cooperative stance with the government, whose major housing initiative has been the sale of council housing. Cooperation to implement government policy may be seen as the quid pro quo for expansion of building society powers. In addition, as Brindley and Stoker note in Chapter 3 of this volume, allowing building societies to engage in development will also further the goals of a government that would like to expand private investment in housing and reduce government expenditure.

SUMMARY AND CONCLUSIONS

Comparing the Experiences of Britain and the United States

There are many parallels between the regulation and operation of the British and U.S. housing finance systems in the decades before 1980. In the United States, federal regulation of deposit rates protected thrifts from an excessive cost of funds but gave them a competitive advantage over commercial banks in attracting deposits. In Britain, the industry's own trade association "regulated" the savings and the mortgage rate, a situation condoned by government. In addition, both nations provided special tax treatments to housing finance institutions. These market protections were justified as a means of insuring financial stability and promoting home ownership. In fact, the segmented markets approach supported institutional inefficiencies that manifested themselves in excessive branching and generous compensation of management. It produced periodic shortages of mortgage capital. Finally, it created a variety of cross-subsidies from depositors to borrowers (and between depositors) that could not be justified by any standards of fairness.

In the United States, inflation was a major force in ending the traditional system; it threatened to undermine the financial solvency of the thrift industry. The British system was less vulnerable to inflationary pressures because it relied on variable-rate loans to balance its rising short-term cost of funds. However, in both nations the tight monetary policies of the early 1980s produced record high interest rates that helped accelerate deregulation in the United States and erode cartel power in Britain.

Changes in British housing finance have not been as dramatic as those in the United States, but the direction is the same—toward integrated capital markets and reduced differences across lending institutions. While these changes promise an end to the problem of artificial scarcity of mortgage funds and adverse redistributions from depositors to borrowers, there are some apparent costs to the new environment, especially in the United States.

The trend toward greater competition in the United States has, at least in the short run, increased instability among thrifts and commercial banks. In the long run, a less volatile macroeconomic environment together with mergers, changes in the deposit insurance system, and a shift away from the mutual form of organization should help to rationalize and stabilize the thrift industry. However, looming on the horizon are future rounds of adjustment as further geographic and interindustry barriers are eliminated and as the specter of the international debt problems threatening the commercial banking sector cast a potential shadow on institutions that could play a significant role in the restructured mortgage industry.

Problems of this magnitude have yet to threaten Britain's housing finance sector. However, the consequences of increased competition in an adverse economic environment may also have been evident in Britain in rising default rates, and rapid changes in the barriers between financial sectors and between British and European financial markets could prove to be somewhat destabilizing in the short run.

For Britain and the United States the question remains whether the trend toward merger that is accelerated in a more competitive environment will result in greater efficiency with benefits passed on to the general public or whether it will eventually result in excessive concentrations of market power. On both sides of the Atlantic, the evidence on the benefits of mergers is mixed, some studies indicating scale economies and others showing no increase in operating efficiency. Moreover, while limits to scale economies are cited as a check on concentration, large firms—heretofore not included in empirical studies—may be able to take over or drive out smaller firms because of economies of scale and scope. Thus, competition in the short run could lead to market concentration in the long run.

The problems of short-run instability and potential long-run market dominance are not reasons to return to the old protected systems. Instead, deregulation should proceed cautiously, with government maintaining or increasing its role in setting prudential standards and monitoring compliance to prevent excessive risk-taking. In addition, there will be greater need to monitor markets for anticompetitive actions by large institutions and to prohibit mergers that are likely to result in excessive market power.

Competitive mortgage markets promise to end the problem of shortages of mortgage capital relative to the demand for funds, as changes in interest rates will direct a balance between the supply of and demand for funds. In the United States, while thrifts will be able to diversify their assets away from home mortgages, their increased ability to attract funds, together with the continuing expansion of secondary markets, should allow the supply of mortgage finance to adapt easily to demand. In Britain, entry of the banks has resulted in a greater supply of funds to the mortgage market. Because of tight constraints on the availability of both council housing and private rental housing in Britain, the ability to expand the supply of funds to the mortgage market is especially important, and thus an end to the building society cartel should be viewed favorably by prospective home owners. However, the government ought to encourage the development of secondary markets to promote further the access of the mortgage market to general financial markets.

Although the end to artificial barriers to the flow of mortgages should eliminate the problem of mortgage availability, deregulation and integrated capital markets will make home owners more vulnerable to general fluctuations in interest rates. In the United States, home owners with fixed-rate mortgages are protected from any upward movement in rates; those with adjustable-rate mortgages, however, may be faced with higher (or lower) rates as market conditions change. In Britain, the power of the cartel—and some government subsidy—moderated the degree of variation in mortgage rates. The loss of cartel power means that the mortgage rate will be more sensitive to market interest rate fluctuations.

What About Housing Policy?

On the whole, changes in the housing finance sectors in Britain and the United States offer a fairer and more efficient mortgage market. However, there are some potential problems that can develop in a situation in which the mortgage rate is subject to fluctuations in market interest rates. What, if anything, should governments do to help home owners in this new environment? Because macroeconomic conditions are always subject to change, governments ought to have policies to buffer households from the temporary problems of very high interest rates or severe unemployment. In Britain, the supplementary benefit for home owners has served the purpose of helping them pay their mortgages when faced with unemployment. However, the government has proposed curtailing this benefit.

One possible new role for the government would be stand-by insurance for home owners in case of cyclical problems (inflation, unemployment) that threaten them.[11] Although a private market for insurance could carry out such a function, it is doubtful that one would develop except after a major crisis among home owners. Such a government program would probably require some degree of subsidy to make it appealing to home owners.

The cost of home ownership will be higher for households in the future than it was in the 1960s and 1970s. Part of this change is an end to the very low and negative interest rates that characterized the 1970s because of errors in anticipating the rate of inflation. This windfall to home owners, particularly in the United States, was part of the threat to the stability of the housing finance system and thus cannot be viewed, from the perspective of the housing market as a whole, as a desirable situation. In Britain, the mortgage rate is also relatively higher than in the past because it is no longer set by the cartel. Higher mortgage rates may pose some barriers to first-time home buyers (although any rise in the mortgage rate may be offset by a fall in house prices). The tools for overcoming barriers to entry already exist in the form of low-start or graduated payment mortgages that are structured to reduce payments in early years in exchange for higher payments in later years when a household is expected to have higher earnings. Such loans require no government subsidy. Direct subsidies to allow households to become home owners hardly seem appropriate on income distributional grounds given the greater relative needs of many renter households who never even approach the economic margin between renting and owning.

It must also be emphasized that problems of inadequate incomes or temporary fluctuations in incomes are faced not only by home owners but also by renters— and it is among the renter population that income problems are more severe. Thus, while schemes to deal with home ownership problems ought to be part of an overall housing agenda, that agenda is acceptable only if it provides equitable support of renters. Yet the distribution of housing subsidies to date has been highly inequitable across tenures and within tenures. In both Britain and the United States tax subsidies to home owners have adverse distributional consequences. Not only are home owners generally better off than renters, but the tax benefits accrue to more affluent households. Moreover, the current trend in both nations is to reduce subsidies for lower-income housing. These spending cuts have been cloaked in the rhetoric of promoting efficiency and fairness in low-income programs. However, these changes in low-income policy together with unchecked growth of tax subsidies to home owners produces an overall policy in which efficiency improvements are minimal and are dwarfed by increasing inequity. The tax reform proposals being considered in the United States in 1986 leave the deductibility of mortgage interest untouched—even with respect to second homes. In 1983 Mrs. Thatcher chose to raise the cap on mortgage deductibility, a rather active courting of the home ownership constituency in direct conflict with her general efforts to reduce public-sector spending. (See Roistacher [1984] for an analysis of low-income housing policy under Reagan and Thatcher.)

While the needs of low-income families should be given a priority, this is not to suggest that it is inappropriate to support the housing of the not-so-needy. Although economists on both sides of the Atlantic argue that favored treatment of home ownership has distorted investment and borne some responsibility for declining productivity in these nations (Downs 1980; Maclennan and O'Sullivan, Chapter 5), a policy that alters the market allocation of resources toward housing can be justified as "socially efficient" if it achieves well-defined social goals— a housing policy that attempts to address the housing needs of its citizens efficiently and equitably. Moreover, policies that assist a broad spectrum of society bolster political support for assistance to the poor.

Unfortunately, housing policy as it has developed has been only weakly directed at household well-being, making it fail on both efficiency and fairness grounds. In particular, the protected housing finance systems of previous periods may have appeared to be pro-home ownership. They were inefficient because the benefits derived by home owners were more costly to society than if a more direct form of assistance had been used. Moreover, they were also unfair, hardly being targeted to those households most in need and denying access to mortgages for certain classes of borrowers and property.

Deregulation of housing finance and an end to the building society cartel provide some opportunity for improving the efficiency in the allocation of mortgages by leaving it to the market. However, without other actions by government—not only to address the specific problems posed by deregulation but also to promote fairness and efficiency in other aspects of its housing-related activities—deregulation cannot be viewed as an attempt to improve housing welfare. The political climate driving deregulation and nonmilitary fiscal austerity has not been conducive to reconstruction of a social housing agenda. Moreover, the importance of special interests in creating a patchwork of irrational and inequitable housing policies, in addition to the broad political popularity of home ownership, do not add to the hope of producing a fair or efficient housing agenda even in a more interventionist political environment.

NOTES

The early stages of this research were supported by a 1982 grant from the German Marshall Fund of the United States. A Queens College Faculty-in-Residence Award provided additional support.

1. The remainder of the originations market is accounted for by life insurance companies and federal agencies.

2. Most thrift institutions are either federally chartered or participants in federal deposit insurance systems, bringing them under federal oversight as well as certain state regulations. As of 1984 there were 3,400 such institutions (Mahoney and White 1985, 154). A few hundred thrift institutions, located in states that maintain their own deposit insurance schemes, are subject only to state regulation.

3. Commercial banks are also eligible for the bad-debt write-off, but the amounts of qualifying assets they are required to hold are lower.

4. Consumer prices rose less than 2 percent annually between 1955 and 1965; they rose 5.5 percent per year in the next decade, and nearly 9 percent per year between 1975 and 1980 (U.S. Executive Office of the President 1985).

5. Distressed institutions are issued nonnegotiable promissory notes by a regulatory agency in exchange for ''net worth certificates'' of an equal amount. This amount is carried on the books of the thrift institution as assets to allow compliance with minimum net worth requirements.

6. Data from the Mortgage Bankers Association show that the proportion of mortgages delinquent 90 days or more has risen quite steadily since 1980, with the delinquency rate for 1984 being 65 percent higher than the average rate for the period 1976–79.

7. The Federal Home Loan Bank Board approved mergers averaging about 2 percent of member institutions annually between 1970 and 1980. In 1981 the figured jumped to 7 percent, and in 1982 to almost 11 percent (Mahoney and White 1985, 154).

8. In order for the composite tax arrangement to provide an advantage to building societies, nontaxpaying depositors would have to be relatively insensitive to interest rates, a reasonable assumption for the large proportion of elderly nontaxpaying depositors, especially prior to the era of high nominal rates. The composite tax arrangement is believed to have redistributed income from nontaxpaying depositors to taxpaying depositors and mortgagors (Foster 1975). Commercial banks have, until quite recently, paid only a gross rate for savings that must be attractive to basic-rate taxpayers.

9. Changes in the personal income tax structure as well as a greater sensitivity of nontaxpayers to interest rates have probably contributed to the increase in the proportion of taxpaying depositors.

10. Property possessions for 1983 were double the level for the 1978–79 period, although only about 25 percent above their 1975 level. For 1983, possessions averaged .123 percent. Loans in six to twelve months of arrears reached .43 percent, nearly three times their 1978 level and about 25 percent above their 1974 level (BSA 1985b, 3–4). By comparison, the Mortgage Bankers Association National Delinquency Survey (1985)

indicated a 90-day delinquency rate of .90 percent and a rate of .20 percent for foreclosures started for 1984.

11. The Canadian government introduced such a program in 1984 (Canada Mortgage and Housing Corporation 1984).

REFERENCES

Bank of England Quarterly Bulletin
1982 "The Supplementary Special Deposits Scheme." 22, no. 1, 74–85.
1985 "The Housing Finance Market: Recent Growth in Perspective." 22, no. 5, 80–91.
Boddy, Martin
1980 *The Building Societies*. London: Macmillan.
Boleat, Mark
1982 *The Building Society Industry*. London: George Allen & Unwin.
Brewer, Elijah, Thomas Gittings, Anne Marie Gonczy, Randall Merris, Larry Mote, Dorothy Nichols, and Alan Reichert
1980 "The Depository Institutions Deregulation and Monetary Control Act of 1980." *Economic Perspectives* (Federal Reserve Bank of Chicago) 4, no. 5, 3–23.
Building Societies Association (BSA)
1983 *The Future Constitution and Powers of Building Societies*. London.
1985a *Building Society News* 5,4.
1985b *Mortgage Repayment Difficulties* (Report of a working group under the chairmanship of Mr. Mark Boleat). London.
1986a Tables. *BSA Bulletin* No. 46.
1986b *Building Society News* 6, 4.
Business Week
1985 "Now Bad Loans are the Thrifts' Biggest Enemy," March 25, 63–64.
Canada Mortgage and Housing Corporation
1984 *Mortgage Rate Protection Program*. Ottawa.
Carron, Andrew
1982 *The Plight of the Thrift Industry*. Washington, D.C.: The Brookings Institution.
1983 "The Political Economy of Financial Regulation." In *The Political Economy of Deregulation*, edited by Roger G. Noll and Bruce M. Owen. Washington, D.C.: The American Enterprise Institute, 69–83.
Downs, Anthony
1980 "Too Much Capital for Housing?" *The Brookings Bulletin* 17, no. 1, 1–5. Washington, D.C.: The Brookings Institution.
Foster, John
1975 "The Redistributive Effects of the Composite Income Tax Arrangement." *The Manchester School* 43, no. 2, 144–57.
Garcia, Gillian, Herbert Baer, Elijah Brewer, David R. Allardice, Thomas F. Cargill, John Dobra, George G. Kaufman, Anne Marie L. Gonczy, Robert D. Laurent, and Larry R. Mote
1983 "The Garn St.-Germain Depository Institutions Act of 1982." *Economic Perspectives* (Federal Reserve Bank of Chicago) 43, no. 2, 3–31.

Gough, T. J.
1979 "Building Society Mergers and the Size-efficiency Relationship." *Applied Economics* 11, 185–94.
1982 *The Economics of Building Societies*. London: Macmillan.
Gough, T. J. and T. W. Taylor
1979 *The Building Society Price Cartel*. London: Hobart Paper No. 83, Institute of Economic Affairs, July.
Hester, Donald D.
1977 "Special Interests: The FINE Situation." Symposium on the FINE Study. *Journal of Money, Credit, and Banking* 9, no. 4, 652–61.
Kane, Edward J.
1983 "The Role of Government in the Thrift Industry's Net Worth Crisis." In *Financial Services: The Changing Institutions and Government Policy*, edited by George J. Benston. Englewood Cliffs, N.J.: Prentice-Hall, 156–84.
Larkins, Daniel
1982 "Recent Developments in Mortgage Markets." *The Survey of Current Business* 62, no. 2, 19–37.
McNulty, James E.
1982 "Economies of Scale: A Case Study of the Savings and Loan Industry." *Economic Review* (Federal Reserve Bank of Atlanta) 67, no. 12, 22–31.
Mahoney, Patrick I., and Alice P. White
1985 "The Thrift Industry in Transition." *Federal Reserve Bulletin* (Board of Governors of the Federal Reserve System) 71, no. 3, 137–56.
Mortgage Bankers Association
1985 National Delinquency Survey. Washington, D.C.: Mortgage Bankers Association, February 28.
Nash, Nathaniel C.
1985 "New Prosperity for Thrift Industry." *New York Times*, August 5, D6.
1986 "U.S. Seeks Changes at Thrift Units." *New York Times*, April 25, D1.
Rhoades, Stephen A.
1985 *The Operating Performance of Acquired Firms in Banking Before and After Acquisition*. (Staff Study) Washington, D.C.: Board of Governors of the Federal Reserve System.
Roistacher, Elizabeth A.
1984 "A Tale of Two Conservatives: Housing Policy under Reagan and Thatcher." *Journal of the American Planning Association* 50, no. 4, 485–92.
U.K. Department of the Environment
1977 *Housing Policy. Technical Volume. Part II*. London: HMSO.
U.S. Department of Housing and Urban Development
1985 Survey of Mortgage Lending (data provided by telephone).
U.S. Executive Office of the President
1985 *Economic Report of the President*. Washington, D.C.: U.S. Government Printing Office.
Villani, Kevin E., and Patric H. Hendershott
1977 *Regulation and Reform of the Housing Finance System*. Washington, D.C.: American Enterprise Institute.
White, Lawrence J.
1986 "The Partial Deregulation of Banks and Other Depository Institutions." In *Reg-

ulatory Reform: What Actually Happened?, edited by Michael Klass and Leonard Weiss. Boston: Little, Brown, 169–209.

Whitehead, Christine

1981   "Housing Finance: A Changing Market." *Public Money* 1, no. 1, 39–41.

1983   "Housing under the Conservatives: A Policy Assessment." *Public Money* 3, no. 1, 15–21.

7

Housing Provision and House Building in Western Europe: Increasing Expenditure, Declining Output?

PETER AMBROSE AND JAMES BARLOW

Abstract. This chapter examines the way very different systems of housing provision in Britain, France, Greece, Italy, Portugal, Sweden, and West Germany have produced *seemingly* similar trends: namely, a general decline in new house building and a shift in the pattern of state support from programs subsidizing the *production* of housing to programs supporting its *consumption*. It details these two basic trends, arguing that in fact they are rather more complex than has previously been thought. It also outlines some possible reasons for the variations in the rate of housing production between the countries.

TRENDS IN HOUSING OUTPUT

Figure 7.1 shows the output of new dwellings (measured as new units built and units added to the effective stock by rehabilitation, and so on) per 1,000 population. Two things can be seen: a long-term decline in new building in most countries and a tendency toward cyclical booms and slumps in output. Whether, of course, this constitutes a general housing crisis is another matter. For the moment it suffices to say that in a number of these countries problems of supply of adequate housing have been a persistent feature during the 1970s and 1980s.

The tendencies toward decreasing and cyclical output are not present in all the countries studied in this chapter.[1] Output over the period has not fallen in Portugal and Greece, and the decline in Sweden has taken place without the booms and slumps characteristic of other systems. Cyclical variations in output are to be expected in any system where the capitalist production of commodities is dominant. But in some countries this effect is heightened because housing production is heavily underwritten by the state. This means that changes in state policy will exert an additional influence on the overall level of production.

We would argue that in most countries three factors are important in influencing the level of new house building: (1) direct capital investment by the state for public housing; (2) state support for production and consumption; and (3) changes in the profitability of house building for production within the private sector. To

Figure 7.1
Dwellings Completed Annually per 1,000 Population

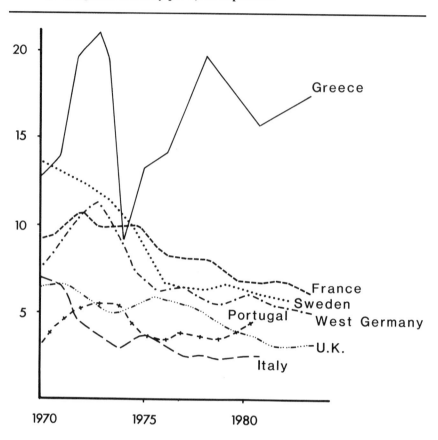

Source: U.K. Economic & Social Council, Economic Commission for Europe, Committee on Housing, Building and Planning, *Survey of the Human Settlements Situation in the E.C. (1983)*.

some extent, in some countries, the third factor may depend on the second. Naturally the balance between production underwritten by public expenditure and production carried out solely for the market will determine where the weight of the explanation lies. Underlying this is the question, which we examine later, of how much of this initial expenditure actually turns into new output.

TYPES OF HOUSING PROVISION SYSTEMS

The countries we have examined fall into five broad categories of provision system:

1. In Greece and Italy nearly all production is carried out under free market conditions.

2. In West Germany and France a large proportion of total production is underwritten by some form of state support (currently about half, although declining in West Germany). Speculative production is limited and new house building in these countries is often carried out on a self-promotion basis for private consumption, that is, by individual consumers contracting a builder.

3. Sweden also has considerable (and since the mid–1970s a growing) level of state support for housing production, but is distinguished additionally by the tight regulation of *consumption* through a system of interest rate and price controls.

4. In Britain there has been a combination of state support for public-sector production (local authority housing), which has been substantially eroded since the mid–1970s, and growing support for private-sector consumption, that is, fiscal concessions for the purchasers of housing. The latter applies indiscriminately to speculatively built new housing and to the existing stock. This form of support has become predominant since 1974/75 (despite the general fall in new private-sector output), although there has also been a growth in new forms of indirect state support for private house builders (for example, through the use of Urban Development Grants).

5. Portugal occupies a position midway between the state-underwritten production systems of France and West Germany and the directly subsidized social housing plus speculative private building system of Britain. However, there is also a considerable ''illegal'' sector, where housing is built without official permission (as in Greece and Italy).

At first sight, the housing finance systems of the seven countries look bewilderingly different. However, despite the national differences in traditions, institutions, political strategies, and so on, it is possible to see common features. In broad terms, housing expenditure can take only a limited number of forms, although there are variations of detail. We have tried to identify the basic pattern of possibilities in Figure 7.2, incorporating all the routes that expenditure on housing can take from the original commitment of the subsidy or investment to the final consumer. Not all countries have flows of money along each of the 14 branches, although this is in theory possible. The next section examines the changes in the balance of flows along the various routes.

RECENT TRENDS IN THE PATTERN OF SUPPORT

In practice it is extremely difficult to disentangle the pattern of expenditure in different countries.[2] In the relatively straightforward case of the United Kingdom, direct public expenditure on the construction of social housing has been drastically reduced in the last decade—between 1979/80 and 1984/85 local authority expenditure on new dwellings fell by nearly 60 percent in real terms (Robinson 1986). There have also been changes in the nature of subsidized production expenditure: A growing proportion took the form of support either for voluntary housing associations (rather than statutory local authorities) or for

Figure 7.2
Possible Forms of State Housing Support

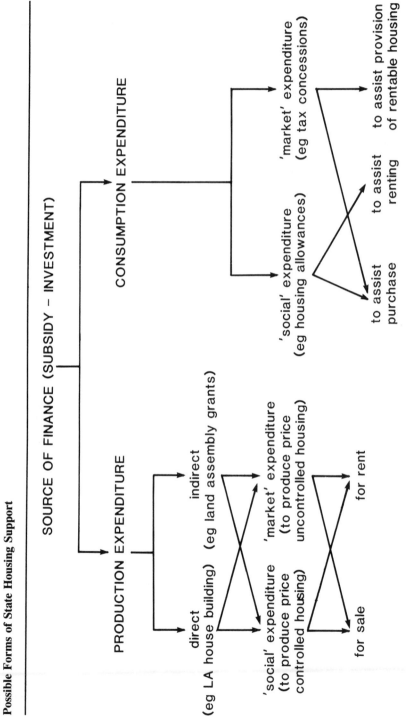

SOURCE OF FINANCE (SUBSIDY – INVESTMENT)

PRODUCTION EXPENDITURE

direct
(eg LA house building)

indirect
(eg land assembly grants)

'social' expenditure
(to produce price
controlled housing)

'market' expenditure
(to produce price
uncontrolled housing)

for sale

for rent

CONSUMPTION EXPENDITURE

'social' expenditure
(eg housing allowances)

'market' expenditure
(eg tax concessions)

to assist
purchase

to assist
renting

to assist provision
of rentable housing

private developers (via Urban Development Grants that underwrite an agreed level of profits). However, by far the largest expenditure on housing in Britain is not on production but on consumption (that is, expenditure on purchase, fiscal concessions for purchasers, and support payments to tenants rather than the production of new housing), although a relatively small part of this is subsidy. This, of course, reflects the high level of transactions in the existing stock. The balance of this consumption expenditure has also been changing, with growing tax subsidies to owner occupiers during the late 1970s-early 1980s, at the expense of rent allowances and rebates. This would be even higher if the discount to purchasers of previously local-authority-owned housing were included.

In France expenditure on new production is considerably greater than on consumption (reflecting the lower level of transactions in the existing stock than in Britain). In fact, by 1979 almost three times as much money was spent on supporting producers rather than users, although this ratio has since fallen. Not only has there been a large rise in total production expenditure, but there was also a 33 percent real increase in state-aided production from 1974 to 1979. State-supported production expenditure formed nearly half of total production expenditure in 1982, although the level in 1970 was over 60 percent. It should also be stressed that a growing proportion of this (from about 25 percent to 45 percent) has been for owner-occupier production, some three-quarters of which is self-promoted (Ambrose and Barlow 1986b).

West Germany's extremely complex system of direct and indirect grants and tax subsidies can make any distinction between production and consumption expenditure somewhat blurred. Nevertheless, the state has been withdrawing its support for both types of expenditure, despite a real increase in the *total* housing subsidy throughout the late 1960s and 1970s. This had reached 18.3 billion deutsche marks (DM) by 1980 (Petzinger and Riege 1981). State subsidized production peaked at about 75 percent of all production expenditure in 1974–75 and had dropped to 45 percent by the early 1980s. There has been a shift toward a reliance on the free market for finance for new building with a reduced role for the building savings premium system and, accordingly, a steadily increasing burden of mortgage tax relief support. Direct support for social housing through the 1st Subsidy System (1 Förderungsweg) has also declined since the early 1970s, although more funds were forthcoming between 1979 and 1982 (Marcuse 1982). This form of expenditure is also buttressed by considerable support in the form of *Wohngeld*, a subsidy to maintain rents below a fixed level. This subsidy in 1983 stood at over 2.5 billion DM, although this has not grown to any great extent since 1975.

For most of the 1970s public expenditure on housing grew rapidly in Sweden. The relatively low *proportion* of government-supported production expenditure (through the system of State Housing Loans and interest rate subsidies) in Sweden actually understates the involvement of the state in housing provision. Total local and central government spending on housing stood at some 27 billion kronor in

1984, over half comprising tax subsidies to owner occupiers and housing allowances, but state involvement extends beyond the supply of grants and subsidies. Most importantly it takes the form of very tight control exerted over land supply and favorable access to land for developers in receipt of State Housing Loans. Some 85–90 percent of single-family dwellings are built within this system (Dickens, et al. 1985).

After the 1974 revolution, Portuguese state expenditure on housing grew threefold in real terms, although sharp fluctuations in housing policy under a succession of different governments can be seen in the uneven levels of expenditure. Here, there has also been a move away from the provision of public social housing, with the introduction of tax concessions to house purchasers and subsidies for private-sector building leading to a boom in speculative production in the early 1980s. By early 1985 some 40,000 newly built units remained unsold and the government was considering how best to incorporate some or all of these into the public sector. Simultaneously, economic difficulties (and the imposition of International Monetary Fund [IMF] controls on public expenditure) have led to a proposed cancellation of all state concessions to purchasers.

Both Greece and Italy have traditionally had very low levels of publicly financed housing. In Greece, the amount of housing provided by the publicly financed Workers' Housing Association (AOEK) is negligible, but the state intervenes in housing provision in other indirect ways. For example, public-sector employees are eligible for short-term low-interest loans and the state matches hard currency remitted by Greeks working abroad, which undoubtedly finds its way into house building. There are now proposals to set up a social housing organization funded by the National Bank of Greece, a move probably partly inspired by the state's desire to reduce the level of private house building.

In Italy, for much of the 1970s, the state became increasingly involved in housing finance: The proportion of wholly privately financed house building fell from about 94 to 80 percent of output between 1970 and 1978, following the housing protests of the late 1960s and the increased role of local authorities in housing provision (see Barlow and Dickens 1984). But this development appears to have been relatively short-lived and there has been an upturn in private-sector output since the late 1970s. State intervention took the form of total subsidies aimed at particular social groups and partial subsidies for house building, comprising grants to agencies specifically set up for public house building (Padovani 1984). More recently, there has been a growth in state support for owner occupation, coupled with sales of public housing, but the extent to which home ownership can be promoted is limited because of restrictions on the total number of loans available (Folin 1985). In practice, then, most housing finance originates from personal savings. Banks make short-term loans and special credit institutions (SCIs) provide longer-term mortgages, but the distinctive feature of the system is the small size of total institutional finance.

In all these countries, therefore, there have been significant changes in the way the state intervenes in housing provision. Some have argued that this can be summarized as a "recommodification" (for example, Harloe 1981), but we believe that this is an unhelpful, oversimple term for what is in fact an extremely complex phenomenon. Recommodification seems to have a different meaning in each country. In Britain, France, and West Germany the tendency has been for a general withdrawal of direct state support for production (for whatever tenure). The opposite has been true of Portugal and Sweden. Leaving Greece and Italy aside, it is also true that owner occupation has grown (Martens 1985) and has been increasingly subsidized in all these countries. This has generally been through some form of consumption support (usually tax relief on mortgage interest payments), although France has yet to introduce such a system and relies largely on production subsidies. The growth of consumption support for owner occupation has often tended to be at the expense of social housing benefits, although in Sweden mortgage tax relief tends to be slightly progressive in its wealth redistributive effects. Even if we conclude that there has been a trend toward the "privatization of consumption" in Sweden, it must be stressed that this has occurred "within the context of essentially *un*changed relationships in the production of housing" (Dickens et al. 1985, 141).

WHY HAS HOUSE BUILDING DECLINED?

Why has the level of new house building fallen in nearly all these countries during the 1970s and 1980s?

In Britain some of the explanation lies in the continuous decrease in investment in the local authority house building program. This started in 1976, when the Labour administration was forced to cut public spending following the IMF loan in 1976/77. Investment in speculative production, about 40 percent of new production during the mid–1970s, has remained relatively constant in real terms apart from the 1970–74 boom years. This has not, however, meant that more speculative housing has actually been built—there has been a long-term decline in output since the mid–1960s, which Ball (1983) argues is the result of decreasing profitability.

Decreasing public expenditure on house building also lies behind the decline in Sweden. This was partly the result of ending the "million program" of massive public investment in house building in the mid–1970s (see Dickens et al. 1985), which led to a considerable drop in the overall number of completions. But unlike Britain, where there is massive unsatisfied demand both from households living in substandard accommodation and from the increasing *number* of households, in Sweden demographic demand is seen to be satisfied (Swedish Ministry of Housing 1985/86 Budget Statement).

The situation in France is less clear. From 1973 to 1979 the vast real increase in production expenditure was not matched by new output. At least some of the explanation for the rapid rise in production expenditure lies in the lack of productivity in the building industry and the inflation of construction costs during the early 1970s (Boyer 1985). The FNPC (Fédération Nationale de Promoteurs-Constructeurs) argues that the Mitterrand government's introduction of value-added tax (VAT) on construction work and a wealth tax are also contributory factors. although the collapse in new building began long before 1981. For much of this period a growing proportion of this was unsubsidized production, financed on the capital market, although this situation has been reversed since 1979. It is clear, therefore, that at least some of this finance is either failing to emerge as new construction or is being translated into larger or higher standard dwellings. We will return to this later.

In West Germany the explanation for the decline can only partly be explained by major shifts in public or private investment policy. Undoubtedly, there has been a drop in effective demand for new housing: There have been considerable changes to the demographic structure, with an overall drop in population and new household formation. The Ministry of Housing also cites the slowdown in the growth of real personal incomes together with the rise in building costs, coupled with the youth of the housing stock, as underlying factors. The sustained growth in the proportion of repairs and maintenance within total housing construction output is clearly one manifestation of this. In fact, by 1985 there was considerable overproduction of new housing: The ZDB (Zentralverband des Deutschen Baugewerbes), representing small building firms, argued that there are as many as 250,000 unsold or unlet newly built units. At least some of these are the result of an increase in speculative building using tax concessions under the *Bauherrenmodell* scheme. This has been an increasingly important sector since the early 1980s and today comprises about 15 percent of annual output. Some of this increase seems to have been produced by the large cash-rich construction companies moving into house building because of cutbacks in the amount of foreign and domestic contracting work, although this is regarded as very much a last-resort strategy in the absence of other work.

Under the Greek self-promotion system the rate of new building is directly linked to the level of remittances and bank credit. Nevertheless, it appears that this mode of housing provision is now reaching some form of limit and there has been reduction in both building for self-consumption and for speculative investment. The explanation for lower levels of owner-building probably lies in rising land and construction costs, together with the decline in the intergenerational transmission of land (which was the key to this method of provision) as controls over subdivision of plots are imposed, and the decline in the flow of remittances. Speculative production has been hit by the rise in costs and recent limitations by the state on sales prices, although this has partly been overcome by the trend toward the intensification of building on each plot.

Rising costs seem to have had the opposite effect in Italy, where the lack of social housing and price inflation in the capitalist housing sector appear to have combined to produce an increase in self-built housing. This has now spread to areas with no tradition of this form of provision.

COMPARING INPUTS AND OUTPUTS

From this review we can conclude that the general decline in housing output appears to be due to factors that are very specific to each country. However, a feature common to many of these countries is a general rise in the level of expenditure (in real terms) on production over the same period. The general picture seems to be that in France (from 1970 to 1980, at least), Britain (especially during the early 1970s boom), West Germany (until 1978), Sweden (1974 to 1981), and Portugal (since 1974) a gap seems to have opened between the level of expenditure on new housing production and the level of housing completions. Why, in most of these widely disparate systems, has this occurred?

One explanation might be that the increase in financial input has led to better *quality*, rather than more, housing. It is, of course, impossible to produce an accurate index of housing quality. While recognizing its limitations, we have tried to use the average size of dwelling as a surrogate for quality (taking into account the variations in the proportion of apartments in the overall number of completions). In West Germany and Sweden there does not appear to have been any change in size standards—the average size of dwelling varies in direct relation with the proportion of multifamily dwellings (MFD) being completed. The situation in Greece and Portugal seems to be improving, with the average size of dwellings up by some 35 percent in Greece and a fall in the level of MFD construction. In Britain, despite a decrease in MFD construction, size standards have been generally declining (BSA 1984). In France, size standards have generally remained static since the early 1970s so the increasing amount of production expenditure does not appear to be have been translated into either more completions or better and larger housing.

Where, then, is this input finance flowing if it is not producing commensurate amounts of new, or larger, dwellings? At what stages in the development process are profits being made? It is to this issue that we now wish to turn.

THE ORGANIZATION OF HOUSING PROVISION

From a public policy point of view, more spending on housing should produce more and/or better housing. However, from the point of view of the various capitalist agents, namely promoters, landowners, builders, and financial institutions involved in housing provision, more spending usually means greater and more varied opportunities for capital accumulation at various points in the complex process of housing production. The actual ways capital accumulation will occur depend on the nature of the housing provision system in each country— that is, the way the relations between the different agents coalesce. The shape of the relations will vary from country to country. The organization of state regulation of provision differs considerably by country, and specific agents (such as multipurpose construction conglomerates) can also be involved at several points in the provision chain. These agents themselves can be associated in a number of ways—for example, banks can be strongly linked with building capital or some types of promoter with builders or finance capital. A preliminary description of these relations was outlined in Barlow and Dickens (1984).

This approach has helped us to identify some of the reasons for the differences between changes in money input and changes in housing output. Some of the ways in which profits can be made through housing provision systems are listed below, together with some empirical examples.

Debt Servicing

Not all money entering the promotion stage (that is, public subsidies plus money from the capital market) goes further along the chain in the form of either investment committed to housing production or to the intensification of the production process. A proportion of it goes back to the lenders in the form of capital repayments and interest on existing loans or as dividends. The balance of these two forms of payment depends on the gearing ratio of the outstanding debt (that is, the ratio of loan capital to share capital). The higher the gearing, the greater the proportion taken as interest and thus the greater the sensitivity both to recent movements (mostly upward) in interest rates and to any tendency toward the contraction of the loan repayment periods. Of course, self-building systems such as those in Italy, Greece, and Portugal are less influenced by debt servicing problems. In this case the ability to initiate construction and acquire materials depends much more on personal cash flow.

Topalov (1985) emphasizes debt servicing problems as an explanation for the mid–1970s collapse in French house building. The combination of increased short-term loans to developers at higher rates of interest and restrained growth in house prices (as the cost of mortgages rose) eventually led to a collapse in new private-sector house building. Similar problems now appear to be facing the small house builders in West Germany who tend to be highly geared and therefore more susceptible to rising interest rates. This sector of the industry has recently been facing competition from large contractors who have more internal resources and thus are less dependent on finance from the capital market. Consequently, they have been able to move into house building relatively easily.

Intuitively it seems quite possible (although we have not carried out any analysis) that at least some of the explanation for the input/output gaps lies in the increased cost of borrowing as real interest rates grew in the late 1970s.

Capitalization Expenditure

In situations where the private house building industry is important in promoting new construction (such as Britain), the ratio of investment in production to investment in capital intensification is significant. The higher the ratio, the greater the likely *short-term* effect of increased spending. But the lower the ratio the greater the gain in productivity and thus the potential of the industry in the long term to turn money invested into housing produced.

Land Prices

In some countries a sizable proportion of investment is given over to the acquisition of development land. The price levels set by the vendors of building land will depend partly on the structure of ownership and the strength and coherence of the landowners and partly on the taxation system. While reliable data on land prices are extremely hard to obtain, it certainly appears that in West Germany, Britain, and for certain forms of housing provision in France there has been a considerable real price increase. One implication for countries with largely private ownership of development land and few or no price controls on land sales is that public authorities seeking to carry out building programs have to compete for land in a market that is, arguably, inflated by other forms of state action (for example, state spending to stimulate demand). Another factor elevating land prices is likely to be the rate and efficiency of the collection of any land development taxes as vendors seek to offset their liability by holding out for higher prices. In Britain this was certainly the case during the 1970s: average plot prices as a proportion of new house prices are today about 80 percent higher than in 1970, and in some areas they have now reached a level such that house builders are reconciled to bidding a price for new sites that may represent 40 percent or more of the value realized by the sale of the completed dwelling. This situation also applied in the early and mid–1970s, a period when production expenditure increased considerably faster than new output.

Development Land Tax has now been abolished in the United Kingdom, without any sign of a fall in the price of development land in many areas. In West Germany, developers argue that the imposition of purchase tax and an infrastructure levy have caused more problems than the considerable rise in land prices. In Sweden, however, land prices have remained at a constantly negligible 1 to 2 percent of new house prices (although in 1982/83 real land prices were 37 percent higher than 1970). In France the land cost element of final house prices has been increasing for single-family housing and particularly for unaided self-promoted building. For the latter, land costs increased from 22 to 29 percent between 1970 and 1982. In contrast, for unaided MFD construction this figure fell from 20 to 14 percent (1973–82). Overall, there does seem to have been a long-term stabilization of land prices since the mid–1960s, following a period of rapid inflation fueled by increases in development profits (Topalov 1985).

Another route by which profit can be taken out of land is through land trading, before construction occurs. In France and West Germany the structure of taxation and zoning control seems to have reduced the potential for this form of speculation. In Sweden virtually all development land is de facto publicly owned, thereby preempting the potential for such profits. In less-well-regulated systems, land trading profit can be made by successfully dealing in potential building land (whether zoned and/or serviced or not) *subsequent* to the sale by the original vendor and *before* construction occurs. In Britain this has happened when liquidated house building companies owning substantial land banks are acquired cheaply or, more generally, when sites acquired in loose control periods attract a greater premium as the rate of land release in Structure Plans tightens up again.

Materials Prices

A proportion of investment money needs to be spent on building materials. The size of this proportion depends to some extent on the degree of oligopoly in the materials supply industry. How have materials prices changed during the 1970s and early 1980s? In Britain and Sweden there has been a considerable real increase in this index, while in France, Greece, and West Germany there has been little or no growth, although Topalov (1985) argues that the sharp increase in construction costs in the early 1970s in France was largely the result of higher materials prices. Clearly lack of demand has stabilized materials prices during recent years in France and West Germany, but despite these conditions in Britain, there has been some materials price inflation. This cannot be entirely explained by the presence of oligopolistic supply conditions, for these are in existence to some extent in all these countries. Sweden, however, must be contrasted with the other countries as its materials industry is monopolistic but, unlike the others, increasingly *integrated* with the building companies (Dickens et al. 1985; Anas et al. 1985).

Labor Costs

In the countries analyzed there is considerable variation in the extent to which building labor is organized. This works in two ways. There may be high or low degrees of unionization, and labor may be permanently employed or organized in a labor-only subcontracting system. Both these systems may theoretically affect the price of labor. It is interesting, though, that in Sweden, West Germany, and Greece building workers' wages have been decreasing in real terms, despite the degree of unionization in the former two countries and their historic political strength in Greece (Barlow and Dickens 1984). In West Germany this is presumably the result of heavy unemployment and short-time working. In France the level of *travail précaire*, that is, short-term contracts, "lump labor," and new work practices (for example, task-and-finish) has risen to the extent that 70 percent of building workers are now employed under such conditions (Tallard and Oeconomo 1983). In Britain, where the lump is increasingly prevalent, earnings for those workers still in work appear to have risen during the late 1970s-early 1980s, although they still remain below the national average. In Sweden there has been a decline in construction workers' earnings owing to two factors. First, the national union policy of solidarity wages, aimed at equalizing intersectoral and interregional differences, has reduced the differential between the construction and other sectors (from about 30 to 15 percent above average). Second, a certain amount of deskilling has occurred as new production techniques have been introduced (Dickens et al. 1985).

Taken as a whole, the evidence does not seem to indicate that the gap between resource input and housing output is primarily the consequence of increased labor costs.

Allocation Profits

Profits can also arise in the market allocation process. These take the form of both an agent's premium on the turnover of properties (whether this is received by the promoter, constructor, or a specialist agent depends on the particular system in question) and of "own account" profits in certain conditions of the speculative market. In systems with a high degree of self-promotion such as Greece, West Germany, and, increasingly, France, there is no initial sale to be handled and no agent's profit arises. The reverse applies in Britain where a combination of very little self-promotion and an agents' cartel ensures that cumbersome and expensive processes are a necessary part of property transactions. This absorbs a proportion of the money devoted to demand stimulation. In this context it is also relevant that the ratio of second-hand to new housing transactions varies very considerably. This is 6:1 in Britain; 0.5:1 in West Germany; 1:1 in France (see BIPE 1984).

What can we conclude from this discussion about the flow of finance for house building through the housing production system? Obviously, whether or not public and private finance committed to house building is actually turned into new dwellings depends on the circumstances specific to a particular system. There is nothing new or surprising about this thought. Housing provision is not a precise, or readily controllable, process. It is, rather, a complex, varied, and inviting field for capital accumulation. The way accumulation actually takes place in each system depends on its organization and on the relative strength of the various interests involved in housing provision. We have sought here to identify as clearly as possible the variety of potential accumulation possibilities and then, by comparing different housing systems, to identify the ways that accumulation seems to occur.

REDISTRIBUTIVE EFFECTS

Politically, it is important to examine the evolution of housing support not just in terms of changes in policy and legislative patterns, but crucially in terms of the progressive or regressive effects they may be having both on the differentials in *access* to acceptable housing and in the long-term *wealth redistributive* effects they produce. While it may well be reasonable to anticipate that a general move toward more market-oriented provision will be accompanied by an increase in housing inequality, the former is only one way in which the latter might occur.

An *increased* level of state intervention can just as surely produce greater inequalities if the intervention has a generally regressive effect. This is undoubtedly
the case with owner-occupier subsidies in the United Kingdom, which have
formed an increasingly important element in state intervention in recent years.
To focus attention primarily on the public/private balance of activity may in fact
draw attention away from the ultimately crucial political point: the net welfare
and wealth redistributive effects of the *total package* of support arrangements.

Marcuse (1982) focuses clearly on this point. He cites evidence from the West
German Federal Ministry of Housing to show that in 1979 households earning
less than 1,600 DM per month (67.8 percent of all households) received a
disproportionately small percentage (51.3 percent) of total government housing
benefits. One of the reasons for this imbalance was probably that tax benefits
as a percentage of all housing benefits went up from 19.8 to 29.6 percent between
1965 and 1980, while social housing subsidies fell 53.2 to 32.1 percent. From
this example it is clear that the net effect of subsidies can change in a progressive
or regressive direction without major shifts occurring in the *pattern* of housing
support, but rather as a result of changes in the financial weight given to each
element in the pattern.

The net redistributional situation in Sweden appears to be considerably different. In 1984/85, total housing subsidies amounted to some 28 billion kronor.
Of this, about 7 billion took the form of interest payment subsidies for new
construction or rehabilitation, and another 7 billion was allocated to owners and
renters alike on the basis of need. Tax relief on mortgages amounted to some
11.2 billion kronor and the rest took the form of other production subsidies. The
combined effect appears to be slightly progressive, but this has perhaps more to
do with the *balance of uses to which the total sum is put* than with the pub-
lic/private balance of funding, promotion, or allocation.

CONCLUSIONS

Two points should be made. First, in light of the complexity revealed by such
comparative analysis it should be stressed that blanket notions such as "com-
modification" need very close examination and cannot be used uncritically. It
is not a question of the balance between private and public finance. Such a
description is often applied only to the *source* of finance—it fails to take into
account the way in which it is channeled and applied. The ratio of private to
public finance is *not* the same thing as a market/social balance of housing *output*
and/or access to that output.

But this is perhaps a red herring. After all, the whole notion of a neat separation
between the private and public sectors of advanced capitalist economies is questionable. Private- and public-sector bodies making investment decisions are simply using previously accumulated money capital and processing personal savings
and tax revenue. What is more important are the *criteria* upon which such bodies
make their decisions—what are the accumulation strategies of privately owned

firms? What are the origins of particular state policies and who had a hand in forming them? What are they aiming to achieve? How precise are their objectives? Are the overall effects of support programs progressive or regressive?

The second point is that the cost of providing housing appears to have grown substantially in most of the countries examined. What are the implications of this? Whether or not increased expenditure actually constitutes a housing problem depends very much on the extent to which housing conditions are improving, an issue too complex to deal with in this chapter. Nevertheless, it does seem that the structure of particular housing provision systems in many countries is such that the stages in the development process provide considerable opportunities for accumulation by the various agents involved. The analytical problem, in the end, is not solely a question of how money leaks from the housing provision system; rather it is to identify as accurately as possible how provision systems actually operate. From the point of view of formulating effective and cost-efficient new housing policies, this sort of understanding is crucial.

NOTES

1. This chapter is based on work carried out during 1984–85 on an exploratory study of seven West European housing systems funded by the Economic and Social Research Council. The research was undertaken by Peter Ambrose, James Barlow, and Peter Dickens. A fuller version of this chapter appears in Ambrose and Barlow (1986a).

2. Details of calculations and sources for all estimates of production and consumption expenditure are elaborated in Ambrose and Barlow (1986a).

REFERENCES

Ambrose, P., and Barlow, J.
1986a "Housing Provision and Housebuilding in Western Europe: Increasing Expenditure, Decreasing Output?" *University of Sussex Urban and Regional Studies Working Paper*, No. 50.
1986b "Alternative Systems and Changing Needs: The "Effectiveness" of European Approaches to Housing Provision." Paper presented at the International Housing Conference, Gävle, Sweden, June.
Anas A., U. Jirlow, J. Gustaffsen, B. Hårsman, and F. Snickars
1985 "The Swedish Housing Market: Structure, Policy and Issues." *Scandinavian Housing and Planning Research* 2, no. 3–4, 169–87.
Ball, M.
1983 *Housing Policy and Economic Power: The Political Economy of Owner Occupation*. London: Methuen.
Barlow, J. and Dickens, P.
1984 "Housing Alliances and Housing Provision in Western Europe." *University of Sussex Urban and Regional Studies Working Paper*, No. 42.
Boyer, R.
1985 "Productivité et Emploi dans le BTP." In *Habitat 88: Emploi et productivité dans*

le bâtiment. Appel de propositions de recherches et d'expérimentations. Paris: Plan Construction et Habitat.

Building Societies Association (BSA)

1984   *BSA Bulletin 39.* London: BSA.

Bureau d'Informations et de Prévision Economiques (BIPE)

1984   *Le Financement du Logement et la Fluidité du Marché Immobilier. Un Essai de Comparison Internationale.* Paris: BIPE.

Dickens, P., S. Duncan, M. Goodwin, and F. Gray

1985   *Housing, States and Localities.* London: Methuen.

Folin, M.

1985   Unpublished paper presented at Conference of Socialist Economists Housing Workshop, London, January 19.

Harloe, M.

1981   "The Recommodification of Housing." In *City, Class and Capital,* edited by M. Harloe and E. Lebas. London: Edward Arnold.

Marcuse, P.

1982   "Determinants of State Housing Policy: West Germany and the United States." In *Urban Policy Under Capitalism,* S. Fainstein and N. Fainstein. Beverly Hills, Calif: Sage.

Martens, M.

1985   "Owner Occupied Housing in Europe: Post-war Developments and Current Dilemmas." *Environment and Planning A* 17, no. 5, 605–24.

Padovani, L.

1984   "Italy." In *Housing in Europe,* edited by M. Wynn. London: Croom Helm.

Petzinger, R., and M. Riege

1981   *Die Neue Wohnungnot. Das Wohnungswunder Bundesrepublik.* Hamburg: VSA-Verlag.

Robinson, R.

1986   "Restructuring the Welfare State: An Analysis of Public Expenditure 1979/80 to 1984/85." *Journal of Social Policy* 15, no. 1, 1–21.

Tallard, M. and H. Oeconomo

1983   *Travail Précaire et Politiques de Gestion de la Main-d'Oeuvre dans le BTP.* Paris: Centre de Recherche pour l'Etude et l'Observation des Conditions de Vie.

Topalov, C.

1985   "Prices, Profits and Rents in Residential Development: France 1961–1980." In *Land Rent, Housing and Urban Policy: A European Perspective,* edited by M. Ball, V. Bentivegna, M. Edwards, and M. Folin. London: Croom Helm.

PART IV

DEVELOPMENTS IN HOUSING TENURE

8

Fiscal Austerity and the Expansion of Home Ownership in the United Kingdom

MICHAEL C. FLEMING AND JOSEPH G. NELLIS

Abstract. This chapter addresses the problems involved in executing in current economic conditions the policy of expanding home ownership in the United Kingdom beyond the existing high levels. It is concerned with the process by which the expansion may be brought about and the characteristics of the households involved. The flow of new entrants to owner occupation in 1983 was studied in order to determine their social, economic, and other characteristics. Particular attention is paid to social class differences, the evaluation of housing choice, and financial factors pertaining to house purchase. Comparisons are made with other buyers.

INTRODUCTION

During the twentieth century, housing tenure in Britain has changed dramatically. Between 1914 and 1983, the owner-occupied proportion of the housing stock has risen from 10 percent to 60 percent while the privately rented sector has declined from 90 percent to around 10 percent, with the balance of around 30 percent in 1983 represented by public-sector rented accommodation (BSA 1983; DOE 1984).[1] The promotion of home ownership has been a policy goal of successive British governments regardless of political persuasion, though particularly of Conservative governments. Currently, it has become the primary goal of housing policy.

The current high level of owner occupation raises fundamental questions as to how the policy of further expansion is to be achieved in practice.[2] The policy also begs several other questions: For which households is a switch from renting to owning feasible? What are the financial implications for mortgage borrowers? Are there lessons for the housing construction industry? These questions provide the immediate stimulus for the work reported here. The aim of this study is to extend and develop our knowledge of the processes at work in the U.K. housing market, and thereby to clarify some of the practical implications of current housing policy.

A major difference between the approach adopted here and that taken in previous studies of the housing market concerns the distinction between the *stock* of existing households and the *flow* of new households. Studies of tenurial change have generally been cross-sectional studies of the stock of households at different points in time, with little or no information about flows. We focus on the flow of new entrants into owner occupation (that is, those becoming owner occupiers for the first time). Central to the analysis is the breakdown of this flow according to social class. This is important because there are marked social differences in housing tenure. We report only results related to the United Kingdom as a whole but it should be appreciated that considerable differences exist at the local level.

Next, we provide a brief profile of the social stratification and other characteristics of existing households according to tenure. Its purpose is to provide a background picture of the ''stock'' situation from which the flows that we analyze originate. The empirical analysis examines (1) the characteristics of new entrants to the housing market in 1983; (2) the relationship between housing choice, housing attributes, and social class; and (3) financial aspects of expanding owner occupation. In a concluding section we bring together the key points of the analysis and comment on the wider debate about the wisdom of a policy of expanding home ownership at the expense of other forms of tenure.

STOCK OF HOUSEHOLDS: SOCIAL STRATIFICATION OF TENURE

Figure 8.1 shows the ''stock'' of households in 1982 according to socioeconomic group and tenure. Clearly, there is a marked social stratification: owner occupation is the predominant form of tenure at the top of the social class scale (that is, professional and nonmanual occupational groups), while renting (both public and private) is predominant at the bottom of the scale (that is, manual workers). At the same time, however, a notable proportion of the skilled manual group is to be found in both tenure categories. The figure also highlights that council house[3] renting increases as one moves down the social class scale, with about two-thirds of unskilled manual workers and about half of those in semi-skilled occupations living in this form of accommodation. About three-quarters of all households living in rented accommodation are public-sector tenants.

Therefore, it follows that the most important source of recruitment for the future expansion of owner occupation is that group of households currently living in rented accommodation and who are in nonmanual or skilled manual occupations. This group constitutes about 15 percent of total households and 42 percent of those in the rented sector alone. Two-thirds of the group are in the skilled manual rather than nonmanual class.

PROFILE OF NEW ENTRANTS

We turn now to the characteristics of new entrants to the housing market, broken down by social class, including comparisons with other buyers where

Figure 8.1
Stock Situation: Social Stratification of Tenure, 1982

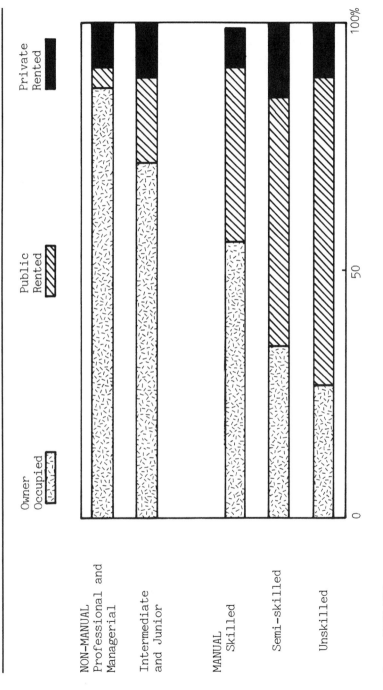

Source: OPCS 1984.

appropriate. An exceptionally large data base is used covering all the house-purchase transactions (over 153,000 after editing)[4] for which the Halifax Building Society[5] made an offer of an advance on mortgage in 1983. This society is the largest building society in the United Kingdom and has good national coverage (Fleming and Nellis 1985b). Almost 40 percent of the total data base involved first-time buyers (that is, new entrants), while the remainder had been former owner occupiers.

The social class grading system used is similar but not identical to that employed for the official statistics (as in Figure 8.1).[6] It is based on a classification of "social grades" used for many market research purposes in the United Kingdom, and groups people into one of six classes on the basis of occupation. Figure 8.2 shows a breakdown of social class, according to this classification, for first-time buyers (FTBs) and former owner occupiers (FOOs).[7]

The Social Classification of New Entrants in 1983

The class distribution of the new entrants splits very evenly between the nonmanual and manual groups. More than 75 percent are drawn from the skilled or lower nonmanual and skilled manual categories. In contrast, two-thirds of other buyers (former owner occupiers) fall within the higher social classes A, B, and C1.

Previous Tenure and Social Class of New Entrants

With regard to the previous tenure of new entrants, an important distinction needs to be drawn between those who are simply new entrants to owner occupation from other tenures and those who are also completely new households entering the housing market for the first time. Half the new entrants in our sample are drawn from the latter category—shown as "living with relatives" in Table 8.1. Of the other new entrants, twice as many are drawn from the private rented sector as from the public rented sector.[8]

Cross-classification of the origin of new entrants by social class is revealing. There is a clear pattern showing that a markedly higher proportion of the new entrants are new households as one moves down the social scale (Table 8.1). Also, the share of the public sector is invariably related to social class. By contrast, those entering from the private rented sector come predominantly from the higher social classes. This is an interesting finding, particularly when coupled with the fact that the average age of new-entrant buyers declines also as one moves down the social scale. The latter may be associated with career progression patterns (that is, because of the time lags involved in reaching higher occupational classes). But it is consistent too with the proposition that the route to higher social classes may require a greater geographical mobility, and that this is facilitated by renting rather than owning accommodation in the early years.

Comparison of the origin of the new entrants by tenure with the stock of

Figure 8.2
Social Classification of House Buyers (Percentage)

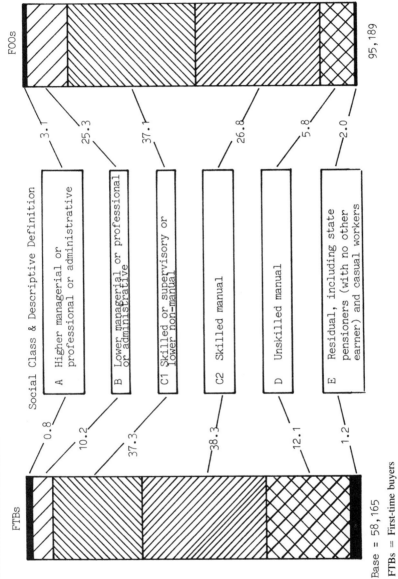

FOOs

95,189

FTBs

| 3.1 |
| 25.3 |
| 37.1 |
| 26.8 |
| 5.8 |
| 2.0 |

Social Class & Descriptive Definition

A Higher managerial or professional or administrative

B Lower managerial or professional or administrative

C1 Skilled or supervisory or lower non-manual

C2 Skilled manual

D Unskilled manual

E Residual, including state pensioners (with no other earner) and casual workers

| 0.8 |
| 10.2 |
| 37.3 |
| 38.3 |
| 12.1 |
| 1.2 |

Base = 58,165

FTBs = First-time buyers
FOOs = Former owner occupiers

Source: Data compiled by the authors.

Table 8.1
Previous Tenure and Social Class of New Entrants (Percentage)

Social Class	Living with Relatives	Private	Rented — Local Authorities & Housing Associations	Other (incl. Rented from Employer)
A	29%	36%	10%	25%
B	35	35	11	18
C1	48	28	11	13
C2	61	17	15	7
D	64	15	17	5
ALL	54	23	13	11

Source: Data compiled by the authors.

households in different tenures is also revealing with regard to the nature of the changes taking place in the structure of the British housing market. Of the stock of *rented* tenures in 1982 held by *economically active* heads of household, three-quarters were local authority tenures (Figure 8.1). But the proportion of new entrants from this sector (excluding subsidized council-house sales) is little more than one-quarter of total entrants from the rented sector as a whole and only about one-half when subsidized council house sales are included. Given the social stratification in these tenures, the flow figures support the fears that are now expressed by several commentators about the process of "polarization" in the U.K. housing market: that is, as the privately rented sector declines in size it is feared that British housing will become polarized between the owner occupied and local authority rented sectors (Hamnett 1984).

Age, Marital Status, Dependent Children, and Social Class

The economic capacity to enter the owner-occupied market is likely to depend on age and social class. Accommodation needs and preferences are also likely to be related to these factors as well as marital status and the number of dependent children.

Age. In each social class new entrants to the U.K. housing market are younger than former owner occupiers, with a mean age of 28 years as against 35.6 years.[9] For *both* groups age increases as class increases.

Marital Status and Dependent Children. Among new entrants only one-third are married compared with four-fifths of former owner occupiers. The proportion of married new entrants tends to be higher among social classes A and B. The mean number of dependent children is lower for new entrants (0.3) than other buyers (1.1). In both groups it is highest among social class A buyers but otherwise it varies little.

HOUSING CHOICE, HOUSING ATTRIBUTES, AND SOCIAL CLASS

Housing choice is determined by an amalgam of factors relating to personal preferences, income, wealth, and family circumstances.[10] Here we are only able to consider choices expressed in terms of the attributes of the houses actually bought. In this section, we examine the relationships between buyer type (FTB or FOO), social class, and the characteristics of the houses purchased in order to shed some light on the possible housing supply implications of the further expansion of home ownership. Details relating to three particular house characteristics—type, size, and age—are presented in Tables 8.2 and 8.3.

House Type

The distribution of choices according to buyer type and social class is shown in Table 8.2. There are some striking differences. Over 40 percent of new entrants buy terraced houses as against 17 percent of other buyers. Only 5 percent of new entrants buy detached houses as against 32 percent of former owner occupiers. This is to be explained in terms of income differences, since detached houses tend to be the most expensive properties and terraced houses the least expensive. The difference in purchasing patterns by buyer type remains pronounced for each social class but becomes less marked as one moves up the scale of social classes with a marked switch in preferences toward detached houses. More than half of class A borrowers buy houses of this type. It is obvious that increasing penetration of the lower social classes into owner occupation will put pressure on particular sectors of the housing market in terms of property types, and it has obvious implications for house builders in meeting demand from new buyers at the lower end of the scale at a price they can afford.

Size of House

Two measures of house size are used: number of habitable rooms and number of bedrooms (Table 8.3). Again, the differences by buyer type and social class

Table 8.2
Housing Choice: Type of House

	FTBs					All FTBs	All FOOs
	SOCIAL CLASS						
Dwelling Type	A	B	C1	C2	D		
Detached House	18.8	11.6	5.5	3.4	2.3	5.0	32.2
Semi-det House	25.4	28.9	29.9	31.8	27.6	30.2	33.2
Terraced House	24.5	28.8	36.7	45.8	56.6	41.8	16.8
Bungalow	7.6	8.0	6.1	6.2	4.4	6.2	13.2
Flat	23.7	22.7	21.8	12.8	9.1	16.9	4.6

Source: Data compiled by the authors.

are pronounced and consistent. New entrants buy smaller houses than other buyers: on average 4.7 as against 5.8 habitable rooms and 2.5 as against 3.1 bedrooms. For both buyer types, mean house sizes increase as one moves up the scale of social classes and the differential by buyer type tends to increase.

Age of House

New entrants, on average, buy older houses than other buyers. This is a general pattern across the social classes. This notable age difference is probably explicable by the fact that new entrants concentrate their purchases on terraced houses and these tend to be the oldest and cheapest properties. However, the relationship between age and house price is not a consistently inverse relationship. Many old houses command a substantial premium over their modern counterparts in the United Kingdom. Table 8.3 shows that there is a tendency for the higher social classes (particularly Class A) to buy older houses—this is especially marked in the case of former owner occupiers. In these cases, incomes are higher and prices are higher too.

Table 8.3
Housing Choice: Size and Age of House

Social Class	Size of House				Average Age of House (years)	
	Habitable Rooms (mean number)		Bedrooms (mean number)			
	FTBs	FOOs	FTBs	FOOs	FTBs	FOOs
A	5.3	7.0	2.8	3.7	51.1	53.6
B	4.9	6.2	2.6	3.4	46.2	41.5
C1	4.7	5.7	2.4	3.1	44.9	36.9
C2	4.7	5.4	2.5	2.9	46.8	35.6
D	4.8	5.2	2.5	2.8	53.8	39.5
ALL	4.7	5.8	2.5	3.1	47.0	38.5

Source: Data compiled by the authors.

FINANCIAL ASPECTS OF EXPANDING OWNER OCCUPATION

We turn finally to the financial aspects of the house-purchase transactions of new entrants in 1983 according to social class. Since all of the transactions studied in this investigation represent "effective" demand (that is, where the desire to purchase has been backed up by the ability to pay and success in obtaining loan finance), all buyers are by definition *intramarginal*. The ability of households living in rented accommodation to enter the owner-occupied sector largely depends upon the relative movement of real incomes as against house prices and mortgage interest rates. In particular, the further expansion of home ownership depends upon the way these factors impinge upon that group of households and potential households who are not currently owner occupiers but wish to become so and, further, on whether any steps can be taken to bring submarginal households into the intramarginal category. The largest sectors of the household population that are not currently owner occupiers are those in the lower social classes. Among these classes the financial problems confronting house purchase are particularly severe, if not insurmountable, at least under current financial arrangements.

House Prices and Social Class

There are very considerable differences in house prices according to social class and buyer type. The mean price paid by new entrants (FTBs) is £14,000 (or 40 percent) less than that paid by other buyers (FOOs). Mean price rises as one moves up the social class scale and the differential by buyer type consistently increases. Class A new entrants pay more than twice as much as those in Class D: £36,229 as against £17,471.

The price comparisons made above are based on *simple* average prices for each category of buyer. Although comparisons on this basis are informative, their interpretation raises a problem because the differentials reflect not only the influence of social class preferences as such, but also differences in the mix of house types and their various other attributes.[11] To bring out the influence of social class we employ regression analysis, holding the influence of other factors on price constant. The results allow us to compute "standardized" price differentials (for technical details, see Fleming and Nellis 1984, 1985b).

Standardization has the consistent effect of reducing the magnitude of the price differentials between classes, regardless of FTB or FOO status. However, the remaining differences are still substantial (Figure 8.3). Thus, new-entrant buyers in Class D buy houses at prices 31 percent less than those bought by Class A buyers as against a difference of 52 percent on a nonstandardized basis. The corresponding figures for existing owner occupiers are 34 and 61 percent. Broadly speaking, all buyers (both FTBs and FOOs) in Class B buy at 10 percent less than those in Class A, Class C1 at approximately 20 percent less, those in Class C2 at about 25 percent less, and those in Class D at about 33 percent less.

Incomes and Social Class

The average income of new entrants is much less than that for other buyers: £7,707 as against £10,125. In each group income rises very considerably with social class, with a two-to-one difference between Class A and Class D buyers.

Financial Ratios: Prices, Incomes, and Advances

Table 8.4 shows ratios between the three financial variables of house prices, incomes, and mortgage advances. For each of the three ratios, new entrants differ markedly from former owner occupiers. In particular:

1. New entrants buy houses priced, on average, at three times their income, compared with a ratio of 3.8 for former owner occupiers.

Figure 8.3
House Price Differentials by Social Class (Standardized [S] and Nonstandardized [N/S])

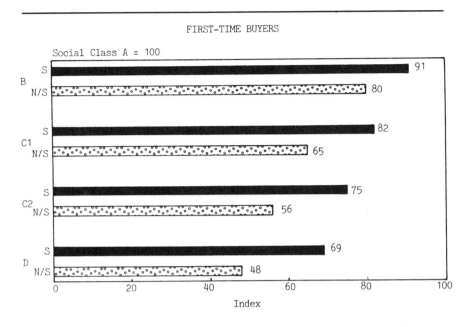

FIRST-TIME BUYERS

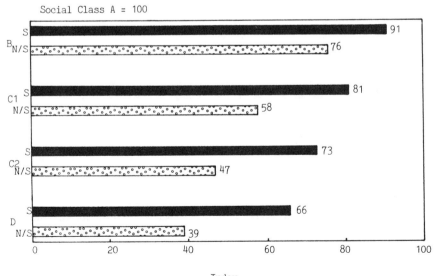

FORMER OWNER OCCUPIERS

Source: Data compiled by the authors.

Table 8.4
Financial Ratios

Ratio	Buyer	Social Class					
	Type	A	B	C1	C2	D	ALL
Price/ Income	FTB	2.82	2.95	3.11	2.98	2.95	3.04
	FOO	3.59	3.70	3.81	3.73	3.88	3.81
Advance/ Price	FTB	0.81	0.83	0.86	0.87	0.87	0.86
	FOO	0.55	0.59	0.62	0.62	0.62	0.61
Advance/ Income	FTB	2.21	2.40	2.61	2.53	2.48	2.54
	FOO	1.85	2.06	2.24	2.18	2.16	2.16

Source: Data compiled by the authors.

2. Despite the difference in price-to-income ratios, new entrants require a much *larger* proportionate advance than former owner occupiers: 86 percent of the purchase price as against 61 percent in the case of the latter.
3. The above patterns are reflected in the advance-to-income ratios: New entrants require advances of two and a half times income against a little over twice for former owner occupiers.

The financial relationship by social class follows a fairly consistent pattern for both new entrants and other buyers. In each group the price/income ratio tends to rise and then fall as one moves down the social scale (with the exception of former owner occupiers in social class D). The advance/income ratios follow a similar pattern. The advance/price ratio tends to rise and then stabilize.

Financial Implications

Important financial implications follow from the analysis:

1. Although new entrants buy cheaper houses, their financing requirement does not decline proportionately because a much larger proportionate advance is required.
2. To the extent to which home ownership is expanded through the recruitment of more and more households in social classes C2 and D (manual workers) in particular, the financing requirements *increase* because they require larger *absolute* advances on average.

3. Further expansion of owner occupation may require the further development of financial schemes to bring households into the market who would otherwise remain submarginal. This development might involve further extension of "low-start" mortgage schemes to deal with the "front-loading" problem,[12] the need for longer repayment periods, possibly greater subsidization for new entrants than exists at present, and possibly the inducement of financial institutions to make larger percentage advances.

DISCUSSION AND CONCLUSION

The stimulus for the work reported here arises from the current housing policy stance in the United Kingdom, which aims to increase the extent of owner occupation. A significant expansion of home ownership has already been achieved. This has been accompanied by the development of a debate about the political, economic, and social significance of owner occupation (see Ball 1983; Merrett 1982; Murie and Forrest 1980; and Gray 1983). Given the high level already attained and the social stratification of housing tenure that exists, the current housing policy raises fundamental questions about how further expansion is to be accomplished. Who are the households that will be induced to shift from one tenure sector to the other? How is the policy to be made operational, if at all, for those in the lower social classes? The answers to these questions have not been spelled out. The basic aim of this chapter has been to extend our knowledge of the process of change involved by focusing on the interface between the rented and owner-occupied sectors at the point where former tenants enter the owner-occupied market.

The salient point about the social class distribution of new entrant households is that they are drawn fairly evenly from the manual and nonmanual classes. But of the new entrants from lower social classes, the main source is new households rather than previous renters. They also tend to be younger, with a smaller proportion who are married and with fewer dependent children—findings that are consistent with the hypothesis that new entrants in lower social classes face the choice of home ownership or starting a family. On the supply side of housing provision, the findings confirm that the increased penetration of owner occupation among the lower social classes will focus demand on the cheaper parts of the housing stock with limited amenities. It seems unlikely that new building will readily provide the means of directly meeting the needs and financial capacity of new entrants in the lower income/lower social class categories. On the financial side, a salient finding is that despite the fact that new entrants buy cheaper houses, those in lower social classes require *bigger* proportionate and absolute advances than former owner occupiers. A principal financial implication is that the further expansion of home ownership involves the need to finance higher advance/income ratios.

The current policy stance does, of course, have wider implications. It is claimed that the desire for home ownership is a natural one (DOE 1977) and surveys have shown a preference for this form of tenure (BSA 1984). However, it may well be that such preferences have been shaped by a system in which the alternative to owner occupation has become council housing (the private rented sector having suffered such a rapid decline under the dual influence of rent controls and fiscal preferences to owner occupiers). Housing is becoming socially polarized between the owner-occupied and public rented sector. The social and political desirability of this development is debatable. There is evidence too that the narrowing of choice in this way has affected fertility by virtue of the financial pressures placed upon young house purchasers (Murphy 1984). Further, the virtual disappearance of the private rented sector has also had unfortunate effects on the labor market in reducing the mobility of labor (Bonnar 1979). Finally, the problem of mortgage default is becoming an important issue (Doling et al. 1985). The latter study suggests that the time is fast approaching when the British government "will need to think more about not only getting people into owner-occupation but also about keeping them there" (p. 51).

These are important issues but they do not form the focus of this chapter. Our purpose has been to shed some light on some of the practical implications of the policy stance and, in particular, its implementation through a detailed study of the process of, and the participants in, the changes taking place in the U.K. housing market.

NOTES

We thank the Halifax Building Society for their cooperation and assistance. Mr. Nellis also acknowledges financial support from Cranfield School of Management.

1. This pattern of tenure varies considerably in different parts of the United Kingdom. For example, Scotland has a higher proportion of public-sector housing or new town homes, with correspondingly fewer owner-occupied homes (53 and 38 percent, respectively in 1983) (see CSO 1985).

2. Apart from the issue of expanding owner occupation, fears are also emerging concerning the ability of current home owners to remain in the owner-occupied sector. In particular, it is reported that an increasing number of home owners are experiencing financial difficulties especially via neglect of repairs and maintenance to their properties and through increasing mortgage arrears and possession. The result is "that although increasing numbers of people are entering owner occupation, increasing numbers are also being forced to leave it" (Doling et al. 1985).

3. That is, housing provided by local government authorities. The terms "council housing," "local authority housing," and "public-sector housing" are used synonymously.

4. The data base was arrived at after excluding properties sold at "nonmarket" prices, such as sales to sitting tenants (for example, sales of council houses and sales between relatives). Council houses are sold at a discounted price under Right-to-Buy legislation.

5. Building societies are mutual savings and loan institutions that specialize in the provision of finance for house purchase in the United Kingdom.

6. Full details of the classification are set out in Monk (1970). A useful comparison

of the classification with that used by the Registrar General and others will be found in Reid (1981).

7. Our discussion pays no attention to category E because of its residual nature covering persons who are not economically active.

8. The inclusion of subsidized council house sales in the analysis would raise the ratio of public-sector buyers to just above that for private-sector buyers.

9. According to a recent survey, Britain has one of the highest levels of young owner occupiers in the world. This survey shows that in 30 percent of households in the United Kingdom, the head of the household is under 25 years old. Among young home owners in other industrial countries, the closest is Australia, where 23 percent of heads of households are under 25; in the United States the figure is 18 percent, Canada 17 percent, the Netherlands 16 percent, France 7 percent, and in West Germany only 4 percent (BSA 1985).

10. For example, the stage of the family life cycle the buyer has reached will have an important bearing on the demand for different sizes of houses (see Donnison 1967, 215–6).

11. For a discussion of U.K. house-price data in this context, see Fleming and Nellis (1985a).

12. That is, a burden of mortgage repayments that is heavy relative to income in the early years but lessens over time under inflationary conditions as the monetary value of the mortgage debt is fixed but incomes rise.

REFERENCES

Ball, Michael
1983   *Housing Policy and Economic Power, The Political Economy of Owner-Occupation*. London: Methuen.
Bonnar, Desmond M.
1979   "Migration in the South East of England: An Analysis of the Interrelationship of Housing, Socio-economic Status and Labour Demand," *Regional Studies* 13, 345–59.
Building Societies Association (BSA)
1983   *Housing Tenure*. London: Building Societies Association.
1984   *Housing Finance into the 1990s*. London: Building Societies Association.
1985   "An International Comparison of Housing Tenure by Age." *BSA Bulletin* 43, July, 7–11.
Central Statistical Office (CSO)
1985   *Social Trends*. London, HMSO.
Department of the Environment (DOE)
1977   *Housing Policy—A Consultative Document*. Cmnd. 6851. London: HMSO.
1984   *Housing and Construction Statistics*. London: HMSO.
Doling, J., V. Karn, and B. Stafford
1985   "How Far Can Privatisation Go? Owner-occupation and Mortgage Default." *National Westminster Bank Quarterly Review*, August, 42–52.
Donnison, D. V.
1967   *The Government of Housing*. Harmondsworth, Middlesex: Penguin Books.

Fleming, M. C. and J. G. Nellis

1984   *The Halifax House Price Index: Technical Details*. Halifax: Halifax Building Society.

1985a "Research Policy and Review 2. House-Price Statistics for the United Kingdom: A Survey and Critical Review of Recent Developments." *Environment and Planning A*, 17, 297–318.

1985b "The Application of Hedonic Indexing Methods: a Study of House Prices in the United Kingdom." *Statistical Journal of the United Nations Economic Commission for Europe* 3, 249–70.

Gray, F.

1983   "Owner-Occupation." Paper presented at a conference sponsored by the Social Science Research Council (SSRC) Environment and Planning Committee under the title "Housing Research in Britain: The Next Decade" held on 12–14 September 1983 at the University of Bristol. London: SSRC.

Hamnett, Chris.

1984   "Housing the Two Nations: Socio-Tenurial Polarization in England and Wales, 1961–81." *Urban Studies* 43, 389–405.

Merrett, Stephen

1982   *Owner-Occupation in Britain*. London: Routledge & Kegan Paul.

Monk, D.

1970   *Social Grading on the National Readership Survey*. London: Joint Industry Committee for National Readership Surveys.

Murie, Alan, and Ray Forrest

1980   "Wealth, Inheritance and Housing Policy." *Policy and Politics* 8, no. 1, 1–19.

Murphy, M. J.

1984   "The Influence of Fertility, Early Housing-Career, and Socioeconomic Factors on Tenure Determination in Contemporary Britain." *Environment and Planning A*, 16, 1303–18.

Office of Population Censuses and Surveys (OPCS)

1984   *The General Household Survey 1982*. London: HMSO.

Reid, Ivan

1981   *Social Class Differences in Britain*, 2nd ed. London: Grant McIntyre.

9

Shared Housing as a Policy Alternative: The Australian Case

PATRICIA KLOBUS EDWARDS, JUDITH A. JONES, AND JOHN N. EDWARDS

Abstract. This chapter discusses current housing problems and public policy restrictions related to shared housing in Australia. Two divergent perspectives that have a potential influence on these restrictive policies are examined: sharing as a wholesome alternative life-style, and sharing as an undesirable consequence of economic constraints. Data from the Australian Bureau of Statistics bearing on these differing perspectives are analyzed. The findings strongly indicate that sharing accommodation generally is not the social problem often alleged. Several options to alleviate the constraints of present policy on shared housing are suggested.

INTRODUCTION

As a result of fiscal problems and governmental austerity, a substantial proportion of Australians are experiencing severe housing problems. High interest rates, increasing construction costs, along with increased unemployment, have made it virtually impossible for many Australians to afford adequate shelter. Homelessness has become a major issue confronting public policy makers (Fopp 1982; Haley 1984).

Because Australia has emphasized private-sector dominance in the housing market (Jones 1983), there is an insufficient supply of public housing to meet current demands. In the State of Victoria alone, the waiting list for public housing numbered about 20,000 applications in 1984, and it was estimated that another 150,000 (about 11 percent of the total households in the state) were eligible for public housing but had not applied.

Graeme Bethune (1983) reports a similar situation concerning the inability of the state government of South Australia to meet the housing needs of its citizens. He cites a variety of demographic and economic reasons for the increasing demands for public housing: the rapid growth of the aged, lone parenthood, and nonaged single-person households; the almost threefold growth of unemployment beneficiaries between 1977 and 1983; the fact that housing costs have risen almost twice as fast as the general inflation rate over the first four years of this decade; and extremely low vacancy rates in the private rental market. In Adelaide, the capital city of South Australia, vacancy rates had reached the alarming level of 1.5 percent by 1983. According to Bethune (1983), those on waiting lists for public accommodation experience severe housing stress, and often manage only by sharing with family or friends.

Sharing residence, however, is generally inhibited by public policy restrictions, as well as social opinion. For the most part, government housing authorities prohibit sharing. Zoning regulations deter sharing in residential neighborhoods, and local councils often refuse to issue more than two parking permits per house. The least-preferred type of tenant after single mothers and their children, according to a survey of real estate agents in Victoria, are house-sharers (Simons 1984).

Whether sharing a house constitutes a social problem or a viable residential alternative remains an unsettled issue to which relatively few empirical data have been brought to bear. In a nation that exhibits an overwhelming preference for home ownership and single-family dwellings, a surprising proportion of Australians share their housing. Approximately one-fifth of all households in 1981 contained adult family members other than the head and spouse, such as an adult child or an elderly parent. Another 9 percent of the households included adult nonfamily members, and 3 percent were occupied by more than one family (Edwards, Jones, and Edwards 1986).

This chapter addresses two questions pertinent to the development of public policy related to shared housing. First, is shared accommodation a housing option desired only by the poor? Second, does sharing simply constitute a means of meeting minimal housing needs? If sharing is a living arrangement found among a broad cross-section of the population without deleterious effects, then it should be treated as a viable housing alternative. Public policies that discourage sharing may be unnecessarily discriminatory, particularly with regard to those who are least able to afford adequate housing on an independent basis.

SOME BACKGROUND: PERSPECTIVES ON SHARING

Two divergent perspectives on shared housing are reflected in the literature: (1) sharing as a means to achieve a wholesome alternative life-style, and (2) sharing as an undesirable consequence of economic constraints. The first perspective, typified by Eric Raimy's (1979) work, emphasizes the virtues of shared accommodation as a mode of residence that mediates the sense of isolation endemic to contemporary industrial society. A wide array of literature, primarily anecdotal in nature and focused on communal living arrangements, has drawn attention to the advantages of sharing a residence with nonfamily members.

Seen from this vantage point, families and individuals who share housing do so voluntarily for a variety of reasons: the desire to create a richer domestic life, the need for emotional and social supports, common or compatibly diverse interests, the convenience of shared household chores, sexual preference, or companionship (Raimy 1979; Baum 1984). While economic motives often can be an important consideration, Raimy suggests that successful shared households are not constituted solely on the basis of economic need. Shared housing allows families and individuals more discretionary income that can be used for other purposes. Those who share housing may achieve a higher standard of living than would otherwise be possible, may divide housekeeping chores, and enjoy a more leisurely life-style as well.

In contrast, the more prominent, antisharing, perspective is not embodied in a well-defined literature. This viewpoint is subtly implied, nevertheless, in numerous studies concerning public housing policy, housing preferences, dwelling satisfaction, and family relations. Shared housing is seen as a problem, reflecting the inability of society to house its population adequately.

The lack of recognition that shared housing may be a preferred life-style for many individuals or families is manifested in Australian government housing programs that, in the past, prohibited the sharing of public housing units. Welfare agencies only recently are looking at shared housing as an alternative for young singles and senior citizens (Simons 1984). Moreover, private housing is designed almost exclusively for nuclear family living (O'Neill 1975). Architects and home builders seldom take into consideration that the nuclear family structure is *not* the predominant family form (Baum 1984), thereby implying that any other type of living arrangement constitutes a deviant residential arrangement.

In a 1980 survey conducted by Cecily Neil, under the auspices of the Commonwealth Scientific and Industrial Research Organization's Division of Building Research, recent survey (1980), 700 respondents, selected from households located in several Sydney suburbs, were asked about their views on sharing the same residence with unrelated families. While almost one-third of the sample believed that living in a home with another family is a good way to share resources and 38 percent felt that it would help children to adapt to others, most respondents reacted negatively to this living arrangement. A large majority of people questioned (69 percent) maintained that shared households are usually not as good as separate family quarters, and over half of the respondents said that it is usually (35 percent) or sometimes (18 percent) true that the situation would be irresponsible if there is any alternative. The strong feelings against shared housing also are evident in the anticipated effects of multifamily residences. A sizable proportion of the sample maintained it would usually lead to arguments (58 percent), loss of self-identity (36 percent), too many rules (39 percent), and would be bad for children (27 percent). In fact, 13 percent of those surveyed believed that shared family housing usually leads to immorality and an additional 18 percent agreed that it would sometimes lead to immoral behavior.[1]

These responses reflect the intensity of social attitudes toward shared living arrangements and suggest that most families and individuals share because of housing shortages and/or insufficient financial resources to establish an independent home. In a British study on housing and public policy, Stewart Lansley (1979, 90–91) suggested it is ''reasonable to assume'' that the great majority of sharing is involuntary, owing to financial exigencies and a lack of housing alternatives.

One of the central assumptions in the housing literature is that a house is more than simply a roof over one's head (Rapoport 1969; Soen 1979). A home, for many families, symbolizes their opportunities and rank within the social system (Jakubowicz 1973; Payne and Payne 1977; Kilmartin and Thorns 1978). Families are accorded status according to their access to housing (Western 1983). Shared housing is thus imputed to have negative overtones for family status.

Housing research indicates that the amount of space and privacy afforded by a dwelling is an important factor influencing resident satisfaction (Young and Young 1976; Rapoport 1971). Neil and Brealey (1982) found that even adequately housed families, using objective measures of crowding, express a desire for at least one more extra room in their present dwelling. The respondents they interviewed maintained that the number of bedrooms is a more important priority than closeness to work, age of the dwelling, or lot size. Research on family relations also suggests that shared housing may have adverse psychological, social, and physical consequences. For example, a number of studies indicate that couples enjoy improved marital satisfaction after their children mature and leave home (Rollins and Feldman 1970; Spanier et al. 1974). Other studies, dealing with the effects of household congestion, have implied that crowding may have a deleterious effect on family relations, mental and physical health, and other aspects of family functioning, but the findings regarding these are quite mixed (Booth and Edwards 1976). Nevertheless, shared housing intimates a lack of privacy, increased stress, and an inhibited family life-style, if it is not a voluntary arrangement.

In net, the reflection of an acceptable social status, the attainment of privacy, and an adequate life-style are generally thought to be unobtainable in shared dwellings. Because private housing is not designed for multifamily use, people who share may live in overcrowded conditions. If low-income families and individuals are disproportionately represented among those who share housing and live in crowded, high-density rental housing, then shared housing is, indeed, a societal problem potentially affecting family health and psychological well-being. However, if our findings do not support this conclusion, efforts should be made to adapt public policy to more adequately address the needs of those who wish to share accommodations.

To shed empirical light on the applicability of these alternative perspectives, we examine the income characteristics and housing status of persons in shared accommodations.

INCOME CHARACTERISTICS OF SHARED HOUSEHOLDS

The data bearing on these issues come from a subsample of 4,560 households drawn from the randomly selected 1 percent Australian Households Sample File of the 1981 Census of Population and Housing (Cameron 1983a). Analysis was limited to heads of all primary and secondary families in the subsample, adult family members other than head or spouse, and adult nonfamily members living as permanent residents in private dwellings.[2]

Table 9.1 provides an examination of the stereotypical notion that low-income individuals and families are disproportionately represented in shared housing. First, the individual income distribution of two categories of single persons who share—namely, adult family members (that is, nondependent children, siblings, or ancestors) and adult nonfamily members—is compared to the individual income distribution of all Australians. These data indicate that the percentages of adult family and nonfamily members that do not have any income whatsoever are half that of the population at large. However, adult family members are overrepresented in the lower income categories. Fully 88 percent of this group make $12,000 (Australian dollars) or less, compared to 74 percent of the adult nonfamily members and 76 percent of all Australians.

The second set of income figures in Table 9.1 compares the family income of primary and secondary families in shared households with that of all Australian families. These data show that the family income distribution for primary families sharing a dwelling with either adult family members, nonfamily members, or secondary families is not substantially different from that of all Australian families. Apparently, a significant proportion of the primary families do not share accommodation as a result of their own financial need. But the proportions of secondary families with no income, or making $6,000 or less, are large relative to other families. In fact, 77 percent of this group report an income of $12,000 or less, in contrast to 49 percent of both the primary families in shared households and all Australians. Sharing a dwelling for many of these secondary families, indeed, may be motivated by economic necessity as opposed to choice.

Our analysis of individual and family incomes in shared households would suggest that while most primary families do not share their homes because of financial distress, economic considerations are quite probably a factor motivating most secondary families, adult family members, and even a sizable proportion of adult nonfamily members to share.

In order to further assess this possibility, we next compared the household incomes between shared and unshared residences. Overall, the total income for those who share is substantially higher than that of other households, with 65 percent or more of all types of shared households having an income in excess of $18,000. Only 32 percent of nonshared households fall into this category. After the sharing of expenses, such as rent and utility charges, then, members of shared households may find themselves with more disposable income than members of nonshared households, although, of course, an even distribution of that income across all members cannot be assumed. Unfortunately, per capita income data are not available.

This examination of the income characteristics of individuals and families who share housing provides mixed support for the hypothesis that sharing is highly associated with economic need. Clearly, there are some families and persons

Table 9.1
Income Distribution of Sample Adults in Shared Households and All Australians
15 Years and Over, 1981 (In Percentages*)

	None	$6,000 and under	$6,001 to $12,000	$12,001 to $18,000	$18,001 and above	Number
Individual income						
Adult family members (excludes head & spouse)	6	39	43	11	1	1,319
Adult non-family members	6	31	37	20	6	381
All Australians**	14	34	28	16	8	10,304,177
Family income						
Primary families in shared households	1	20	28	22	29	1,420
Secondary families in shared households	5	44	28	7	15	81
All Australian families	1	23	25	21	30	4,512,147
Household income						
Households with primary families only	1	21	25	22	32	2,887
Households with secondary families	0	0	11	20	69	70
Households with primary families and adult family members	0	2	13	19	65	862
Households with primary families and adult non-family members	0	3	14	18	65	373
All Australian households	1	16	21	20	41	4,285,939

*Percentages based on nonmissing data cases only.

**The figures for individual income for all Australians include individuals living in nonprivate dwellings, whereas the sample includes those in private dwellings only.

Source: 1981 Census sample data and ABS Summary Characteristics of Persons and Dwellings, Australia 1981, Cat. No. 2443.0.

for whom sharing is economically essential in lieu of public assistance. For others, sharing may be economically advantageous: allowing some saving, a less-meager existence, or perhaps a better standard of accommodation and a more desirable location than any one party could afford alone. For still others, while economics may have been a consideration in deciding to share, it does not appear to have been the primary concern.

THE HOUSING STATUS OF SHARED HOUSEHOLDS

We have ascertained that for many families and individuals, shared housing has the potential, at least economically, of providing a better standard of accommodation. Yet there are a variety of other issues bearing on the housing status of shared households and whether such household arrangements constitute a social problem. Are families in shared accommodation more likely to live in rental housing than other Australian families? Do they tend to live in different housing types? Do they live in more crowded situations? Are families who share disadvantaged in terms of housing costs relative to other families? The negative connotations ascribed to shared housing would suggest that sharing can provide only a minimal standard of shelter.

Nature of Occupancy

It is well known that Australia can claim one of the highest owner-occupancy rates among industrialized nations. "The ideal of home ownership is enshrined as Australia's principal national value, expressed as 'the Great Australian Dream' " (Kemeny 1981, 112). Home ownership, however, is positively correlated with socioeconomic status. In Australia, approximately 80 percent of high-income earners are buying (or own) their home, compared to 55 percent of low-income earners (Kemeny 1981). Thus, living in a purchased, as opposed to rental, home can be a symbol of status even in shared households.

While it is probably rare that adult family members and secondary families living in shared housing actually participate in the ownership of a dwelling, all household members can derive benefits from home ownership. As Kilmartin and Thorns (1978, 107) point out, "ownership gives a greater sense of security because one cannot be evicted, and a greater opportunity to develop a sense of identity."

Table 9.2 shows the nature of occupancy among different household types for the sample data and all Australian households. Inspection of these data indicates that extended households—those composed of a primary family and adult family members—have a higher owner-purchaser rate (82 percent) than that of unshared households. These findings, in part, may be a function of the age of the family head. In the sample, 88 percent of the heads of extended family types are over 40 years of age, compared to 53 percent of the sample heads of

Table 9.2
Nature of Occupancy by Household Type, Structure of Dwellings, Sample Data, and Australian Totals, 1981 (In Percentages*)

Household type	Nature of occupancy				Number
	Owner	Purchaser	Private rental	State housing	
Primary family only	34	40	20	7	2,891
Primary family and adult family members	46	36	9	9	935
Primary family and adult non-family members	20	24	53	3	379
Multi-family households	40	30	25	5	116
All Australian households	36	38	22	5	4,343,346

Household type	Structure of dwelling**				Number
	Separate house	Medium density	Flat over 3 stories	Other housing	
Primary family only	79	18	2	2	3,037
Primary family and adult family members	90	9	1	1	957
Primary family and adult non-family members	63	32	2	3	389
Multi-family households	92	7	1	0	127
All Australian households	80	17	2	1	4,602,063

*Percentages based on nonmissing data cases only.
**Medium-density dwellings include semidetached, row or terrace, or other medium-density housing.
Other housing includes caravan, houseboat, improvised home, or flat attached to shop/office.
Households were coded missing if they did not state the structure of their dwelling unit.

families that do not share. The former group, perhaps, have had more opportunity to accrue savings toward the purchase of a home.

Conversely, private rental dwellings are most common for primary families sharing with adult nonfamily members. The relatively low proportion of owner-purchasing for this group (44 percent) may be attributed to the fact that 69 percent of these households accommodate young singles. Our findings probably reflect the difficulty this group has in obtaining housing loans or may indicate the temporary and fluid nature of such households, as is the case, for example, with a group of students or unemployed youth sharing.

Finally, the owner-occupancy rates of multifamily households are only slightly lower (70 percent) than that of the Australian norm. With the exception of households that include adult nonfamily members, the housing status of shared households with regard to home ownership is not disadvantaged according to national standards.

The Structure of Dwellings

Dwelling structure has implications for residential density and the socioeconomic composition of a neighborhood. Thus, the distribution of shared households among different types of dwellings is an indicator of the kinds of neighborhood environments that typically foster shared accommodation.

Table 9.2 also presents the distribution of household types by dwelling structure and demonstrates that the most common form of dwelling for any household type is the separate house. We find that among the shared household types, only the primary family with adult nonfamily members are disadvantaged in not having a separate dwelling. However, since the majority of this group are head-only families living with other adult singles, the high proportion located in medium density housing (32 percent) may be a function of choice, offering opportunities for social contacts that may not be otherwise attainable.

Crowding

Kemeny (1981, 127) maintains that "there is a vast gap" between Australian households that have a shortage of housing space and those that have a surplus of rooms. He estimates that in 1971 about one in five Australians lived in overcrowded dwellings despite the fact that, overall, the housing stock was sufficient to provide a density of less than one person per room. Since housing is typically not designed to accommodate extended or multifamily households, it is generally assumed that shared dwellings are overcrowded (Baum 1984).

Two measures were used to provide an estimate of the extent of crowding in the different types of households. The first, shown in Table 9.3, uses a level of more than two persons per bedroom as an indicator. According to this measure, a higher percentage of shared households are crowded, compared to unshared households in the sample and all Australian households. The proportion of households with more than two persons per bedroom is particularly high with respect to multifamily residences (17.5 percent) when contrasted to all Australian dwellings (2.6 percent).

The second crowding measure used in Table 9.3 consists of the number of persons per room. Once again, multifamily households appear most crowded; 16.3 percent have more than one person per room, compared to 2.0 percent for unshared households in the sample and 3.3 percent for all Australians. Shared dwellings that include adult nonfamily members have the highest incidence of the maximum crowding category, but at 1.5 percent this is still a very small proportion. The consequences of sharing, therefore, do not seem to include crowding for most Australians.

Housing Cost

The social pressures for home ownership and the lack of suitable alternatives may force some families into taking extreme financial measures to buy their own home (Kemeny 1981). Table 9.4 presents monthly mortgage payments by household type for those households purchasing a dwelling. Some 60 percent of the households consisting of primary family with adult family members are in the lowest category, paying less than $200 per month on their mortgage repayments. These are the households where the head is likely to be older and hence have repaid more of the mortgage than is the case for younger families. The highest repayments, $399 or more per month, are more usual for multifamily households and for households having a primary family with adult nonfamily members (21 and 20 percent, respectively). The percentage of family income (combined income of head and spouse) expended on mortgage repayments also varies by household type: 14 percent of primary families sharing with nonfamily members spend more than 30 percent of their family income on repayments,[3] compared to 5 percent of households with a primary family only, 6 percent of households having a primary family with adult family members, and 9 percent of multifamily households. A small proportion of households, therefore, have made a substantial financial commitment to purchasing a home in either absolute or percentage terms.

Table 9.4 also shows weekly rental payments by household type for those households renting a dwelling. The most expensive housing, at $80 or more per week, is most favored by households having a primary family with nonfamily members (20 percent) and multifamily households (17 percent). Households having a primary family with adult family members have the highest proportion (27 percent) in the lowest rental category of less than $29 per week, followed by households with a primary family only (25 percent) and multifamily households (23 percent). As with home purchasers, multifamily households and those with primary family and nonfamily members are most likely to be paying higher prices for rental housing. In terms of the percentage of family income paid for rent,[4] multifamily households and those with a primary family and nonfamily

Table 9.3
Percentage of Households with More Than Two Persons per Bedroom and Number of Persons per Room by Household Type, Sample Data, and Australian Totals, 1981

Household type	More than 2 persons per bedroom*	persons per room**			Number
		More than 1.50	1.01 to 1.50	Less than 1.0	
Primary family only households	1.7	.3	1.7	98.0	3,052
Households with adult family members	3.8	.7	3.8	95.5	960
Households with adult non-family members	5.1	1.5	3.5	94.9	395
Multi-family households	17.5	1.3	15.0	83.7	80
All Australian households	2.6	.6	2.7	96.7	4,596,072

*Percentages based on nonmissing data cases only.
**The maximum category for number of rooms is "8 or more." Where more than eight persons were in a dwelling of eight or more rooms, that household was, conservatively, placed in the "less than 1" category.

Table 9.4
Monthly Mortgage Payments and Weekly Rental Payments by Household Type, Sample Households, and Australian Totals, 1981 (In Percentages*)

Household type	Monthly mortgage payments ($)				Number
	Less than 200	200-398	399 and over		
Primary family only	46	42	12		1,090
Primary family and adult family members	60	31	8		308
Primary family and adult non-family members	33	48	20		86
Multi-family households	30	48	21		33
All Australian households	48	41	11		1,487,657

Household type	Weekly rental payments ($)				Number
	Less than 29	30-49	50-79	80 and over	
Primary family only	25	34	32	8	735
Primary family and adult family members	27	39	27	7	159
Primary family and adult non-family members	9	22	49	20	209
Multi-family households	23	31	29	17	35
All Australian households	25	34	32	10	1,137,217

*Percentages based on nonmissing data cases only.

members again pay the most, with 33 percent paying more than 30 percent of their income. This suggests that part of the housing costs, at least, is being met from the income of secondary families or unrelated adults. Overall, renters who share accommodations pay a higher proportion of family income for their accommodation than do their counterparts who are purchasing a home, a factor that has implications for their ability to save a deposit for a home.

CONCLUSIONS

While the prevalence of house sharing among Australians is rather substantial, involving almost one-third of all households, there is very little evidence in the data we have examined to suggest that the sharing of accommodation constitutes a large-scale social problem. In viewing the income characteristics of shared households, a very mixed picture is presented. Sharing appears to be an economic necessity for only a small proportion. For most, this type of household arrangement seems to have economic advantages, potentially increasing the standard of accommodation that would be otherwise attainable and permitting alternative uses for the disposable income available.

Certainly, sharing one's dwelling has little effect on the propensity to own a home. Only young singles seem to be disadvantaged in actualizing the general preference for home ownership. Nor do we find that shared accommodations differ significantly from unshared ones in the type of dwelling occupied. Moreover, with the possible exception of multifamily residences, shared households are not unusually crowded. Furthermore, in terms of housing costs, it is only a relatively small proportion of those who share that pay an undue amount of their income on home purchase or rental.

In sum, our findings, with the exceptions noted, do not indicate that those who share are the most poverty stricken or that shared accommodations represent only minimal housing. The data suggest that viewing shared housing as a widespread social problem is unwarranted.

As Jones points out (1983, 252–53), "Australia between 1976 and 1981 built a new dwelling for each 1.36 people added to the population; there were fewer persons per dwelling and fewer persons per room since 1945. All indications suggest that Australia is a well housed country, better housed than at any other time in its history." But this overlooks the fact that existing housing is not necessarily evenly distributed in relation to need and there may be selective shortages in certain type of housing stock.

Uneven distribution and selective shortages of both public and private housing necessitate exploring new forms of residential arrangements. Established home owners with relatively low mortgages have become locked into their properties. Many older householders find themselves with surplus space but are financially unable to move to smaller homes. Yet, as previously mentioned, utilization of surplus space in private housing is generally constrained by zoning regulations, building codes, and even informal marketing practices. The South Australian

Planning and Development Act, which stipulates that residential zones are primarily constituted to accommodate single-family dwellings, typifies Australian zoning policy. Even "granny" or "mother-in-law" apartments are restricted under this legislation as a consequence of the limited definition of what constitutes a family (Baum 1984). According to Baum, in theory, residents who wish to share a home must apply for permission to change the use of a dwelling, but in practice this is rarely done because of public objections.

Evidence of a widespread extralegal response to increased housing demands also can be found in the United States in the form of converting underutilized rooms and attic or basement spaces into accessory apartments (Goetze 1985). The benefits of these apartments, Goetze maintains (p. 24), accrue to both the provider and seeker in terms of:

- increasing the supply of small apartments for both young and old households seeking rental housing that is more affordable;
- providing supplemental income for older homeowners;
- enhancing the security of older homeowners from fear of criminal intrusion or personal accidents when alone;
- companionship; and
- enabling older homeowners to stay comfortably in homes they might otherwise have to leave.

Research should be undertaken to determine if these conversions actually undermine surrounding property values—a concern that undoubtedly influences public opinion toward shared accommodation. The public is also affected by media judgments on housing problems. As Goetze (1985) observes, the perceptual differences between "double up" or "entering shared living" are vast. Labels shape public attitudes toward sharing accommodation and, consequently, affect housing policy agendas.

Despite public resistance, efforts are being made to institute new approaches to shared housing in Australia. Private organizations and social service agencies are initiating accommodation services matching people in need with those who are willing to share (Baum 1984). Some agencies are instituting congregate housing for pensioners (Simons 1984). But more attention needs be given to developing zoning laws that will enhance and, at the same time, effectively regulate accessory conversions. Goetze (1985, 29) suggests:

allowing conversions only in principal structures over a certain size or age; limiting them by floor area or to a certain percentage of the house; requiring owner occupancy or that occupants of the two units be related; requiring that one or the other of the occupants be over 65 years of age; regulating exterior alterations; or limiting the total number of conversions in a town or specific neighborhood.

These provisions are only illustrations of the options local jurisdictions can consider in refining their zoning regulations to accommodate shared housing in a more positive vein. In times of fiscal austerity, they demand serious consideration.

NOTES

1. The Sydney survey includes a representative sample of 500 and an additional sample of 200 renters. It is conceivable the views expressed about shared accommodation are influenced by current tenure as well as anticipated housing tenure, all other things being equal. This is a separate research question that merits exploration. We thank Dr. Cecily Neil of the Division of Building Research, Commonwealth Scientific Industrial Research Organization, for the use of the data from the Sydney Suburban Household Sample.

2. The Australian Bureau of Statistics (ABS) definitions of adult family members and adult nonfamily members are used throughout this chapter. Adult family members, according to ABS, may be a lone parent, sister (in-law), brother (in-law), or nondependent child of the household head or spouse. This specifically excludes the household head and spouse. Adult nonfamily members are relatives who belong to a family unit outside the household (that is, married sons or daughters), boarders, or any other lone individual 16 years of age of over (Cameron 1983b).

3. Because categories rather than actual income were used by ABS in coding family income, the maximum value of the category range was used in calculating the percentage of income spent on mortgage payments. Where both income and repayment were in the maximum category, repayments were classified as less than 30 percent of income. These constraints may contribute to an underestimate of those paying more than 30 percent of family income in repayments. An additional problem is that the primary family, whose income was used in the calculations, may not in fact be the family purchasing the dwelling.

4. Percentage of family income paid in rent was calculated in the same way as for mortgages, with the same constraints applying.

REFERENCES

Australian Bureau of Statistics
1981   "Summary Characteristics of Persons and Dwellings." *Census of Population and Housing*. Canberra: Australian Government Publishing Service.
Baum, F. E.
1984   "Shared Houses: Some Ideas for Planners." *Australian Planner* 22, 13–15.
Bethune, G.
1983   "Population Trends and Public Housing." Paper presented for seminar on Impact of Population Trends on Demand for Housing, Adelaide, Australia.
Booth, A., and J. N. Edwards
1976   "Crowding and Family Relations." *American Sociological Review* 41, 308–21.
Cameron, R. J.
1983a "Households Sample File Technical Details, Australian Bureau of Statistics." *Census of Population and Housing*. Canberra: Australian Government Publishing Service.
1983b "Dwelling, Household, Family." *Information Paper*, No. 2150.0, Australian Bureau of Statistics. Canberra: Australian Government Publishing Service.
Edwards, P. K., J. A. Jones and J. N. Edwards

1986   "The Social Demography of Shared Housing." *Journal of the Australian Population Association* 3, 130–43.

Fopp, R.
1982   "Unemployment, Youth Homelessness and the Allocation of Family Responsibility." *Australian Journal of Social Issues* 17, 304–15.

Goetze, R.
1985   "Shared Housing and Other Innovative Living Alternatives." Proceedings of a meeting held in Boston, February 13–15.

Haley, K.
1984   "Houses, Houses Everywhere." *The Age*, Monday, April 24, 2.

Jakubowicz, A.
1973   "Some Sociological Aspects of the Sociology of Housing." *Architecture in Australia* 62, 74–76.

Jones, M. A.
1983   *The Australian Welfare State: Growth, Crisis and Change*. Sydney: Allen and Unwin.

Kemeny, J.
1981   *The Myth of Home Ownership*. London: Routledge and Kegan Paul.

Kilmartin, L., and D. C. Thorns
1978   *Cities Unlimited*. Sydney: Allen and Unwin.

Lansley, S.
1979   *Housing and Public Policy*. London: Croom Helm.

Neil, C. C. and T. B. Brealey
1982   "Dwelling Space: Expectations and the Housing System." *Australian Journal of Social Issues* 17, 62–72.

O'Neill, J.
1975   "Social and Sociological Aspects of Housing Patterns in Australia." In *An Intergenerational Housing Project and the Development of New Housing Patterns in Australia*. Melbourne: Australian Frontier.

Payne, J., and G. Payne
1977   "Housing Pathways and Stratification: A Study of Life Chances in the Housing Market." *Journal of Social Policy* 6, 129–56.

Raimy, E.
1979   *Shared Houses, Shared Lives*. Los Angeles: J. P. Tarcher.

Rapoport, A.
1969   *House Form and Culture*. Englewood Cliffs, N.J.: Prentice-Hall.
1971   "Man and Environment." In *Design for Living*. Melbourne: Victorian Family Council.

Rollins, B. C., and H. Feldman
1970   "Marital Satisfaction over the Family Life Cycle." *Journal of Marriage and the Family* 32, 20–27.

Simons, Margaret
1984   "The New Families." *The Age*, Tuesday, February 28, 11.

Soen, D.
1979   "Habitability—Occupant's Needs and Dwelling Satisfaction." *Ekistics* 275, 129–34.

Spanier, G. B., R. A. Lewis, and C. L. Cole
1974   "Marital Adjustment over the Family Life Cycle: The Issue of Curvilinearity." *Journal of Marriage and the Family* 37, 263–76.

Western, J. S.
1983   *Social Inequality in Australian Society*. Melbourne: Macmillan.
Young, S., and M. S. J. Young
1976   "Social and Psychological Needs Related to Residential Diversity and Housing Form." *Technical Paper* No. 13. Canberra: National Capital Development Commission.

PART V

HOUSING SUBSIDIES

10

The Aims and Effects of Housing Allowances in Western Europe

MICHAEL J. OXLEY

Abstract. Using evidence from West Germany, France, the Netherlands, the United Kingdom, and Denmark, this chapter considers whether housing allowances give most help to those in greatest need, result in improved housing conditions, and give a more equitable distribution of aid than alternative policy instruments. It is suggested that the less housing policy is viewed as a question of production and the more one of distributional justice, the greater is the emphasis on individual subsidies. The more distributional justice is seen simply as a distribution-of-income problem, the greater is the emphasis on income supplements and the less on subsidies tied to housing consumption.

INTRODUCTION

As governments in Western Europe have tried to cut public expenditure, housing programs have been a prime target for reductions. These reductions have often been presented in terms of concentrating help where it is most needed by switching aid from buildings to people. This has meant that there is more emphasis on housing allowances. In light of this changing emphasis this chapter examines questions about the aims and effects of housing allowances using evidence from West Germany, France, the Netherlands, the United Kingdom, and Denmark. Much of the material was gathered as part of a wider investigation into housing policy in Europe (Oxley 1983).

Housing allowances are payments to households intended to reduce the costs of housing consumption. In order to make this definition more explicit and to contrast housing allowances with other housing policy instruments, it is useful to identify four basic types of housing subsidy. Two are subsidies to consumers and two are subsidies to suppliers:

1. Pure Subject Subsidies. Also known as income supplements, these are payments to households, in any tenure, that depend only on household size and income.

2. Conditional Subject Subsidies. Also known as housing allowances, these are payments to households that depend on household size, household income, and the price of housing services consumed. Some writers refer to housing allowances as price reductions, but this is a misleading description. Housing allowances are typically cash payments, although for purely administrative purposes the money is sometimes paid to landlords who then reduce the rents they require from tenants accordingly.

3. Pure Object Subsidies. These are payments to housing suppliers that contribute to building, management, or interest costs. They are unrelated to the characteristics of the occupants of the dwelling. It might be argued that British Exchequer subsidies to local authority housing have taken this form, although in allocating dwellings authorities may apply their own criteria that take account of household circumstances.

4. Conditional Object Subsidies. These are payments to housing suppliers given on the condition that (1) the occupants of the dwellings are in certain economic or social groups; and (2) they are charged prices or rents within certain limits. Many of the subsidies given to nonprofit housing associations in Europe are of this type. The case for housing allowances thus involves the case for subject as opposed to object subsidies, and the case for conditional, as opposed to pure, subject subsidies.

Although payments to households to help meet housing costs have existed in France since 1948, the *aide à la personalisée au logement* (APL) dates from the recommendations of the Barre Report in 1975 (see Local Finance 1977, 10–23). Denmark has had a system of housing allowances (Boligsikring) since 1967. The Netherlands' *Individuele Huursubsidie* dates from 1970, although the principle of a rent subsidy was used as early as the Housing Act of 1901 (Howenstine 1986, 2). Individual household subsidies were introduced in West Germany in 1965 but the present *Wohngeld* is a result of expansions of the system in 1970 and 1971. The British system of rent rebates (public sector) and rent allowances (private sector) was introduced in 1972 and amalgamated in the Housing Benefit System in 1983, but there were earlier limited and localized rent subsidy schemes.

The money value of housing allowances is generally an increasing function of household size and asking rent and a decreasing function of money income. Allowances are limited by mechanisms and rules that vary from country to country. There are (variously) income limits above which the allowance is not paid, a maximum eligible rent, or simply a maximum subsidy.

In the late 1960s and 1970s there was, in many European countries, a switch in the balance of government housing expenditure away from object and toward subject subsidies, which became more significant as rental markets became less constrained by rent controls. Housing allowances as a proportion of direct subsidies, involving payments from the Exchequer, have increased in recent years in each country as has the number of recipients. In 1982 over 20 percent of households in the United Kingdom and France were in receipt of housing allowances. For Denmark the figure was about 13 percent and for the Netherlands and West Germany about 13 and 8 percent, respectively (Howenstine 1986, Table 10, 106–7).

THE AIMS OF HOUSING ALLOWANCES

Housing allowances are often associated with a view of the housing market that reflects a desire for a free interaction between demand and supply subject to assistance being provided for those on lower incomes. In the Netherlands, for example, it has been argued that the *Individuele Huursubsidie* was introduced at a time when the "government's guiding principle was that the housing market should begin to operate as a free market . . . on the basis of supply and demand" and housing allowances were to "correct the consequences of an unequal distribution for the poorest members of society" (Wiewel 1979, 2); similar views have been expressed with respect to the desirability of introducing housing allowances in the United Kingdom (Pennance 1969, 29).

The aims of housing allowances should be seen in the historical context of a relaxation of rent controls while simultaneously a "rent-gap" problem remained. Where rent-gaps existed some rents were related to historic costs. There were thus higher rents for newer than for older dwellings, especially in West Germany, the Netherlands, and Denmark. In this situation, with housing costs varying in a random manner between households, there was a situation that can be described as "inconsistent pricing." Governments introduced policies designed to encourage consistent pricing but they also used housing allowances to compensate for inconsistent pricing.

Housing allowances can provide a method of helping households bid for higher quality accommodation or a method of reducing the proportion of household income spent on rent. Alternatively, housing allowances may be seen as a reaction to the failure of object subsidies to distribute aid according to some criterion of need. Supportive arguments have often stressed the necessity of a rational basis for housing subsidies, gearing them to income, family size, and housing costs.

There has been a close relationship in Western Europe between moves toward subject subsidies and the elimination of crude housing shortages. Typically this has been fostered by the notion that the emphasis should move from production to redistribution. In the distributional process governments have claimed to prefer allowance systems because they help most those in greatest need. In fact, the shift away from object subsidies has conveniently allowed governments to reduce their total budget allocations to housing, as extensions of housing allowance schemes have moved in tandem with reductions in aid to nonprofit or public housing.

Summarizing, housing allowances have at least three aims: (1) an increase in the quality of housing consumed by certain households; (2) a reduction in the proportion of income that some households spend on housing; and (3) improved equity in the distribution of housing aid.

Arguments by critics of housing allowances may be summarized as follows:

1. Housing allowance schemes do not result in significant increases in housing consumption or housing quality because these depend on supply-side factors, which allowances leave unaltered.
2. The distributional consequences are not as advocates claim and allowances do not concentrate help on those in greatest need. This is because in specific schemes the payments are not sensitive enough to incomes, housing costs, or household size and many of those in "need" fail to claim the allowance. Furthermore, allowances can result in price and rent increases so that benefits accrue to landlords.
3. Housing allowances are inferior in welfare terms to income supplements, which do not depend on the price of housing services.

The first two counterarguments claim that housing problems are not simply income distribution/housing cost problems, while the third claims that they are *only* income distribution problems.

The aims and counterarguments, given above, yield three questions that will be examined in the rest of this chapter:

1. In practice, do housing allowances give most help to those in greatest need?
2. Do the payments received result in greater housing consumption and improved quality or do supply-side constraints prevent this?
3. Do housing allowances produce a more equitable distribution of housing subsidies than either object subsidies or income supplements?

HOUSING ALLOWANCES AND HOUSING NEED

Housing allowance schemes measure "need" by taking account of a number of factors. The following observations are based on an examination of the way certain schemes operated in the late 1970s. In Denmark, the Netherlands, and the United Kingdom, for any rent, the level of subsidy fell as income rose. In the Netherlands and the United Kingdom rents had to be at least twice the average rent at above-average incomes before an allowance was paid, but in Denmark rents had only to be just above average. In the United Kingdom and the Netherlands, allowances increased substantially as rents rose above the average, while in Denmark they increased little. The Danish system was geared to ensuring that households could afford the average rent but did not encourage households to seek more expensive dwellings. The Dutch system concentrated benefits on low-income households paying above-average rents and both the Dutch and British systems compensated for relatively high rents paid by low-income families to a greater extent than the Danish system did. If the rent was high enough, people with above-average incomes could obtain a subsidy in the United Kingdom. In contrast, the Dutch and Danish systems were more concentrated in their effects. The Dutch allowances were significant only at above-average rents and below-average incomes and the Danish allowances made only a small contribution at above-average income levels.

The systems were further compared by examining their effects on the percentage of income devoted to rent. A major contrast between the British and the other two systems was the effect on the rent quota as incomes rose for a given rent level. As incomes increased from low to average, the proportion of income that had to be spent on rent in the United Kingdom rose, but it fell in Denmark and the Netherlands. (In the latter case it was simply because no subsidies were paid.) The large rent quota reductions for those on the lowest incomes in the United Kingdom were at the expense of a large increase in the rent burden as income rose. This much-observed problem for means-tested benefits was ameliorated in the Danish system by very low rates of benefit reduction as income rose up to the average income level, but by sharply reducing rates at above-average incomes. At average income levels the rent quota was reduced only for those with above-average rents. In this respect the three schemes were similar, although the percentage reductions were higher in the United Kingdom and Denmark than in the Netherlands. Also in the Netherlands the proportion of recipients with low quotas increased dramatically after subsidy and the proportion with high rent quotas was greatly reduced. There was also a gradual increase in the rent quota after subsidization as income rose.

It is clear from the evidence that the largest subsidies did not go to those with the lowest incomes. Housing allowance schemes have to cope with the inequalities of two distributions: one relating to incomes, the other to rents. If there was little variation in rent levels from one location to another and rents adequately reflected the standard of accommodation, policy makers could rationally decide that the "need" for assistance was mainly a function of income.

Such a situation is, however, hypothetical, for rents varied considerably within each of the countries considered. In Denmark, for example, there were differences associated with the age of properties. Despite these variations, housing allowance payments varied less with rent levels than in the other countries. The Danes were clearly relying on a "rent harmonization policy" to reduce the rent differences rather than simply using housing allowances to compensate for the differences. In contrast, the Dutch government faced with a similar "rent-gap" problem gave substantial help to households with high rents. This was partly a recognition of the failure of other policies to reduce rent-gaps. It can be argued that the West German *Wohngeld* exhibited insufficient variation with rent levels and location and, therefore, the scheme gave unequal treatment by region because the same rent level bought accommodation of different quality at different locations. Thus, those in the highest rent cities were helped less than those in lower rent areas. As a result, eight of the federal states of West Germany introduced supplementary income-related assistance to compensate for particularly high rents. (Bundesministerium für Raumordnung, Bauwesen und Stadtebau 1977, 9–12). If rents vary with location, what is sufficient to buy adequate accommodation in one area will be insufficient in another, and rent will be a poor proxy for quality. There are five policy options for governments in these circumstances:

First, to accept rent as a market signal and a proxy for a package of attributes including the quality of the dwelling and the general desirability of the area. Rents may then be said to represent quality as long as "quality" is redefined to include all these attributes. This policy option stresses the allocative functions borne by rent variations.

Second, do nothing if high rents in some locations are a result of local policy decisions. In these circumstances the central government might claim that the local government should accept the consequences of its decisions and introduce, if it wishes, local housing allowance schemes to help low-income households.

Third, the central government could choose to vary allowances with location.

Fourth, the government could attempt to reduce rent differences between areas by variations in subsidies to housing suppliers and by setting rules for the public or nonprofit sector that enforce consistent pricing.

Fifth, the government could define quality in terms of a minimum provision of facilities for households of different sizes, and then by means of rent regulations and/or housing allowances relate the amounts paid by individual households to both the quality of the dwelling and household circumstances.

The first option is most frequently selected. Elements of the second option are found in West Germany, where there are locally financed supplementary allowances, and in Britain, where local authorities with rents that are a specified amount above the average can apply for central government authorization to make more generous payments. Neither the West German nor the British situation amounts, however, to a nationally organized and financed system of local variations in housing allowances equivalent to the third option.

There are some examples of the fourth option. In France, object subsidies vary with location. There have been attempts to place nonprofit-sector rents in France, West Germany, and Denmark on an internally consistent basis. In the Netherlands a "points system" of rent determination has been adopted to relate quality to asking rent. In Britain the brief move in the early 1970s to a national "fair rents" system in the public sector was another attempt at consistency at the expense of local autonomy.

Although the fifth option has not been adopted in any of the countries, the allowance systems in France and Denmark do require dwellings to be of a minimum standard for any allowance to be paid. Furthermore, the "points system" in the Netherlands has attempted to reflect varying standards in the asking rent. If policies to achieve consistent pricing were successful, a major reason for adopting rent allowances in preference to income supplements would no longer be valid. However, in none of the countries investigated have the necessary conditions obtained.

Housing allowances alone cannot, of course, ensure that "most help goes to those in greatest need," for other aspects of housing policy can work against an equitable distribution of subsidies. For example, subsidies to owner occupiers tend to increase with income, especially in those countries with open-ended forms of mortgage interest tax relief. Even in France and West Germany, where the housing allowance schemes formally extend to owner occupiers, very few home owners benefit, mainly because households on low incomes are unable to obtain the necessary loans.

Low rates of take-up mean that housing allowance schemes fail to reach many of those eligible for benefit. The Dutch scheme had an estimated take-up rate of only 76 percent despite what is claimed to be "extensive advertising" in newspapers and on television (Wiewel 1979, 4 and 8). The Department of the Environment estimated the take-up of rent rebates in England and Wales in 1979 to be 72 percent and for rent allowances 50 percent.

In Britain, West Germany, and the Netherlands a high proportion of allowances is paid to pensioners. In West Germany "the allowance is principally a means of providing assistance to those who are not in employment" (Bundesministerium für Raumordnung, Bauwesen und Stadtebau 1977, 9). When a high proportion of recipients are in a particular social group and that group is already in receipt of state subsidies (for example, pensioners, unemployed), it may be administratively cheaper to combine housing allowances with these other payments. This might also increase take-up rates.

A household must lose some benefit as income rises if allowances are to give most help to those on lower incomes. However, if this "taxation" is large there may be consequences for household behavior that governments consider undesirable. It has been claimed that high "marginal taxation rates" implicit in housing allowance schemes affect the willingness of workers to obtain additional earned income and thereby reduce the supply of labor (Dick 1977, 22). This raises the question: Are significant reductions in benefit as income increases a necessary feature of housing allowance systems? Examination of marginal taxation rates for the Danish, British, and Dutch systems gave a partial answer. The progressive nature of the taxation in Denmark contrasted with the regressive nature in the other two countries where there were lower tax-rates at higher than at lower income levels. Furthermore, many housing allowance recipients did not face the question: "Shall I or shall I not acquire more income?" Many were pensioners and many were unemployed.

Whether or not housing allowances are distributed according to need clearly depends on what definition of need is used. Governments offer no definitions but allowance systems imply that need is some function of income, housing costs, and household size. If housing allowances are not sufficiently sensitive to variations in these items they clearly will not ensure that payments are distributed in an equitable fashion. The treatment of housing costs poses major problems that could be alleviated by consistent pricing and/or systematic variations in allowances with location. Low take-up rates, and the exclusion from schemes of owner occupiers and those without any independent accommodation, prevent housing allowances providing some consistent measure of assistance to households. In practice a high proportion of housing allowance recipients are elderly or unemployed. With the Danish example this shows that it is possible to structure housing allowances so that any weak disincentive effects due to the concentration of aid on lower-income households are likely to be insignificant.

HOUSING ALLOWANCES AND THE SUPPLY OF ACCOMMODATION

Within a free market framework, the effect of housing allowances on the quantity of housing services consumed depends on the following:

1. *The demand-increasing consequences of the allowance.* This will be a function of the price and income elasticities of demand for accommodation (given that housing allowances can be viewed as selective price reductions and income supplements). Unfortunately there is very little direct empirical evidence of these elasticities for recipients of housing allowances.
2. *The elasticity of supply of accommodation.* There is some limited information about improvements in housing circumstances but there appear to have been no attempts to develop and apply a methodology for specifically testing the supply response.

Some have argued that housing allowances may not lead to any improvements in the quantity or quality of accommodation consumed because rents and prices will rise and only landlords and landowners will benefit (see, for example, Nevitt 1966, 154; Donnison 1967, 264–65). This will, of course, be true only if supply is perfectly inelastic. It has also been argued that rents will rise only to the extent that the recipients of housing allowances use them to bid themselves into more preferred positions and "only the landlords of (better) accommodation in increased demand would be able to raise rents." (Pennance 1969, 30). However, it would be the landlords of accommodation in increased demand and inelastic supply that would be able to raise rents the most. There is no reason to assume that their accommodation is "better." Zeyl (1973, 151) has suggested that reliance on housing allowances "would be a gamble by the market" and without adequate competition, an abundant supply and complete mobility within the stock housing allowances will "be very costly for the community." With supply inelasticity, elements of price control and incentives to low-cost building are seen as essential.

In theory, housing allowances may lead to higher rents without any increase in quality, relieve the strain on recipients' budgets without changing housing quality, or lead to housing improvement through landlord repairs or by encouraging recipients to move to better housing. Rent controls can, of course, prevent rent inflation from occurring.

In the Netherlands, such rent increases have not occurred, probably because of the stabilizing influence of a large percentage of units owned by nonprofit organizations. Rent increases in controlled areas have been mainly to maintain or improve the return on capital rather than for housing improvements. The Dutch system is likely to lead to improvements only if recipients move to better housing and the mix of housing improvement and budget relief that results from housing allowances depends on the mobility of tenants. While there have been no longitudinal studies, available evidence on the consequences of Dutch housing allowances "suggests a considerable potential for mobility among low-income residents of low rent housing" (Wiewel 1979, 8). Of a sample of recipients living in "older" housing, 10 percent said they would not have moved into their current accommodation if they had not been eligible for a subsidy; for recipients in "newer" housing the proportion was 20 percent. Answers to other questions suggested that, on the average, recipients were prepared to pay 0.73 Dutch florins (DFl) more rent for every 1 DFl increase in allowance.

A high proportion of West German recipients live in newer (high-quality) accommodation. This is partly a function of the rent gap: Newer dwellings have higher rents. There is, however, evidence that suggests that the payment of housing allowances has been associated with improved standards of accommodation (Bundesministerium für Raumordnung, Bauwesen und Stadtebau 1977, 16–17). Other West German sources suggest that the housing allowance has very little effect on the demand or the supply of housing (Pfeiffer and Stahl 1975).

Housing allowances will have more influence on supply,

1. the higher the mobility of tenants, implying faster forward shifts in demand;
2. the higher the average vacancy rate in the stock in the short run, and the higher the elasticity of supply in the long run, implying reductions in transfers to housing owners;
3. the more differentiated the quality structure of newly constructed housing, especially in the lower quality brackets, implying a higher elasticity of supply in these quality brackets;
4. the more efficient the administration of the housing allowance scheme, including its adjustment to changing income and rent levels.

Pfeiffer and Stahl conclude that in West Germany there is insufficient tenant mobility, elasticity of supply, and efficiency in administration for the housing allowance scheme to have important supply-increasing consequences.

In the Netherlands, Denmark, and West Germany some economists who consider the housing problem mainly in terms of a requirement for increased supply are opposed to a large-scale use of housing allowances. It has been argued that housing allowances cannot deal with those factors that restrict the supply of housing, such as the provision of finance, and that object subsidies are necessary to increase the profitability of building. The Danish economist Sondergaard (1978) has suggested that moves toward subject subsidies have gone too far. He stresses the ability of object subsidies to give a better control over the supply of accommodation and to encourage both new building and modernization, and argues for a "re-allocation of subsidies from consumer aid to investment aid (p. 7)." In West Germany some have argued that the housing problem is mainly one of low-income minorities living in low-quality accommodation in large cities, necessitating improvement and rebuilding in city centers. While housing allowances may have distributional advantages, they will not help solve these "production" problems.

Conflicting propositions about the consequences of housing allowances (to what extent will there be higher prices or more supply?) arise out of conflicting assumptions about the price elasticity of supply of accommodation. However, the very concept of price elasticity is of varying significance from country to country. Much of the rented stock in Western Europe is in the nonprofit or public sector. Supply here is not necessarily a function of market demand and price.

Supply-side constraints do clearly inhibit the effectiveness of housing allowances in increasing the quantity and quality of housing consumed. Many of the objections to housing allowances arise from alternative perceptions of housing problems. Proponents of allowances consider housing problems mainly in terms of income levels and income and rent distributions rather than in terms of supply. Housing allowances clearly cannot solve problems on the supply side caused, for example, by financial or institutional restrictions. Some of the more naive advocates of housing allowances have argued that supply problems have been solved since crude housing shortages ceased to exist. Those policy instruments that are used to tackle supply problems will influence both the role that subject subsidies are to perform and the level at which they are to be paid.

HOUSING ALLOWANCES AND EQUITABLE DISTRIBUTION OF HOUSING SUBSIDIES

The evidence of the previous section suggests that supply-side restrictions prevent housing allowances giving any guarantee of distributional superiority over object subsidies.

Some economists view housing allowances as price reductions and thus see them as inferior in welfare terms to income supplements, which give consumers more choice and, for a given Exchequer cost, allow consumers to reach higher levels of utility than are possible with housing allowances (see, for example, Richardson 1978, 352–55; Stafford 1978, 68–69).

This analysis assumes that there are no restrictions on the supply of accommodation and households can make a free choice about how much housing they consume. Some households will be better able to bid themselves into situations of greater utility and/or greater housing consumption than others. Discrimination or entry conditions set by public- or private-sector landlords work against the reality of this assumption.

The analysis is sometimes used in an attempt to support the general proposition that current housing payments are not relevant in assessing how much assistance to give any household. Implicitly, this assumes that equal increases in income give equal increases in utility for any household at a given income level, and income supplements therefore satisfy the conditions for horizontal equity. This will be the case only if the relative prices of housing and nonhousing are the same before subsidy for all households who are to receive assistance. In practice this will not be the case because housing services are available at different prices to different households. The evidence shows that rents vary, for example, with the age of properties and location. If housing services are not priced on a consistent basis, income supplements of equivalent size have different conse-quences for both utility and housing consumption for households with equivalent incomes who face differing prices per unit of housing.

Housing allowances increase household resources and allow greater expend-iture on housing or nonhousing. In this sense they do not restrict choice. Although the receipt of housing allowances is tied to housing (in that the amount obtained is related to the price of housing services consumed) the spending is not. There are good reasons for linking the qualification for benefit to housing costs, es-pecially when housing costs vary from household to household in an indiscrim-inate fashion. Housing allowance schemes acknowledge the significance of variations in both incomes and housing costs as factors affecting the ability of households to improve their housing conditions.

Supply constraints can prevent housing allowances from achieving a more equitable distribution of aid than that achieved by object subsidies. If there are indiscriminate variations in housing costs and housing allowances are sufficiently sensitive to housing costs, they have the potential to give a more equitable distribution of aid than pure income supplements.

CONCLUSIONS

Proponents of subject subsidies believe that low levels of income or the dis-tribution of incomes in relation to costs is at the root of the housing problem. However, if too low a level of production or capital market shortages and high interest rates are deemed to be the central issue, object subsidies may be used to achieve production increases or cost reductions. If an inefficient or inequitable allocation of the stock is a major issue, housing allowances may have a part in improving the relationship between some measure of housing need and the size and quality of accommodation occupied, by supplementing the incomes of those with high needs but low incomes. However, overconsumption of housing by high-income groups with low needs will not be altered unless the allowance scheme is accompanied by some sort of tax on the use of accommodation by high-income earners. Only in this situation is a significant redistribution of the stock likely. This thinking was behind a proposal in the Netherlands in 1974 for an "assessment levy" to be paid by tenants with high incomes but low rents. The proposal was, however, rejected by Parliament and has not been revived. A similar *sur loyer* proved politically unpopular in France in the 1960s and was abandoned. A significant allocation problem arises out of the relationship between rents and the quality of accommodation. A satisfactory relationship between the two can be sought by means other than housing allowances. Housing allowance schemes do, however, tend to assume, implicitly, that asking rent is a suitable proxy for quality.

In recent years an increasing emphasis has been attached to housing allowances as a means of avoiding or correcting some of the alleged deficiences of object subsidies. The lack of discrimination in aid to buildings is supposedly avoided by personal subsidies that give most help to those in greatest need. There are some similarities between countries in how need is measured and thus in the basic structure of housing allowance systems, but there are important differences in the rates at which benefit is withdrawn as income rises and in the variability of the allowance with rent levels. Some schemes are more like general income supplements than others that more directly tackle the issue of household budget relief necessary as a result of high rents.

The experience in the different countries provides evidence relevant to the propositions detailed in the beginning of this chapter. These propositions raised questions about the relationship between housing allowances and (1) the need for household subsidies; (2) the supply of accommodation; and (3) an equitable distribution of housing subsidies.

Housing allowance schemes measure need with respect to household incomes, household size, and housing costs. The relative importance of these factors varies from country to country. Where rents vary significantly with the age of properties or location, allowances may not show sufficient variation to adequately help those with very high rents. Many households on the lowest incomes are ineligible for benefit because they do not have independent accommodation, have very low rents, or they are owner occupiers. Those in the greatest need may not qualify or may not claim assistance. The effective incidence of personal subsidies will be such that some of the benefits are shifted to suppliers.

Evidence suggests that housing allowances can lead to an improvement in the quality of accommodation occupied but it is likely that supply inelasticities severely limit the ability of housing allowances to induce major increases in supply, especially in the short run. Much of the rented accommodation in the countries studied is, furthermore, in the non-profit or public sector where additional supply will not necessarily be a function of increased expected profits resulting from increased demand.

The distributional consequences of housing allowances and the housing allowances versus income supplements debate are crucially affected by the degree of consistency in the pricing of accommodation. A lack of consistent pricing has been a powerful argument against income supplements. The introduction of housing allowances cannot, in isolation from other measures, promote an equitable distribution of housing subsidies if other subsidies and regulations that arbitrarily distort housing consumption continue. This is especially true where allowances apply only to the rented sector and income-regressive subsidies to owner occupiers are maintained.

Housing allowances fill a gap between an acceptable housing payment by the household and the cost of decent accommodation. Before deciding in favor of housing allowances and determining the form the allowance is to take, governments have to take a view on what is acceptable and what is decent and how, in the rented sector, the asking rents for decent accommodation are to be determined: market rents, cost price rents, rents according to quality points, local authority discretion, or something else? If the resulting rent level is too low, an insufficient quantity of new housing units will be provided by market forces. How in these circumstances is the government to encourage supply? If allowances are extended to owner occupiers, governments have to decide whether mortgage costs or some other imputed measure is to serve as the indicator of housing costs. If the government is willing to allow market rents and prices to be the basis for consumer charges and for determining the level of output, the case for an exclusive use of housing allowances is stronger than if the government has alternative aims regarding the determination of rents, prices, and the level of output.

One cannot prove that housing allowances are better than object subsidies or inferior to general income supplements. The relative merits of policy instruments must be judged in relation to their aims and with the aid of an analysis of the factors that impede the achievement of those aims. The less housing policy is viewed as a question of production and the more a question of distributional justice the greater is the emphasis attached to housing allowances. The more distributional justice is seen simply as a distribution of income problem the greater is the emphasis on personal income supplements and the less on personal subsidies tied to housing consumption.

The structure of housing allowance schemes will vary with their aims. If housing allowances are to be a means of redistributing incomes they must be judged in relation to other redistributive mechanisms. If housing allowances are to be a means of compensating for inconsistent pricing one needs to question why inconsistent pricing exists and what can be done about it. If there are efficient redistributive mechanisms at work and there is consistent pricing in the housing market the case for housing allowances rests only on arguments about encouraging households to consume more of a specific commodity that the state considers desirable.

REFERENCES

Bundesministerium für Raumordung, Bauwesen und Stadtebau
1977 *"Wohngeld und Mietenbericht,"* part translation "Report on Rents," Part C, British Library RTS 12382A.
Dick, E.
1977 "Distribution of Housing Costs between the Public Sector and Individuals." *Proceedings* of UNECE Seminar on Housing Policy, Turku, Finland, July.
Donnison, D.
1967 *The Government of Housing.* London: Penguin.
Howenstine, E. J.
1986 *Housing Vouchers: A Comparative International Analysis.* New Brunswick, N.J.: Center for Urban Policy Research.
Local Finance
1977 "Reform of Housing Finance in France: Barre Report." *Local Finance* 6, no. 1, February 1.
Nevitt, A.
1966 *Housing, Taxation and Subsidies.* London: Nelson.

Oxley, M. J.
1983 "Housing Policy in Western Europe: An Economic Analysis of the Aims and Instruments of Housing Policy in the United Kingdom, West Germany, France, the Netherlands, Denmark and Ireland." Unpublished doctoral dissertation, Leicester University.

Pennance, F. G.
1969 *Housing Analysis and Policy*, Hobart Paper 48. London: The Institute of Economic Affairs.

Pfeiffer, U., and K. Stahl
1975 "Housing Finance Policies in Germany." Paper supplied in translation by West German Federal Ministry for Regional Planning, Building and Urban Development.

Richardson, H. W.
1978 *Regional and Urban Economics*. London: Penguin.

Sondergaard, J.
1978 *Direct og indirect tilsud til boligsforbruget*, SBI Report 107, part translation "Direct and Indirect Housing Subsidies," British Library RTS 12384A, 12385A, 12387A.

Stafford, D. C.
1978 *The Economics of Housing Policy*. London: Croom Helm.

Wiewel, W.
1979 "Housing Allowances and the Dutch Rent Subsidy Program." *Rand Corporation Paper*.

Zeyl, N.
1973 "Systems of Individual Subsidies." In *Proceedings* of UNECE Seminar on Financing of Housing. Geneva: UNECE, August.

11

The Impact of High Rent-Income Ratios on Other Consumer Expenditures

SHERMAN HANNA AND SUZANNE LINDAMOOD

Abstract. To target limited rental assistance funds more effectively, information is needed on the impact of high rents on other consumer expenditures. This chapter analyzes a sample of renter households in the 1980/81 Survey of Consumer Expenditures conducted by the U. S. Bureau of Labor Statistics. Expenditures on five nonhousing spending categories were regressed on household income, household size, age, rent-income ratios, and all quadratic terms. Controlling for income, household size, and age, rent-income ratios were positively related to expenditures in the categories examined for almost all households with annual incomes over $3,000.

INTRODUCTION

Housing policies in many countries have been based partly on the goal of helping families avoid having to pay too high a proportion of income for housing expenses. Along with the primary housing policy goal of providing decent housing and neighborhoods, the goal of holding down housing cost for low- and moderate-income families is reflected in many housing assistance programs. Starting with observations over 100 years ago that workers tended to pay a week's wages for a month's rent (Feins and Lane 1981), the rule of thumb has been that families should not spend more than 25 percent of income for housing. This guideline seems sensible, as obviously families must buy food, clothing, and other items that provide for physiological and psychological comfort.

Presumably, families who must spend a high proportion of their incomes on housing must compensate by reducing other spending, or by reducing their savings, liquidating assets, or borrowing. If families with high proportions of income devoted to housing cut back on necessities such as food or health care, there would be a social justification beyond the direct improvement of housing and neighborhoods for providing housing assistance. Obviously, families cannot continue for long periods of time to live off assets or credit.

It is possible that families base their spending on long-run expected income rather than current income. In terms of either Milton Friedman's (1957) permanent income theory or Franco Modigliani's (1986) life cycle theory, families set their spending levels as a proportion of their permanent income. A family that temporarily has low income will spend a high proportion of income for all spending categories.

If Friedman's or Modigliani's theories are valid, rent-income ratios will be positively related to spending-income ratios in nonhousing categories. If a household's income drops, it can try to reduce housing expenses by moving and cut back on other expenses, or maintain spending at usual levels in anticipation of a return to a normal income level.

Variability in real income frequently occurs due to changes in jobs, self-employment income, family membership (divorce, death, and so on), and other causes. Studies of the University of Michigan Panel Study on Income Dynamics have found that many U.S. households have significant (more than 5 percent) increases or decreases in real income levels over a five-year period (Lane and Morgan 1975). Only 40 percent of households were in the same income quintiles in both 1978 and in 1971 (Duncan 1984). Changes of more than one income quintile between 1971 and 1978 were experienced by 23 percent of households (Duncan 1984). Only about 11 percent of households in poverty in one or more years between 1971 and 1978 were in poverty during all eight years (Duncan 1984). Low-income households have greater income variability than do middle- and upper-income households (Mirer 1973).

Given the variability of relative household income, traditional policies of rental assistance programs, based on current income for periods of a year or less, may be inappropriate. If households do have a planning horizon of a year or less, then very high rent levels relative to income might lead to sacrifices in other spending, which in turn might cause problems for health or other aspects of the quality of life. If, on the other hand, households have a longer planning horizon, as suggested by Friedman and Modigliani, high rent-income ratios may be accommodated by borrowing or dissaving rather than by sacrifices in nonhousing expenditures. The impact of high rent-income ratios on household spending patterns is relevant to key questions about housing allowance programs, such as ''Do housing allowances give most help to those in greatest need?'' (See chapter 10 by Oxley in this volume).

The purpose of this chapter is to ascertain the impact of high rent-income ratios on other consumer expenditures. For a sample of renters, spending in each of five categories is regressed on the rent-income ratio and household characteristics. If families tend to cut back on other spending to compensate for a high rent-income ratio, a high rent-income ratio should be related to lower spending in nonhousing categories.

METHODS

Variables

Expenditure Categories. Six expenditure categories are defined: food, housing, transportation, health care, clothing, and all other current consumption. The housing category includes rent plus insurance, fuel and other utilities, repairs, improvements, furnishings, and equipment. An advantage of using a broad definition of housing is that housing expenditures of families in different situations can be more accurately compared. For instance, rent for a furnished apartment with all utilities included should not be compared to rent for an unfurnished apartment with no utilities included in the rent. By defining housing expenditures as the total of all housing-related expenses, comparisons between different households are more valid. However, the comprehensive housing expenditure amounts and rent-income ratios reported here are higher than the rent-income ratios that are based only on contract rent.

Transportation includes expenditures for all forms of transportation, except for vacations. Health care includes all medical insurance, plus all expenditures for doctors, dentists, hospitals, medicines, and such. All other current consumption expenditures are lumped together. Important components of the other category include alcohol, tobacco, insurance, gifts, vacations, recreation, and education.

Independent Variables. The independent variables are annual after-tax household income, household size, age of householder, the rent-income ratio, and all quadratic terms. The rent-income ratio is total annual housing expenditures as a percentage of annual after-tax household income. (Results using pretax income were similar to those reported here.)

The Sample

The data for this analysis are the most recent available to us from the public-use tape file from the expenditure data collected in the quarterly interview component of the 1980/81 Consumer Expenditure Survey of the U.S. Bureau of Labor Statistics. Only renter households with four quarters of data were included in this analysis.

RESULTS

Descriptive Statistics

The median rent-income percentage was 36; see Table 11.1 for other percentiles of the rent-income distribution. Eight percent of the households reported zero or negative after-tax incomes, so for those households, the rent-income ratio was calculated as if income equaled one dollar. Obviously, as income approaches zero, the rent-income ratio becomes very large. Therefore, percentiles of the rent-income ratio for households with after-tax incomes greater than $3,000 are also presented in Table 11.1.

Based on a means test, the subgroup of renters differed significantly from all renters only in terms of age and income (see Table 11.2). Renters with incomes

Table 11.1
Distribution of Rent as a Percentage of Income, 1980/81

	Rent as % of Aftertax Income	
	All Renters	Renters with Incomes Greater Than $3,000
5th percentile	13%	13%
25th percentile	24	22
50th percentile (median)	36	32
75th percentile	59	44
95th percentile	297,193*	74
99th percentile	*	106
Maximum	*	242
Mean	*	36
n	1,182	986

*These levels are not meaningful, as they represent ratios based on very low incomes.

Source: Prepared by the authors, based on analysis of computer tapes for the 1980/81 interview component of the U.S. Bureau of Labor Statistics, Survey of Consumer Expenditures.

over $3,000 had a mean age of 43, compared to a mean age of 45 for all renters; and they had a mean income level of $13,127, compared to $11,055 for all renters. Surprisingly, there were no significant differences between the two groups in any of the spending levels.

Regressions

For each of the five nonhousing expenditure categories, a stepwise regression was run.[1] In each spending category, predicted spending increased as the rent-income ratio increased. For two spending categories—apparel and health care—predicted spending increased with the rent-income ratio, then decreased, but the negative relationship existed only at very high levels of rent-income ratios that existed for less than 1 percent of the renters with incomes over $3,000 per year.

Table 11.2
Means and Standard Deviations of Household Size, Age of Householder, Rent, After-Tax Income, and Spending, 1980/81

Variable	All Renter Households		Renter Households with Incomes > $3,000	
	Mean	Standard Deviation	Mean	Standard Deviation
Household Size	2.3	1.6	2.4	1.6
Age of Householder	45	20	43	19
Annual Gross Rent	3,802	2,159	3,856	2,082
Aftertax Income	11,055	9,775	13,127	9,399
Total Spending	11,301	7,038	11,691	6,965
Nonhousing Spending	7,499	5,484	7,835	5,471
Food	2,503	1,466	2,543	1,458
Apparel	663	680	690	677
Health Care	551	955	572	1,012
Transportation	2,043	2,631	2,168	2,723
Other	2,291	2,339	2,434	2,279

Source: Prepared by the authors, based on analysis of computer tapes for the 1980/81 component of the U.S. Bureau of Labor Statistics, Survey of Consumer Expenditures.

Figure 11.1 shows the predicted relationship between spending in each of five nonhousing categories, and rent as a percentage of income, at mean values of income, household size, and age of the householder. It should be noted that the 99th percentile of rent as a percentage of income was 106 percent, yet the relationship between spending and the rent-income ratio becomes negative for apparel only when the ratio exceeds 138 percent, and for health care only when the ratio exceeds 115 percent. Therefore, for over 99 percent of the subsample, the relationship between predicted spending and the rent-income ratio is positive.

The regressions for the five nonhousing spending categories provide inefficient estimates.[2] An efficient estimate can be obtained by using total nonhousing spending as a dependent variable. The relationship between predicted nonhousing spending and rent as a percentage of income is shown in Figure 11.2, assuming

Figure 11.1
Predicted Annual Spending by Rent-Income Percentages at Mean Values of Income, Age, and Family Size

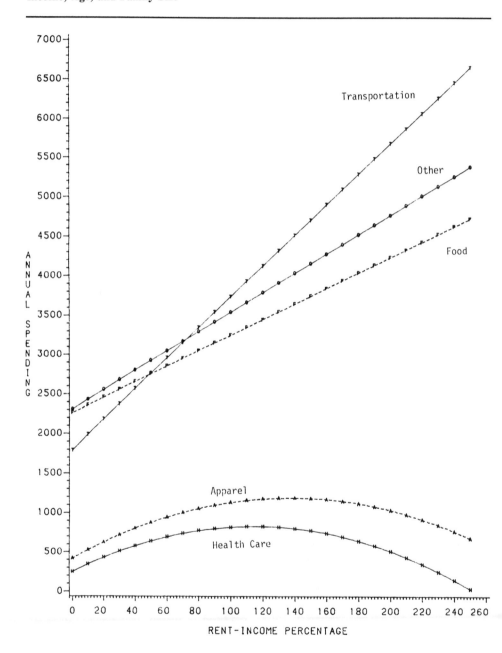

Source: Data compiled by the authors.

Figure 11.2
Predicted Annual Nonhousing Spending by Rent-Income Percentages at Mean
Values of Income, Age, and Family Size

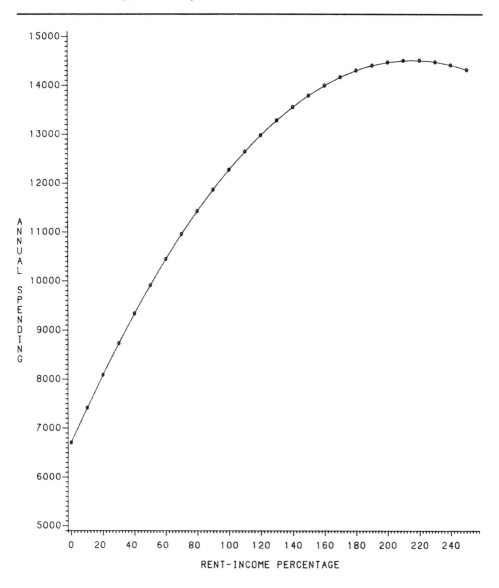

Source: Data compiled by the authors.

mean values of income, household size, and age of householder. This relationship is positive for rent-income ratios lower than 215 percent, or over 99 percent of the subsample.

DISCUSSION

One should be cautious in making inferences from this cross-sectional analysis, but there seems to be some evidence that most households with high rent-income ratios do not have lower nonhousing spending than similar households with lower rent-income ratios. It seems plausible to conclude that households tend to deal with high rent-income ratios by overspending and dissaving, rather than by cutting back on nonhousing spending.

Given the austerity being imposed on many government housing programs, and the need to focus assistance on the truly needy, it would seem wise to examine rental assistance formulas carefully. One step in this direction would be to focus on longer time periods in evaluating the resources of families in need. Many households may move in and out of poverty in terms of current income (Duncan 1984), without suffering great hardships. Other households may have long-term poverty associated with aging, disability, or other problems, and thus be in greater need of rental assistance than temporarily poor households.

The findings of this study indicate that nonhousing spending stays high as the rent-income ratio increases up to very high levels. Our results seem to be consistent with Friedman's permanent income theory and Modigliani's life cycle theory, in that households seem to have related their spending more to some long-run measure of income rather than current annual income, and thus nonhousing spending-income ratios were positively related to rent-income ratios. More efficient estimating techniques should be applied to this data set, as well as more recent data from the United States and from other countries.

NOTES

1. Variables could enter the regression only if the impact on the dependent variable was significantly different from zero at the .01 level, and if the mimimum tolerance was 0.1. (A variable could not enter the regression if the independent variables already in the regression could account for more than 90 percent of the variance in that independent variable.) The regression results are shown below:

Variable	Food	Apparel	Health Care	Transpor-tation	Other	Total Non-housing
Income	0.111	0.064	0.035	0.268	0.180	0.664
Income Squared	-8.76E-7	-4.88E-7		-2.96E-6		-5.00E-6
Age Squared		-0.050	0.106	-0.194	-0.150	-0.349
Family Size	396.017				-126.933	252.307
Rent % of Income	9.907	11.174	10.033	19.470	12.326	72.565

Rent % Squared		-0.041	-0.044			-0.168
Constant	6.976	-246.830	-402.936	-864.324	258.374	-1759.742
Adjusted R^2	0.462	0.322	0.089	0.257	0.512	0.567

Source: Prepared by the authors, based on analysis of computer tapes for the 1980/81 interview component of the U.S. Bureau of Labor Statistics Survey of Consumer Expenditures.

2. The regressions for the five nonhousing expenditure categories provide inefficient estimations, as applying ordinary least squares regressions separately to each equation does not use all of the information available about the system of equations. The total of the six expenditure categories equals total current consumption expenditure, which is available separately. While there are more efficient estimation techniques available that could be applied to a system of equations (Pindyck and Rubinfeld 1976), simply regressing total nonhousing spending on the same set of independent variables provides an efficient constrained estimate of the effect of rent-income ratios and other variables on total consumption. The results of that regression indicate that total nonhousing spending increases as the rent-income ratio increases, up to the point that rent equaled 215 percent of after-tax income.

REFERENCES

Duncan, G.
1984   *Years of Poverty, Years of Plenty: The Changing Economic Fortunes of American Workers and Families*. Ann Arbor: Institute for Social Research, University of Michigan.
Feins, J. D., and T. S. Lane.
1981   *How Much For Housing?: New Perspectives on Affordability and Risk*. Cambridge, Mass.: Abt Books.
Friedman, M.
1957   *A Theory of the Consumption Function*. National Bureau of Economic Research. Princeton, N.J.: Princeton University Press.
Lane, J. P., and J. N. Morgan.
1975   "Patterns of Change in Economic Status and Family Structure." In *Five Thousand American Families: Patterns of Economic Progress*, Vol. III, edited by G. J. Duncan and J. N. Morgan. Ann Arbor: Institute for Social Research, University of Michigan.
Mirer, T.
1973   "Aspects of the Variability of Family Income." In *Five Thousand American Families: Patterns of Economic Progress*, Vol. II, edited by J. N. Morgan. Ann Arbor: Institute for Social Research, University of Michigan.
Modigliani, F.
1986   "Life Cycle, Individual Thrift, and the Wealth of Nations." *American Economic Review* 76, 297–313.
Pindyck, R. S., and Rubinfeld, D. L.
1976   *Econometric Models and Economic Forecasts*. New York: McGraw-Hill.

PART VI

STATE POLITICS AND HOUSING

12

Scarce State Resources and Unrestrained Processes in the Socialist City: The Case of Housing

BRONISLAW MISZTAL AND BARBARA A. MISZTAL

Abstract. In this chapter we investigate the nature of the relation between economic development and social needs under state socialism. We argue that housing is one of the principal commodities sought by the citizen and controlled by the state. Social housing policies in Poland are then reviewed, and it is concluded that the socialist state has withdrawn from its earlier welfare promises regarding availability of housing for every member of socialist society. Subsequently, housing has become a scarce resource, subject to market regulations and not to social policies' control. We link this new situation not only to the fiscal strain experienced by the socialist state, but also, to a considerable degree, to the profound restratification of socialist society, in the course of which egalitarian ideals were mostly abandoned and replaced by consumerist ones. Together, those factors contributed to inefficiency and chaos of urban development, releasing a peculiar mixture of uncontrolled and unrestrained processes that have become a structural feature of the socialist economy.

INTRODUCTION

Socialist state systems, unlike capitalism, do not create a developed private sector. Market forces in their pure form are not supposed to play a role of economic regulation. The principal factor of social organization under socialism is the state. Its major premises are that social forces are to be controlled, and that social development should become a rational process subject to control by the state. Such control should introduce the logic of the system into the process of social development. A key element of socialist macro-logics is a system of values according to which the costs and rewards of the implementation of developmental scenarios are split equally among segments in society. Such is the egalitarian principle of the socialist state according to recurrent political rhetorics. Ideology is the ultimate organization to oversee the controlled course of social processes and their congruence with the superior value system.

The state, therefore, is responsible for the magnitude and level of social consumption including housing. Whereas for capitalism the political meaning of the urban question is reduced to tensions between "private sector profitability and social needs" (Saunders 1981, 267), for the socialist system the urban question means tensions between state developmental strategy and social needs. The aim of this chapter is to investigate the nature of the relation between economic development and social needs as mediated and controlled by the socialist state, with special reference to housing.

HISTORICAL BACKGROUND

Among many various goods that are desired and that become an object of unfulfilled aspirations, housing is for two reasons definitely at the top of the list in Poland. Decent living conditions in one's own apartment have always been a rather unattainable value for a majority of Poles. Until 1939, the living standards of the population varied greatly, and only the richest strata were able to afford decent urban housing. A majority of Poles, however, had very poor living conditions, since the program of industrial modernization had started only shortly before World War II. When the war ended, its disastrous effects were seen first of all in the area of housing. More than 60 percent of the urban stock had been destroyed. Therefore, not only was Poland backward as far as housing standards were concerned, it also suffered a specific handicap because of the war damage.

The developmental strategy adopted by the authorities in the postwar period was based on the premise of rapid industrial growth. The cities remained outside the focus of this policy, since they were seen as a by-product of industrial development. The demand for housing grew along with the implementation of the forced industrialization policy. However, limited state expenditures on the urban infrastructure in industrialized centers have been responsible for a continuation of serious housing deficiencies (*Zycie Gospodarcze* 1985). Adverse effects of limited urbanization and inconsistent state housing policies were exacerbated by two further processes: continuous migration to the cities and three baby booms (in the early 1950s, in the 1960s, and in the 1980s). This led to an increasing gap between a rising demand for housing and shrinking possibilities of the state to deliver the needed apartments.

In 1970 there was a shortage of 1,295,000 apartments, measured by the number of households exceeding the number of apartments available statewide. The housing stock would have to grow by 16 percent in order to fill the gap between demand and supply of housing in 1970. During the next 15 years the gap between the needs and the possibilities of satisfying them deepened. In 1982 the housing shortage reached 1,800,000, or 18.3 percent of the available resources. While in 1970 every fourth household in Poland did not have an apartment of its own, in 1982 this percentage had increased to 28 percent (*Zycie Gospodarcze* 1985). The housing shortage and the absence of social control over state housing policies have resulted in several unrestrained processes by which Polish society tries to cope with this problem.

THE UNRESTRAINED PROCESSES UNDER STATE
SOCIALISM

Socialist societies are generally perceived as positively overcoming the un-restrained character of social development. With the exception of Poland, the state exerts full control over property and production relations. Social life and economic development are subject to planning by specialized governmental agen-cies. The planning process itself is supposed to be controlled and mediated by society. It is believed that these planned social processes are superior to those that take place spontaneously. This theoretical principle is fully embodied by the idea of the so-called socialist city.

The theoretical notion of the socialist city emerges from analytical studies by Polish urban sociologists, planners, architects, and urbanists. The main assumed feature is that its development does not occur spontaneously, but is directed by central plans. The socialist city, therefore, was expected to embody major face values of socialist ideology. One would expect, thereby, the emergence of ad-vanced egalitarianism processes, the withering away of sociospatial segregation, and optimal satisfaction of urban dwellers' basic needs.

In actual fact, the functioning of cities in the socialist countries diverges greatly from this ideological model. Urban development has become increasingly com-plicated and uncoordinated. Despite the efforts of an egalitarian housing policy in the 1950s, when apartments were granted to various social strata, spatial segregation already existed and it was further intensified as "migrants from rural areas took rooms in working class districts" (Hamilton 1979, 253). In the 1970s, the city of Warsaw showed considerable sociospatial segregation: "compared to the downtown and central zones, the external zone . . . indicated different social structure, containing twice as many blue collar workers than the intelligentsia" (Ciechocinska 1975, 225). The relegation of the working class to ecologically worse, peripheral districts, with poor-quality housing, a sparse public transpor-tation network, and so on, was due to several reasons.

First, a large group of worker-tenants agreed to change their residence into more distant locations when offered significant cash refunds by those willing to move into old, central districts. Second, the impoverished residents of the old housing estates could no longer afford the costs of maintenance, or the costs of modernization of their apartments, and they, too, moved to more convenient but distant locations. Third, the bill reestablishing private ownership of small multi-apartment houses was introduced by the power elite in their search for luxurious housing. New, powerful owners displaced old tenants to the municipal housing stock and took over old villas of petite bourgeoisie, so proudly nationalized in 1944. Indeed, the most recent research indicates increasing areas of privilege and deprivation and deepening social distance between the rich and the poor in the socialist city (Sieminski 1980–86).

Since Polish cities consist of several disorderly monofunctional zones (indus-trial, residential, and commercial), severe social problems arise such as lengthy commuting, incomplete infrastructure of new housing estates, and a shortage of basic urban services. Consequently, a wide range of private, entrepreneurial initiatives substitutes for the nonexisting or unavailable services that were supposed to be provided by the socialist welfare system—for example, private nursery schools (payable) and private day-care centers (payable) have emerged at distant housing estates.

Limited availability of labor is also responsible for urban social problems, some of which affect the housing situation. Two different political decisions have had a particularly sharp impact on housing. First, in the 1950s, it was decided to transform the social structure of existing urban populations by adding new industrial sites. The objective was to counterbalance the nonproletarian tradition and to supplement the city with new working class districts. Examples are the Nowa Huta steel mill, located in a Cracow neighborhood, and the Huta Warszawa steel mill in Warsaw.

Second, the status of a "closed city," with sealed off administrative borders, was invented to bar prospective migrants and to control social structure in the most important urban-industrial centers. Not surprisingly, industry was the most powerful actor to break down the restrictive policies with counteractions, which were, in fact, unrestrained processes.

By the mid–1970s, two major processes affected Polish cities. First, reforms of the state administration system have abolished the relative autonomy of some centers and undermined the financial basis of all towns. Their budgets were to be set centrally by allocation of funds from state resources. At the same time, the part of industry that previously was subordinated to the urban administration was included into the state-controlled "key-industry" system. The local industry used to be the sole contributor to the cities' budgets. With the absence of local or regional taxation of individuals and businesses, the cities became entirely dependent on state allocation of funds. The centralized system of appropriation and distribution of locally produced surplus value did not reflect local or regional contribution to the state budget.

Second, the overwhelming economic crisis created an unprecedented shortage of raw materials, construction materials, and other commodities necessary for reproduction of urban infrastructure. When confronted with such shortage, the state authorities decided to maintain the priority of supply for key or strategic industries, at the expense of curbing supply of those materials to the cities. The centralized system of administration, along with the previously achieved dismantling of relative local independence (through the so-called reform) helped to implement several austerity measures that affected cities. For example, the former process led to shutting down local brick factories as inefficient and the subordination of the remaining plants to the construction industry. The latter process deprived cities of a central supply of construction materials.

The fiscal crisis of cities had a feed-back effect on industry. In fact, major industrial sites were either located within urban agglomerations or otherwise dependent on the urban infrastructure for housing and transportation of its employees. With a staggering urban economy it proved to be impossible to fully use existing industrial capacities. For example, in the late 1970s the president of the city of Gdansk reported that several factories were operating on a one- or two-shift system instead of a three-shift system because the city was unable to house enough labor.

The fiscal strain and austerity measures experienced by cities and industry led to the emergence of several informal and spontaneous measures to cope with the crisis. Wherever the industrial sector in the cities was powerful and affluent enough it offered to undertake common endeavors, financed by industry, and frequently also based on the use of industry's resources (construction materials, trucks, excavators, and manpower). Several housing projects, as well as roads, shopping, medical, and health care facilities, resulted from such cooperation. Obviously, industry demanded some concessions in return for investment participation. Usually it requested that restrictions on residence permits be lifted for the new employees of contributing plants, and that apartments in new estates be allocated to persons designated by industrial administration and not by cooperative self-management.

According to research conducted in Warsaw in the 1970s, the annual increase of housing units was more or less equal to the number of residence permits granted and to the increase of jobs—approximately 12,000 per year (Misztal 1979). It was the industry that overwhelmingly consumed the housing increase for its newly hired people. These people were brought to the city despite restrictions, and urban authorities were forced to grant both resident and housing permits if they were to profit from financial and management aid provided by industry.

These dynamics of urban industrial forces did away with the planned character of urban development. Urban growth in general, and housing in particular, were a result of accidental and uncoordinated decisions by different branches of industry. There was a vacuum in planning and administering urban processes caused by political, financial, and bargaining weaknesses of the urban authorities, and if the industry had not taken over, several functions would have collapsed. This is evident from the fact that 72 percent of the day-care centers, 30 percent of the nursery schools, 69 percent of the district cultural centers, and 33 percent of the movie theaters were founded with funds that came from industry.

The same processes continue to operate in the 1980s. However, the scope of the economic crisis and the austerity measures taken by the military authorities since 1982 have severely limited the scale of informal operations, which usually means abuse of budgets or by-passing of existing regulations. The effort has been made to create some opportunities of housing investment for the most powerful industrial actors. The authorities allowed registration of more than 2,000 of the so-called small cooperatives, being, in fact, groups of industrial-sector employees sponsored by their respective factories or branches. These new cooperatives, unlike earlier projects, are managed without participation of city authorities (especially regarding size of apartments and allocation of tenants).

The industrial or particularistic impact on urban development, along with lack of social control over this process, have magnified the differentiation of living conditions in and between the cities. Inequalities exist mostly in the sphere of housing and urban facilities, dividing big and small towns, industrial and non-industrial cities. Egalitarianism of housing was never effectively implemented.

THE CASE OF HOUSING

Since housing is mediated through economic and social policies of the state, it is this field of social consumption where deprivation is experienced most strongly. Since the 1940s the Polish housing situation has been serious. The politically based developmental strategy, favoring the goals of immediate production over the fulfillment of social needs, had its impact on housing policies. Housing policies of the state have been inconsistent: While social pressures and uprisings forced the state to increase housing expenditures temporarily, or to distribute them more equally, such periods were usually followed by a sharp drop in the level of collective consumption. The level of housing investments fluctuated subject to changing conceptions regarding state control over the housing economy. The original premise of full and perfect control over housing and of the protective welfare function of the socialist state was gradually abandoned and replaced by the concept of privatization of housing, allowing a free housing market to emerge.

Immediately after World War II, the authorities allowed private investments in the reconstruction of destroyed buildings in order to promote individual initiative in the improvement of the housing situation. Those who decided to invest in housing were guaranteed that they could retain renovated apartments or houses. This process ended in 1950, when up to 15 percent of all funds came from private hands, leading to considerable improvement of the housing stock of the cities.

Since the late 1940s, the cornerstone of the state's social policy was that major social services were to be provided by the state itself, housing included. Full socialism was to be achieved by the involvement of state capital, an increase in centralized control, and nationalization of all property. In 1951, all privately renovated housing was taken over by the state's urban administration, and the centralized system of allocation, administration, and disposition of housing was established. The state authorities also issued norms, prescribing an allowed maximum apartment size in municipal housing construction. This stage corresponded with the period of intended equity in the whole of the system. No private property was possible. Even the cooperatives from before the war were taken under compulsory state control. At this time, the authorities even used to allocate several families to previously privately owned apartments. The allocation of apartments took place through the state-operated employment system—that is, a person had to get a housing permit from his or her employer. Rents were extremely low, the costs of maintenance and construction were borne by the state, which exerted full control over the otherwise financially helpless citizen. When the housing authority noticed a household whose apartment was larger than the prescribed average of square meters per capita, it either forced the family to move to another, smaller apartment, or if there was an extra room, the authority would allocate it to another family. Such was the meaning of controlled social processes in housing. Despite its leveling character, this process helped to improve considerably the housing situation of thousands of people who otherwise would have had to live in slums. Throughout the 1950s an effort was made to provide a separate apartment for every family and household by the late 1970s.

By the mid–1960s, however, the processes of restratification of society had already started, and the costs of forced industrial growth were consuming an overwhelming portion of the state's investment capital. The state was simply unable to afford intensive industrialization and the subsidized housing model simultaneously. More and more migrants came to the cities, more traditional town people lined up for new apartments, while considerably fewer funds were available. On the other hand, the financial standing of part of the population made certain social groups willing to divert their earnings into housing investments, provided this would shorten their waiting time. At that time, however, the restoration of private property was not possible for ideological reasons, since this would be at odds with facade slogans of state socialism. The state was confronted with the dilemma of how to reshift to the private sector the costs of housing and to retain control over the allocation process of this important social good. By the mid–1950s, the parity of private investments in housing reached the dangerous volume of 40 percent. Further relaxation was not possible without significant concessions regarding property relations.

POLICY CHANGES

To solve the dilemma, the authorities launched an extensive cooperative housing program, based mostly on private investment, but via the cooperative financial system. Unlike municipal housing, which was cheap and subsidized in full, cooperative housing was based in part on private funds. The state established new norms and standards, restricting municipal housing to the poor and underprivileged. All families with average incomes who wished a new apartment had to apply for a cooperative apartment.

This significant shift in state social policies took place around 1960, as evidenced by the proportion of housing investments in the state's general spendings: 21.0 percent in 1958, 16.1 percent in 1961–65, and 14.0 percent in 1966–70. In other terms, the state withdrew from its former function of providing housing, making individual people responsible for the fulfillment of this need. Gradually, state subsidies to housing were further limited, and the cooperative system monopolized the process of production and distribution of apartments.

The cooperatives did not emerge freely, but were subject to strict control by the authorities. A system of preferences, norms, and prescriptions specified the conditions under which the cooperative could grant an apartment to a person designated by the authorities, usually skipping the waiting list. Therefore, despite organizational relaxation and the socialization (that is, reshifting) of construction costs, the state could still exert control over housing, and the construction distribution process was still subject to restrictions that effectively curbed the play of free market forces.

Also the cooperative housing system established in the 1960s is based on the tenant cooperative principle according to which the property is in collective hands and not hereditary. Consequently, no market transactions are possible, since an apartment returns to the collective owner when a tenant dies or when a tenant moves to another apartment.

Along with the restratification of society that took place in the 1970s, the state modified its housing policies. The tenant cooperatives did not solve the housing problem, since waiting lists were long (at that time about five to six years after the down payment); apartments—to comply with prescribed norms—were tiny. Many people whose financial standing improved found that their rising housing aspirations could not be fulfilled by the existing system. To meet these needs the owners' cooperative system was implemented with the intention to skim the richest and the most impatient from the housing market, to whom apartments would be delivered sooner, with fewer restrictions regarding size, but for considerably more money. Blooming of the owners' cooperatives in the 1970s was further promoted by an unprecented move, when the state allowed mixed-status cooperatives and approved the sale of previously constructed, state-owned apartments. This step, taken in 1973, meant a reestablishment of private real estate property under the state socialist system. An apartment previously owned by the state could now be bought by a tenant, who would be allowed to rent it out, sell it, or exchange it against any other type of real property. Also, any state-owned apartment could be changed into a privately owned one within the same cooperative, usually by an administrative procedure that involved payment of a lump sum to the cooperative. At the same time, there remained a need for municipal or state housing, because some layers of Polish society were too poor to afford such a status conversion.

Since the reprivatization of the housing system, the state has abandoned its former premise of full control over housing. In 1980, owing to subsequent increases in the prices of construction materials and manpower, the costs of housing delivered through cooperatives has tripled, compared to the 1970 level. Also the state increased the prices of apartments put on sale from the municipal stock; its price in 1985 was six times more than what it was in 1973. The state managed to reshift to the private sector the overwhelming portion of housing costs.

CURRENT DEVELOPMENTS AND CONDITIONS

Shifting economic and social policies of the state regarding housing did not result, however, in significant improvement of the housing situation in Poland.

There is still a considerable apartment shortage. During the economic crisis of the 1980s, the drop in housing construction was sharper than the drop of production in any other sphere of the economy. In 1984 the volume of apartment construction was about 25 percent lower than in 1979 (Lutokanski 1985). At present, the level of housing construction in Warsaw does not exceed that of 1956. The volume of newly constructed apartments is about 8,000–9,000 per year, while the waiting lists include 250,000 households, more than 110,000 of which are in urgent housing situations (*Polityka* 1985).

Comparative statistics for some European socialist countries indicate how serious the Polish housing problem is. For example, during the 1976–80 period the volume of newly constructed apartments per 10,000 inhabitants was 485 in the German Democratic Republic, 428 in Czechoslovakia, 425 in Hungary, and 374 in Poland. In 1983 alone, the same index was 118 in the German Democratic Republic and 54 in Poland (*Zycie Warszawy* 1985).

The situation is further exacerbated by the cutback in funds for the renovation of existing housing. In total, Poland should spend up to 90 billion zlotys per year, while current spending does not exceed 1.5 billion (*Zycie Warszawy* 1985). The centralist system of management and the monopolistic position of the state-owned contractor contributes to the problem, since the contractor is able to dictate technical, financial, and architectural conditions of housing investment. There is neither competition in nor social control of the housing market. Furthermore, the pressure of thousands on the waiting lists and the primacy of industrial construction mean that new housing construction is of even poorer quality than it used to be. The housing industry is also extremely inefficient. It currently employs 1,100,000 people who produce 200,000 apartments per year, while in the German Democratic Republic a similar number of apartments is produced by half of this labor force (*Zycie Warszawy* 1985).

Another barrier to housing effectiveness lies within the model of cooperatives. Since the 1970s they have become highly bureaucratized organizations, where the distance between rank-and-file members and the cooperative's executive body alienates both members and administrators. With no say in the everyday running of the cooperatives, the members are silent witnesses of the apartments being given up to the contractor, of plans being changed, and of the violation of sound economic principles.

Another important problem is the poor quality of existing housing. At the end of 1978, according to the most recent governmental sources (*Zycie Gospodarcze* 1985), more than 42 percent of the Polish population lived in apartments where the density exceeded even the official state standard (that is, more than 1.5 persons per room).[1] More than 14 million people live below the official norm, more than 11 million live in apartments without running water, and 16 million (48 percent of the population) live in apartments without a toilet. Also, more than half of the existing housing stock is at least 50 years old and heavily used.

The changes proposed in the state's economic plan indicate that housing expenditures would increase within the next 15 years (1985–2000) from 2.1

percent of an individual household budget in 1985 to more than 10 percent in the year 2000. Rents have already gone up by 15 to 45 percent in late 1985, and the costs of new construction are extremely high. As the result of the privatization of the housing system a relatively free housing market has emerged, in which the prices of new real estate are equivalent to prices elsewhere in Western Europe, around $200–300 per square meter, although Polish incomes are much lower than those in Western Europe. The authorities try to curb the free market without providing more housing to those in need. Recent regulations have increased value-added tax for the apartments that are put on sale and imposed several restrictions with no apparent effect on prices.

The increase in housing costs did not go along with a further relaxation of restrictions regarding the allowed maximum size of an apartment. Nor did the waiting lists get any shorter. Right now the waiting times exceeds 10 years (after the down payment is made). In some cities it takes 16 to 18 years to get an apartment. It is commonly known that new-born babies become waiting members of housing cooperatives; even then their chances of getting an apartment when they reach maturity age (18) are bleak. Political authorities are afraid of losing control over the material basis of societal existence, since such control is the sole source of power. Under state socialism the economic domination constitutes the material basis for political and social domination (Heller et al. 1983). Growth of the private housing sector would amount to an increase of the uncontrolled sphere, thus posing a threat to state power monopoly. Thereby, it is against the fundamental interest of the authorities to invest in the private consumption sphere. To the contrary, investments in the state-owned sector and accumulation increase state power monopoly.

For political reasons even the current situation in housing would not lead to relaxation of legal restrictions imposed by the state. Individual housing projects are extremely rare, especially in big cities, and it takes several years, frequently a decade, to construct an individual house. Unlike other countries, credit is very limited and usually does not cover more than 15 percent of the official construction costs. The state administration, on the other hand, continues construction of individual dwellings, apartment buildings, or housing estates restricted to state officials and their clients. Regardless of the continuing economic and housing crisis, this still is a group that is not affected by shortages.

CONCLUSION

The controlled social processes under state socialism are supposed to contribute to a better economy and to fulfill societal needs. These needs are predicted in advance and then included in national plans. Housing is one of these national needs. Owing to its universal character, it is subject to political control by the state.

The restraints imposed by the state over social processes result from its aim to maintain the monopoly on developmental scenarios. The political legitimacy is drawn from the presumed efficiency of current control and not from democratic mechanisms. One of the most important sources of power of local authorities is their say in the distribution of housing. Therefore, the allocation of apartments remains a significant mechanism of buying political conformism.

Because of the worsening of the economy in Poland and the restratification of its society and the greater affluence of certain segments of the population, the state had to loosen its previously tight control over the housing system by allowing gradual relaxation of its strict policies. When granting these freedoms the state was also under pressure of its own power elites who wanted to consolidate their political, financial, and social statuses. Therefore, the relaxation had a rather relative character. When the housing resources of the state were put on the market in the early 1970s, incomes were still very limited and relatively few people were able to buy real estate. Among the early buyers were many members of the power elite, who could afford the state prices. When this first wave ended, the regulations changed, and so did the prices, thus making ownership practically unavailable to a majority of the working class. The socialization of the costs of housing did not result in improved housing. A deepening gap between objectively emerging social needs and politically established housing policies undermined the planned character of urban development, increasing the inefficiency and chaos in the urban sphere. In housing, it led to a mixture of uncontrolled and unrestrained processes, some of which were simply the response to an overcentralization of social life and others resulted spontaneously in the economic system.

NOTE

1. It is worthwhile noting that current Polish standards do not distinguish between bedrooms and other rooms, which means that 1.5 persons per room may mean three persons occupying a two-room flat, or a one-bedroom apartment by American standards.

REFERENCES

Ciechocinska, Maria
1975   *Problemy ludnosciowe aglomeracji Warszanskiej*. Warsaw: P.W.N.
Hamilton, Ian
1979   "Spatial Structures in East European Cities." In *The Socialist City. Spatial Structure and Urban Policy*, edited by Ian Hamilton. London: John Wiley.
Heller, Agnes, Ferenc Feher, and Gyorgy Markus
1983   *Dictatorship over Needs*. London: Croom Helm.
Lutokanski, K.
1985   *Odrodzenie*. February 15.
Misztal, Bronislaw
1979   "Social Problems of the City of Warsaw." Unpublished paper presented at the conference of Polish Sociological Association on social problems in Warsaw.
Polityka

1985   Interview with General Debicki, the President of the City of Warsaw,'' no. 3 (January 19), 7.
Saunders, Peter
1981   *Social Theory and the Urban Question*. London: Hutchinson.
Sieminski, Waldemar
1980–86 Unpublished research papers on old housing districts. Research carried out within the Institute of Environmental Studies, Warsaw.
Zycie Gospodarcze
1985   "Elementy Prognozy Przemian Konsumpcji," no. 11 (March), 5–7.
Zycie Warszawy
1985   Editorial statistical information, no. 16.
1986   Editorial statistical information, no. 216.

13

Conservative Government Housing Policy in Britain, 1979–85: Economics or Ideology?

CHRIS HAMNETT

Abstract. Since the election of the first Thatcher administration in Britain in 1979, the Conservative government has embarked on a major council house sales program and sharply cut expenditure on state housing. It is argued that this policy was adopted more to further the political ideology of home ownership than for reasons of financial expediency.

INTRODUCTION

The direct provision of state subsidized public housing in Britain commenced in 1919 with the introduction of Lloyd George's "Homes Fit for Heroes" policy to build half a million new houses at affordable rents for the working classes. Although this policy was a direct product of the high level of social and political unrest over poor housing conditions and the perceived threat to state stability and was sharply cut back in 1923 when political circumstances changed, it marked a historic watershed in terms of British government policy toward housing and the rejection of what Lord Shaftesbury termed "The Mischief of State Aid."

The subsequent history of public housing in Britain was characterized by a series of similar political vissicitudes depending on economic circumstances and the nature of the party in power. For most of the following 60 years, however, both Conservative and Labour governments continued, albeit with varying degrees of reluctance and enthusiasm, the policy of expanding the public housing sector. There was a broad, though highly uneven and very variable, political consensus that subsidized public housing had an important role to play in the provision of adequate housing for a substantial proportion of the population. Labour support for council housing has generally been stronger than that of the Conservatives, who have traditionally viewed state housing with suspicion as a necessary, if somewhat undesirable, social expedient. The Conservatives, however, reluctantly accepted the continuing existence of council housing and the council sector in Britain continued to grow, albeit very unevenly, under both

Labour and Conservative governments to the point where, by 1979, it housed over 30 percent of British households (Merrett 1979).

This broad policy consensus was not to last. Since its election in 1979, the Conservative government in Britain has presided over the greatest single attack on the direct provision of state housing since its inception in 1919. Elected on a program of "rolling back the frontiers of the state" (Thompson 1984), the Conservatives set out to reduce systematically the size of the council sector and to promote the growth of owner occupation. To this end, they embarked on a four-pronged policy involving large cuts in the level of finance available for new council building, large increases in council house rents, a restructuring of local authority finance designed to encourage councils to make a profit on their housing stock, and, perhaps most importantly, a major program of council house sales to tenants at a substantial discount and with guaranteed mortgage finance. In addition, the 1983 budget raised the maximum level of mortgage eligible for income tax relief from £25,000 to £30,000 (Prentice 1985; Crook 1986; Forrest and Murie, chapter 2 in this volume).

As a result of these policies, the level of new council house building has fallen to its lowest peacetime level since the 1930s. The government has made considerable reductions in the level of capital spending on council housing and many local authorities now find that as a result of the council rent increases the council sector is now a net source of revenue income that can be used to subsidize the local rate account. Finally, the introduction of the mandatory Right to Buy policy, under the terms of the 1980 Housing Act, has resulted in a total of almost 1 million council house sales by 1986, a drop in the total size of the council sector approaching 15 percent. As Forrest and Murie have pointed out, council house sales from 1979 to 1984 were more than double the sales in the previous 40 years.

The housing expenditure cuts began in 1976 under a Labour government but it is argued here that the scope and impact of the policies under the Conservatives has been quantitatively and qualitatively more severe than the cuts initiated by Labour. While Labour initiated capital expenditure cuts, the Conservatives carried them far further and added large rent increases, council house sales, and changes in the local authority housing revenue account. The cumulative impact of Conservative policies since 1979 has been such that the state housing sector in Britain has been stopped dead in its tracks and thrown into sharp reverse for the first time in 60 years. As Murie (1982, 34) has argued:

The late 1970s and early 1980s are an important watershed in policy. The developments imply more than just a speeding up of existing trends. They also imply more than simply a new period of retrenchment and concentration on special needs. They imply a new era for council housing . . . which . . . involves a reassertion of the role of the market backed by a minimal poor law service.

The goal of this chapter is to attempt to explain this dramatic shift in state housing policy in Britain. In doing so, particular attention will be paid to the relative influence and importance of economic, political, and ideological considerations in shaping Conservative policies toward housing since 1979. First, however, it is necessary to consider some more general questions regarding the nature and determinants of state housing policy formation in capitalist economies. This in turn necessitates consideration of different theories of the state for, as Merrett (1979) and Ball (1983) have rightly pointed out, the analysis of state housing policy is necessarily dependent upon some theory of the state in capitalist societies.

THEORIES OF STATE INTERVENTION IN HOUSING

It is possible to identify at least three common interpretations of the role of the state in capitalist economies. The first interpretation, which Marcuse (1978a, 1978b, 1982) has aptly termed the "myth of the benevolent state," implicitly underpins many liberal analyses of state housing policies. Viewed from this perspective, the state is commonly seen as a "socially neutral entity which rationally and equitably presides over a harmonious and conflict free society" (Ball 1983, 242). State policies are seen as essentially corrective and ameliorative in nature, and the history of housing legislation is perceived as "a process of groping towards a technical solution that provides a social optimum" (Ball 1983). As Marcuse (1978a, 21) summarized it:

In brief the myth is that government acts out of a primary concern for the welfare of all its citizens, that its policies represent an effort to find solutions to recognized social problems, and that government efforts fall short of complete success only because of lack of knowledge, countervailing selfish interests, incompetence or lack of courage.

The second major perspective is the essentially pluralist one of the neutral or representative state (Saunders 1979). This recognizes the existence of conflict between competing interest groups but sees the state as a neutral ringmaster independent of specific interests. No single interest group is able to dominate state decision-making processes and the state's "housing actions (or failures to act) are caused by the interplay of conflicting pressures from groups and interests swirling around it" (Marcuse 1978b, 397). Finally, there is the simple Marxist instrumentalist view that sees the state "as a tool of capital, as an apparatus formed to carry out the instructions of the capitalist class" (Merrett 1979, 277). This view—which Marcuse has termed the "myth of the malevolent state"—has resulted in a number of highly deterministic functional theories of state intervention in which the state is seen as intervening in a consistent and relatively unproblematic fashion in the interests of capital or its dominant factions. Pickvance (1978) has termed these "tight-link" theories, in the sense that the requirements of capital and the response of the state are tightly linked together with little scope for variation or autonomy of action on the part of the state.

Each of these perspectives is fatally flawed, hence Marcuse's characterization of them as "myths." The crippling weakness of the first perspective is its failure to recognize that "conflicts are central to events, not marginal to them" (Marcuse 1982, 84). Marcuse argues that the historical analysis of government actions and inactions affecting housing in America reveals no evidence of a benevolent state acting consistently toward the amelioration of housing problems and he rejects the notion of the benevolent state in regard to housing as "radically and demonstrably false." Marcuse similarly rejects the notion of "housing policy" on the ground that it misleadingly implies "the underlying existence of a government thrust towards the solution of the social problem of housing" (Marcuse 1978a, 21).

While Marcuse's blanket rejection of the idea of state housing policy can be challenged in the British context, Gauldie (1974), Merrett (1979), and Steadman-Jones (1971) have all convincingly shown that, far from being benevolent and ameliorative, state intervention in housing in nineteenth-century Britain was undertaken only with the greatest reluctance and in response to threats to public health from cholera, perceived threats to middle-class safety from the slums, or fear of working-class unrest. As Merrett (1979, 8) has pointed out, "it was not by accident that in 1840 the first debate held in the House of Commons on the subject of health and housing went under the title 'Discontent among the working classes.' "

If the notion of the benevolent state must be rejected on the grounds that it fails to identify the centrality of conflict in the determination of housing policies, the pluralist notion of the state as a "neutral ringmaster" between competing interests must be rejected on the grounds that it fails to recognize that capitalist societies are necessarily class societies with all their associated economic and political conflicts and that the state will generally act to maintain capital accumulation and the political legitimacy of the state and the existing social order. Foster (1979) goes so far as to argue that several key late nineteenth-century slum clearance measures were initiated on behalf of the property-owning landlord class in the face of oversupply of housing and falling profitability. While this interpretation has been queried by Yelling (1982), there is clear evidence that the introduction of rent control in 1915 (Byrne and Damer 1980; Englander 1983; Melling 1980) was a direct response to the high level of working-class unrest and the threat this posed to the war effort.

Merrett (1979) and Swenarton (1981) have also provided detailed official evidence to support the view that the origin of direct state intervention in housing provision during World War I and immediately after was intended to support the stability of the state in the face of widespread social unrest over poor housing conditions. The introduction of directly subsidized state housing in 1919 was seen, as the Parliamentary Secretary to the Local Government Board put it in 1919, as "an insurance against bolshevism and revolution" and when Lloyd George outlined his proposals to the Cabinet he declared: "Even if it cost a hundred million pounds, what was that compared to the stability of the state"

(Swenarton 1981). It is significant, however, that although the proposals received wide acceptance, the Treasury was unhappy about the cost of the program. Thus, when in 1921 the economy went into severe postwar recession and the dreaded "triple alliance" of miners, dockers, and railway workers collapsed (and with it the threat to state stability from organized labor), the program was sharply curtailed on the grounds of economy and rising costs. As the Secretary to the Local Government Board cynically put it: "Now that the risk has disappeared, the insurance policy could be terminated" (Swenarton, 1981).

If the idea of the benevolent state is a myth, the weaknesses of the simple instrumentalist structural Marxist view of the state have also come under growing attack in recent years on a number of grounds. First, they have been criticized for their "tight link" and highly functionalist perspective (N. Duncan 1982). All they tended to offer was a "tautology which asserts that the capitalist state exists to serve capitalism" (Harloe 1978, 593). The second weakness of Marxist structural-functionalist analysis was that it generally ignored the variety of state policies toward housing both over time and between different capitalist societies. The problem, as Szelenyi (1981) recognized, was that whereas such analyses tended to examine the capitalist mode of production in a pure form, capitalism does not exist in a pure form. As a result, structuralism "was locked into a sort of determinism which meant that it was unable to conceptualize the problems of social alternatives" (Szelenyi 1981, 3). Similar criticisms have been voiced by Harloe and Martens (1985) among others, and S. S. Duncan (1981, 247) has commented that "nothing can actually be deduced from such abstractions about the form, extent and nature of state intervention in any one society."

Simple instrumental "capital logic" theories of the state have also tended to ignore the conflicts of interest between different factions of capital (such as property and industrial capital) and between capital and labor. Capital has been seen as a single, undifferentiated entity and the objective requirements of capital have been treated as straightforward and unproblematic. Little or no attention was paid to the mechanisms by which the requirements of capital were allegedly translated into state policy (Dunleavy 1986) or to the role of class conflict and resistance. The state is treated as the executive committee of the capitalist class and, where apparent working-class gains have been made, these are often interpreted as being in the long-term interests of capital (Dickens 1978). But, as Dunleavy (1986) has argued, this approach effectively ignores or dismisses the role of politics, and Byrne and Damer (1980) and Ball (1983) have also argued that major housing reforms in Britain (such as the advent of rent control in 1915, state subsidized housing in 1919, and the large council building program in the 1950s) have been dependent on the strength of working-class power and the prevailing balance of class forces. By focusing on the necessity of the state to support capital accumulation and the reproduction of labor power, this kind of highly functional and economistic analysis also tended to ignore the dual, and often contradictory, roles of the state in fostering capital accumulation and maintaining social and political order (Harloe 1978).

THE DETERMINANTS OF STATE HOUSING POLICIES

It is clearly necessary to reject economistic structural-functionalism as both theoretically and empirically inadequate. The state does not function consistently in the interests of capital accumulation in a uniform and a priori predictable way from one country and one period to another. On the contrary, any state possesses a variety of potentially contradictory objectives that extend far beyond the sphere of housing. Marcuse suggests these wider conflicts are likely to involve several interrelated concerns, including the maintenance of profitability and capital accumulation within the economy as a whole and the maintenance of social and political legitimacy. The state has several roles to play in the resolution of such conflicts and Marcuse (1982, 87) argues that the specific form of state policies affecting housing is a product of "the tension among and within these basic roles." But Marcuse argues that the outcome of these tensions is structured rather than random. While consumption issues and the distribution of profits will determine short-term housing policies, continued accumulation and profit maximization will generally be the most important long-term determinant of housing policies, while the need for stability and legitimation will take precedence in periods of political crisis. As he puts it,

conflicts around long-term accumulation and political stability are the underlying determinants of housing policy: within the broad parameters allowed by their resolution, the interests of housing producers, housing consumers, and the state apparatus will determine the specific shape a policy will take (p. 88).

This recognition of the relative autonomy of the state in the determination of policy within the broad constraints imposed upon it by the requirements of accumulation and legitimation is useful and Marcuse goes further to argue that "The state itself . . . has a history and a set of determinants governing its actions that must be taken into account. The representatives of the state are not simply pawns in the games of others but players themselves" (p. 86).

THE IMPORTANCE OF POLITICAL AND IDEOLOGICAL CONSIDERATIONS IN THE DETERMINATION OF STATE POLICIES TOWARD HOUSING

Marcuse's recognition that the state is not just the passive executive arm of the interests of capital, and that the state may also have policy goals and objectives of its own, represents an important advance over past tight-link and deterministic theories. The position to be argued here is that while the state in capitalist economies is not, and cannot be, wholly independent of the social and economic relations of capitalism, it is relatively autonomous. Thus, while state policies are unlikely to run directly counter to the long-term need for continued capital accumulation and the maintenance of social legitimacy, the specific policies adopted by any given government in the short term will reflect not only the tension between these and other goals, but also the wider political and ideological goals of individual governments and key individuals within them and the overall balance of class forces.

These wider goals may be only a partial and imperfect reflection of the interests of capital and labor, not least because political parties do not necessarily reflect or represent material interests in any simple and direct way. On the contrary, they not only have a strong vested interest in being elected or reelected to power, but they also carry what Short (1982, 4) has termed "ideological baggage from past times, memories of the past and an intellectual articulation of their position relative to other parties." Thus, although political parties are not completely independent of material interests, they express them only indirectly through the medium of political representation and through the filter of different political ideologies regarding, among other things, the desirability or otherwise of different forms of social and economic organization and activity. As Short (p. 4) puts it,

the economic context does not fix set courses for state action. There is no one path set by external economic conditions. The state of the economy affects policies through the filter of political action. The constraints and opportunities afforded by the economic background will be perceived differently according to the balance of political forces. There is no inexorable policy course set by economic logic above the domain of politics.

Short's assessment of the importance of political and ideological factors in the determination of state policy is strongly endorsed here and it is argued that the policies pursued by different governments will, within the broad constraints set by economic, social, and political conditions, broadly reflect the ideological predispositions and political objectives of the party in power and the views of key individuals within that party. Thus, although both Labour and Conservative governments undertook a high level of new council building during the interwar period, their goals were very different and the scale of the program varied markedly. As Merrett (1978, 61) has pointed out,

For capital and the Conservatives state housing was seen as a means of reproducing the capacity to labour and of securing the perceived legitimacy of the social order. For the working-class movement municipal house building was a means for advancing the material interests of the class. . . . As a result of these marked differences in the degree of political commitment, local authority housing output was extremely unstable between the wars as output responded (in a lagged fashion) to shifts in the strength of the trade union movement and in the control of the state.

The same argument can be made regarding the postwar period until 1979. Although both Conservative and Labour governments continued the policy of new council house building, the level of support was contingent on both economic and social conditions and the party in power. As Boyne (1984, 183) has pointed out, "changes in the governing party have invariably caused changes in the quantity and quality of new construction, the basis and level of subsidies, and the level of rents."

The argument to be advanced in the remainder of this chapter is that the 1979 and the 1983 Thatcher Conservative governments in Britain have pursued policies toward housing that have been based as much or more on political and ideological goals than economic ones. This is not to say that the government's policies toward housing have not had a strong economic dimension to them—they have— but that the government's decision to cut council housing expenditure and sell council houses was shaped more by their wider political and ideological goals for housing than it was by external economic requirements. Although, as Forrest and Murie stress in Chapter 2 of this volume, the sale of council housing and the cuts in state subsidies for council housing have come to play a key role in the development of the government's economic strategy, the policy did not emerge as a result of financial calculation. Its initial motivation lay in the Con- servative party's long-standing antipathy to council housing and was primarily one of political ideology. Indeed, there is a strong argument to be made that the government's drive to reduce public expenditure and the Public Sector Borrowing Requirement (PSBR) have been determined more by political and ideological objectives than by external economic pressures (Keegan 1984).

CONSERVATIVE POLICIES TOWARD HOUSING IN BRITAIN, 1979–85

Since the Conservatives came to power in 1979, public spending on housing has been cut sharply—from £6.6 billion in 1979/80 to £3.0 billion in 1983/84 at 1983/84 prices, and housing's share of public spending has fallen by 55 percent in real terms. As a result, new council house building has declined to its lowest peacetime level since 1925 and central government subsidies to local authority housing revenue accounts have fallen dramatically. Expenditure on housing has borne the brunt of public expenditure cutbacks—over 75 percent of the projected 4 percent cut in public expenditure between 1979/80 and 1983/84 according to the House of Commons Environment Committee (Harloe and Paris 1984; Forrest and Murie, Chapter 2 in this volume).

The facts are clear, but the key question that needs to be answered is why the housing program was singled out for such severe cuts. A similar question can be posed over the Conservative government's motivation for council house sales. In each case two principal explanations can be identified: one economic and one rooted in the political and ideological goals of the ruling party.

Among the principal exponents of the economic explanation for the cuts in housing expenditure are Harloe and Paris (1984). They argue that the economic crises of the mid–1970s led to considerable pressures for the reduction of state welfare expenditure in most Western countries and that "most of what has occurred in Britain is the result of the international economic crisis" (p. 73).

While they accept that the attack on collective consumption has been pushed further and faster by the Conservatives than it was by the previous 1974–79 Labour government and that public housing has been most severely affected "to a degree that would be unlikely under Labour" (p. 78), they point to the fact that the first major recent cuts in housing expenditure took place in 1976 under Labour in the wake of the sterling crisis. They argue from this that the principal motive for the cuts was financial and that capital expenditure on council housing offered a relatively easy target that (unlike health or education spending) affected only a relatively small minority of the electorate. They conclude that cuts in housing expenditure have not been solely products of the New Right Conservative government, but have been a crucial element in the monetarist policies pursued by both Labour and Conservative governments since 1976. They are therefore

very cautious about suggesting that a sharp political break occurred in 1979. Rather it seems that the attack on collective consumption has gathered pace under both right-wing Conservative and right-wing Labour governments since the mid-seventies. Essentially, this is a result of economic circumstances and a common acceptance by both Labour and Conservatives of the need for, inter-alia, reductions in public expenditure (p. 78).

While Harloe and Paris are correct to point to the fact that the cuts in housing expenditure started under Labour, the principal objection to their argument is, as they acknowledge, that the cuts have been carried much further and faster under the Conservatives than under Labour. In seeking to highlight the similarities in the economic situation faced by both parties, they underemphasize the quantitatively and qualitatively different nature of the policies pursued by the two parties. Whereas Labour undertook the cuts in housing expenditure with reluctance as an essentially short-term response to a financial crisis, the Conservatives cut expenditure on council housing with enthusiasm as part of their wider goal of rolling back council housing in favor of owner occupation. It is important in this context to note Dunleavy's (1986) argument that the cabinet decision to implement spending cuts in 1976 in the wake of the sterling crisis and the International Monetary Fund intervention was by no means an economically inevitable conclusion. He argues that a cabinet majority was opposed to the cuts and that "in a marginally different conjuncture political events could well have run a different course" (p. 133). More generally he argues that "any large-scale policy shifts must . . . be mediated through a structure of political and administrative mechanisms. The operation of this political intermediation cannot be taken for granted, and always has an inescapably contingent element—a level of underdetermination by external influences" (p. 133).

The financial explanation for council house sales can be simply stated. Council housing has proved a greater source of revenue to the Conservatives than all other public asset sales combined. The sale of council houses raised £6.4 billion over the period 1979/80–1984/85 compared to the £3 billion raised from the privatization of British Telecom. This revenue has not only indirectly funded and offset other Conservative housing expenditure, it has also enabled the government to keep the budget deficit and the PSBR lower than would otherwise have been possible without raising taxes (Forrest and Murie, Chapter 2 in this volume). There is no doubt that the sale of council housing has become an important element of the government's wider financial strategy. The crucial question, however, is not whether the policy is currently beneficial, but whether the financial benefits arising from council house sales constituted the principal rationale for the policies toward council housing adopted by the Conservatives in 1979. It is contended that they did not.

Although there appears to be a direct correspondence between the financial benefits derived from the Conservatives' policies toward council housing and local authority finance and their wider public expenditure goals, we cannot simply infer that the financial outcome of their policies provides an explanation of their origins. To do so would be to fall into the trap of inferring causes from their effects. The argument advanced here is that an adequate explanation of government policy toward housing must necessarily locate the policy decisions within the framework of the government's wider political and ideological housing objectives as well as their wider economic objectives. The financial aspects of Conservative policies toward housing were secondary to their political and ideological goals. Although the cuts in capital expenditure on council building, substantial assumed rent increases, and the sale of council houses all made a significant contribution to the Conservatives' overall goal of cutting public expenditure, these policies were not undertaken solely or even primarily for financial reasons. On the contrary, it is suggested that the expansion of owner occupation at the expense of the council sector was seen as a key policy goal and that the revenue from council house sales represented a secondary bonus for the government's wider economic policies.

We shall attempt to support this argument in two ways. The first point to make is that although the sale of council houses has produced major short-term financial gains for the government, the Department of the Environment calculated in 1978 that sales would result in long-term losses. In a subsequent report produced for the Conservatives in 1980, these losses were transformed into net gains by using dubious alternative assumptions regarding, among other things, the likely rate of rent increases (Kilroy 1980, 1982). The conclusion appears to be that the Conservatives adjusted the assumptions to produce a predicted financial outcome favorable to their policy goal of council house sales. It is ironic that the subsequent high rent increases assumed by the Conservatives have made council sales appear far less profitable in the long term. Long-term financial benefits appear to have been sacrificed for reasons of short-term political ideology.

The second point that needs to be stressed is that the housing expenditure cuts adopted have been highly selective rather than across the board. As Forrest and Murie point out in Chapter 2, there has been a major reorientation of state housing expenditure away from direct subsidy toward council housing and toward increased subsidies for owner occupation and means-tested housing benefits. It follows, they argue, that "either there has been little systematic application of notions of what the country can afford, or the view is that the country can afford substantial support for home owners but not for housing investment or for other housing subsidies." Either way, it "would be misleading to attribute changes in housing policy as logical and inevitable outcomes of fiscal restraint." On the contrary, the changes are the result of a series of explicit Conservative policy decisions to support owner occupation at the expense of council renting.

If we accept the premise that the main goal of Conservative government housing policy from 1979 onward was the reduction of public expenditure on housing, there were a number of potential options open to them. The government could have cut tax relief on mortgage interest to owner occupiers, which currently amounts to some £5 billion a year. Although tax foregone does not constitute public expenditure, the abolition or reduction of the tax subsidy to owner occupiers would have increased government tax revenue and reduced the PSBR. It would also remove one of the major distortions in the housing market. It is significant that when this option was raised by Mrs. Thatcher's economic policy advisors soon after the 1979 election, it was immediately dismissed as politically unacceptable and Mrs. Thatcher subsequently pledged that mortgage interest tax relief would remain as long as she was prime minister. Instead, the government chose to cut capital expenditure on council housing and reduce central government subsidies to local authority housing revenue accounts. While it can be argued that cutting or abolishing tax relief on mortgage interest would have been politically suicidal for a Conservative government, it would have been possible to restrict tax relief to the basic rate of tax and abolish higher rate tax relief as this benefits only a relatively small number of higher income taxpayers. This was not done and, in 1983, the maximum size of mortgage eligible for tax relief was actually increased from £25,000 to £30,000 against Treasury advice. Not only did this cost the Exchequer an additional £60 million in the first year of operation, it also substantially weakened the possibility of stabilizing the long-term burden of mortgage interest tax relief by allowing the value of tax relief to be eroded by rising house prices and mortgages. This policy reflects a conscious decision to support subsidized owner occupation at the expense of council housing and council tenants who faced rapidly increasing rents. In addition, improvement grant expenditure—most of which is geared toward home owners—increased sixfold between 1979/80 and 1983/84 and the proportion of net government housing expenditure on housing associations increased from 15 to 48 percent of a much smaller cake over the same period (Back and Hamnett 1985). The result, as Forrest and Murie show, is that while central government spending on council housing has fallen sharply, the overall level of central government spending on housing has been reoriented rather than cut.

Viewed from a narrowly economic perspective, this reorientation of government housing expenditure toward continuing and enhanced support for owner occupation could be seen as a failure of public expenditure policy. Had the government been committed to cutting the PSBR and rolling back the frontiers of state intervention at all costs, then, logically, they should have committed themselves to removing mortgage interest tax relief. The problem with such an interpretation is that it fails to appreciate the importance of the government's policy of promoting owner occupation at the expense of council housing almost irrespective of cost. Whitehead (1983) quotes Michael Heseltine, the then secretary of state for the environment, as stating to the House of Commons Select Committee on Public Expenditure, that "as a matter of policy they [the Government] want to encourage owner occupation and give very substantial fiscal incentives to do that." The same point applies to the sale of council housing at a substantial discount on its market valuation. Both discounted sales and mortgage interest tax relief may appear inconsistent for a government committed to the operation of market pricing but, as Farmer and Barrell (1981, 329) have commented, "the apparent inconsistency arises from an attempt to elide two quite distinct policy objectives: that of developing a vigorous free-market economy with as little government interference as possible, and that of guaranteeing the fundamental conditions for the existence of such an economy."

To the extent that the expansion of home ownership and the creation of a mass property-owning democracy is seen by the Conservative government as a fundamental political prerequisite of a successful free market economy, there is "no necessary inconsistency in the Thatcher administration's advocacy both of less government interference in the market process in general and yet of government intervention to increase homeownership" (Farmer and Barrell 1981, 329).

The remainder of this chapter will seek to show that while the promotion of owner occupation and reluctant support for council housing have comprised long-standing elements of Conservative housing policy, it is only from 1979 onward that these attitudes have crystallized into a clearly defined political ideology of tenure and an associated "tenure policy" (Malpass 1986).

THE IDEOLOGICAL BASIS OF CONSERVATIVE HOUSING POLICY

The Conservatives have always been opposed to the expansion of state housing on principle. While they have countenanced council building in conditions of major national shortage, it has commonly been viewed as a temporary and undesirable social necessity to be cut back as soon as possible in favor of private provision and the continued growth of owner occupation. The Conservatives have always been reluctant collectivists. Although new council house building reached its highest-ever level under a Conservative government in the mid-1950s, this represented the culmination of the postwar housing drive initiated by Labour and the policy was only pushed through by Harold Macmillan, the then minister of housing, in the face of considerable opposition from the right wing of the

party. Macmillan subsequently presided over a sharp reduction in council building in favor of owner occupation.

When Labour regained power in 1964, they immediately embarked on an
expansion of council house building. Meanwhile, Conservative hostility to state
housing was steadily reasserting itself and, when the Conservatives were reelected in 1971, they introduced the 1972 Housing Finance Act. This was designed, among other things, to raise council rents and reduce Exchequer subsidies
to council housing. It is significant that tax relief to owner occupiers remained
untouched.

The Housing Finance Act was repealed by the 1974–79 Labour government,
but the dispute over the cost and equity of subsidies to council tenants and owner
occupiers continued and was intensified both by the rapid inflation in council
housing building costs during the mid-1970s and by Labour's decision to hold
down council rent increases below the level of inflation as part of its anti-inflation
strategy. As a result, the proportion of gross rents to the total cost of council
housing fell from 69 percent in 1968–69 to 55 percent in 1975–76 (Craven 1975)
and the climate of opinion against council housing within the Conservative party
hardened decisively.

With the election of Mrs. Thatcher as leader of the Conservative party in
February 1975, the Conservatives embarked on a major reappraisal of policy
that culminated in the publication of "The Right Approach" in 1976. This
document outlined the Conservatives' commitment to a general policy of "rolling
back the frontiers of the state" and a reassertion of the role of the market as a
means of increasing individual freedom of choice. In housing, this meant the
expansion of owner occupation to as many people as possible and the sale of
council housing was a perfect vehicle for this policy. It killed two birds with
one stone. Both Kemeny (1981) and Boyne (1984) have pointed out that the
continuing decline in the size of the privately rented sector and the decline in
new building for owner occupation during the 1970s meant that the two principal
sources of additional owner-occupied dwellings were contracting. Only council
house sales offered the possibility of a continuing rapid increase in owner occupation. To the extent that Kemeny and Boyne are correct, the expansion of
owner occupation necessitated the sale of council housing on a large scale.

The importance of the sale of council housing and the growth of owner
occupation for the Conservatives cannot be stressed too strongly. It underpinned
their whole approach to housing and it was a policy they were willing to pursue
at almost any cost. As Julian Amery, a former Conservative minister for housing,
stated in 1978: "what I care about is that we should aim to make house purchase
not merely attractive but irresistibly attractive to the council house tenant." The
Conservatives set about this task in two principal ways. First, they introduced
a policy of selling council houses at a discount, which increased with length of
residence, of between 30 and 50 percent of their assessed value. In 1983, in
response to a declining rate of sales, the Conservatives increased the maximum
discount to 60 percent and relaxed the financial penalties on resale within five

years. In 1986 the maximum discount on the sale of flats was further increased to 70 percent and the limitations on resale were reduced to two years.

The second aspect of their policy involved a series of large but nonmandatory rent increases that raised the average council rent (before rebates) from £6.40 per week in April 1979 to £13.50 per week in April 1982—an increase of 110 percent in three years and half as large again as the rate of inflation. The assumed level of council rents was raised by nearly 50 percent in 1981 alone. Although the rent increases were nonmandatory (local rent policies being the prerogative of local government), they were assumed to have been implemented for the purposes of calculating the level of central government subsidy required by each local authority. Central government subsidies were thus reduced on the basis that the increases had been implemented irrespective of whether or not they had. If a local authority chose not to make the increase it would have to increase the level of subsidy from the local rate fund. This was clearly a powerful inducement to rent increases and the level of assumed rent increases was such that many of the smaller rural authorities who had carried out little recent building and thus had a low debt burden found that if they increased their rents by the assumed amount they would go into surplus on their Housing Revenue Accounts (HRAs). This was permitted only under the terms of the Housing Act of 1980. Previously councils had been under a statutory duty to balance the books on their HRAs. While many local councils were reluctant to run a surplus on their council housing, the government's 1982 decision to limit local authorities to an overall 4 percent increase in spending for 1983/84 meant that many smaller authorities were forced to increase rents and apply the surplus to reducing their overall spending lest they fell into the government's overspending penalty zone and suffered a cut in their central government rate support grant. While it must be said that the principal objective of this policy was a reduction in the level of central government subsidy to council housing, the resultant rent increases served as a considerable inducement to purchase for those who were financially able to. The same can be said of the reduction in the level of new council building from the already low figure of 107,000 in 1978 to just 37,000 in 1981—little more than one-fifth of the figure in 1975 and the lowest peacetime level since the 1930s. As new house building fell, the housing waiting list increased sharply and the pressures to buy increased for all those who were able to purchase (Fielding 1984).

The importance of owner occupation for the Conservatives cannot be too strongly stated. It has been such a recurrent theme in the Conservative statements on housing since 1979 that it may be more accurate, as Malpass (1986) has suggested, to talk about Conservative tenure policy rather than housing policy. As Crook (1986) has put it: "Since 1979 . . . the increase in owner occupation has been the central feature of the Conservative Government's housing policy" (p. 641).

In the debate on the Queen's speech in May 1979, Mrs. Thatcher stated that the policy of council house sales will be a giant stride towards making a reality of Anthony Eden's dream of a property owning democracy. It will do something else—it will give more of our people that freedom and mobility and that prospect of handing something on to their children and grandchildren which owner occupation provides.

In a 1983 interview on BBC radio with Jimmy Young, Mrs. Thatcher declared: "What I am desperately trying to do is to create one nation with everyone being a man (sic) of property."

There are a variety of reasons why the creation of a property-owning democracy is seen as important by the Conservatives, but at root they all boil down to the belief that home ownership fosters greater independence and self-reliance as well as giving people a stake in the system and a greater commitment to social stability and sound (that is, Conservative) government. Mrs. Thatcher's second minister of housing, Ian Gow, commented before the Building Society Association in 1985: "We should set no limit to the opportunity for owner occupation in Britain. . . . In those societies where property is widely owned freedom flourishes. But where the ownership of property is concentrated in the hands of the State freedom is in peril."

The Building Societies Association made a similar point in the mid–1970s:

The point where more than half the houses in the country have become owner occupied was a significant milestone because even a small stake in the country does affect political attitudes. The greater the proportion of owner-occupiers the less likely are extreme measures to prevail (quoted in Boddy 1980, 24).

Views such as these have permeated deeply into Conservative thinking. Whether they are correct is largely immaterial for the purpose of analyzing the determinants of policy. The point, as Boyne (1984) rightly observes, is that the Conservatives believe them to be correct. To this extent, their policies are constructed on the basis of a political ideology of tenure.

CONCLUSIONS

It has been argued in this chapter that housing policies in capitalist societies cannot be interpreted in terms of benevolent and conflict-free altruism. Nor can they be interpreted in terms of some mechanistic and functionalist response to the overriding requirements of capital. While state policies under capitalism cannot ignore the necessity to maintain the economic base of the system and its social and political legitimation, there is no one policy path set by these requirements. On the contrary, there is likely to be a tension between these various requirements and the state possesses considerable autonomy of action in responding to these conflicts. In addition, the policies pursued by individual governments are likely to reflect, within broad constraints, the political and ideological objectives of the party in power. This aspect of state policy formation has unfortunately been neglected in the literature but it is of considerable importance in helping to explain variations in housing policy both between different countries and within the same country over time.

Although the cuts in housing expenditure began in 1976 under a Labour government faced by a sterling crisis and IMF demands to restrain public spending, it is argued that the policies pursued by the Conservatives since 1976 have been both quantitatively and qualitatively different. While the cuts initiated by Labour can be argued to have been undertaken with reluctance, it is argued that the Conservatives have set out to create systematically a mass property-owning democracy at the expense of the council sector. Within their largely self-imposed constraints on public expenditure and the PSBR, the Conservatives pursued a set of policies toward housing that had the explicit goal of reducing not just spending on council housing but the size of the council sector itself. It is therefore argued that Conservative policies toward housing represent a sharp political break with the past rather than the speeding up and development of policies initiated by the 1974–79 Labour government as a short-term response to economic circumstances.

REFERENCES

Back, G., and C. Hamnett
1985 "State Housing Policy Formation and the Changing Role of Housing Associations in Britain." *Policy and Politics* 13, no. 4, 393–411.
Ball, M.
1983 *Housing Policy and Economic Power: The Political Economy of Owner Occupation*. London: Methuen.
Boddy, M.
1980 *The Building Societies*. London: Macmillan.
Boyne, G.
1984 "The Privatisation of Public Housing." *Political Quarterly* 55 (April/June), 180–87.
Byrne, D., and S. Damer
1980 "The State, the Balance of Class Forces, Early Working Class Housing Legislation." In *Housing Construction and the State*, Political Economy of Housing Workshop of the Conference of Socialist Economists, No. 3. London: Conference of Socialist Economists.
Craven, E.
1975 "Housing." In *Social Policy and Public Expenditure*, edited by R. Klein. London: Centre for Studies in Social Policy.
Crook, A. D. H.
1986 "Privatisation of Housing and the Impact of the Conservative Government's Initiatives on Low-Cost Homeownership and Private Renting between 1979 and 1984 in England and Wales: 1. The Privatisation Policies." *Environment and Planning A* 18, 639–59.
Dickens, P.

1978   "Social Change, Housing and the State." In *Urban Change and Conflict*, edited by M. Harloe. Proceedings of the 1977 Centre for Environmental Studies Conference, York.

Duncan, J. S., and D. Ley
1982   "Structural Marxism and Human Geography: A Critical Assessment," *Annals, Association of American Geographers* 72, no, 1, 30–58.

Duncan, N.
1981   "Home Ownership and Social Theory." In *Housing and Identity: Cross-Cultural Perspectives*, edited by J. S. Duncan. London: Croom Helm.

Duncan, S. S.
1981   "Housing Policy, The Methodology of Levels and Urban Research: The Case of Castells." *International Journal of Urban and Regional Research* 5, 231–54.

Dunleavy, P.
1986   "The Growth of Sectoral Cleavages and the Stabilisation of State Expenditures." *Environment and Planning, D* 4, 129–44.

Englander, D.
1983   *Landlord and Tenant in Urban Britain, 1838–1918.* Oxford: Clarendon Press.

Farmer, M. K., and R. Barrell
1981   "Entreprenurship and Government Policy: The Case of the Housing Market." *Journal of Public Policy* 1, 307–32.

Fielding, N.
1984   "Who Is Subsidising Whom?" *Roof*, March/April, 11–14.

Gauldie, E.
1974   *Cruel Habitations: A History of Working Class Housing, 1780–1918.* London: George Allen and Unwin.

Harloe, M.
1978   "Housing and the State: Recent British Developments." *International Social Science Journal* 30, no. 3, 591–603.

Harloe, M. and M. Martens
1985   "The Restructuring of Housing Provision in Britain and the Netherlands." *Environment and Planning, A* 17, 1063–87.

Harloe, M., and C. Paris
1984   "The Decollectivisation of Consumption: Housing and Local Government Finance in England and Wales, 1979–81." In *Cities in Recession*, edited by I. Szelenyi. Beverly Hills, Calif.: Sage.

Keegan, V.
1984   *Mrs. Thatcher's Economic Experiment.* New York: Penguin.

Kemeny, J.
1981   *The Myth of Home Ownership.* London: Routledge.

Kilroy, B.
1980   "From Roughly Right to Precisely Wrong." *Roof*, January 16–17.
1982   "The Financial and Economic Implications of Council House Sales." In *The Future of Council Housing*, edited by J. English. London: Croom Helm, 52–95.

Malpass, P.
1986   *The Housing Crisis.* London: Croom Helm.

Marcuse, P.
1978   "Housing Policy and the Myth of the Benevolent State." *Social Policy*, January/February, 21–26. (a).

1978   "The Myth of the Benevolent State: Notes Toward a Theory of Housing Conflict."
       In *Urban Change and Conflict*, edited by M. Harloe. Proceedings of the 1977
       Centre for Environmental Studies Conference, York. (b).
1982   "Determinants of State Housing Policies: West Germany and the United States."
       In *Urban Policy Under Capitalism*, edited by N. I. Feinstein and S. S. Feinstein.
       Beverly Hills, Calif.: Sage.
Melling, J., ed.
1980   *Housing, Social Policy and the State*. London: Croom Helm.
Merrett, S.
1979   *State Housing in Britain*. London: Routledge.
Murie, A.
1982   "A New Era for Council Housing?" In *The Future of Council Housing*, edited
       by J. English. London: Croom Helm.
Pickvance, C.
1978   "Explaining State Intervention: Some Theoretical and Empirical Considerations."
       In *Urban Change and Conflict*, edited by M. Harloe. Proceedings of the 1977
       Centre for Environmental Studies Conference, York.
Prentice, R.
1985   "What Has Happened to Housing Under the Conservatives?" *Housing Review*
       34, no. 5, 163–65.
Saunders, P.
1979   *Urban Politics: A Sociological Interpretation*. New York: Penguin.
Short, J.
1982   *Housing in Britain: The Post-War Experience*. London: Methuen.
Steadman-Jones, G.
1971   *Outcast London*. Oxford: Oxford University Press.
Swenarton, M.
1981   *Homes Fit For Heroes*. London: Heinemann.
Szelenyi, I.
1981   "Structural Changes of Alternatives to Capitalist Development in the Contem-
       porary Urban and Regional System." *International Journal of Urban and Regional
       Research* 5, no. 1, 1–14.
Thompson, G.
1984   "Rolling Back the State? Economic Intervention 1975–82." In *State and Society
       in Contemporary Britain*, edited by G. McLennan, D. Held, and S. Hall. Cam-
       bridge: Polity Press.
Whitehead, C.
1983   "Housing under the Conservatives: A Policy Assessment." *Public Money*, June,
       15–21.
Yelling, J. A.
1982   "L.C.C. Slum Clearance Policies, 1889–1907." *Transactions of the Institute of
       British Geographers* 7, no. 3, 292–303.

PART VII

POLITICS AND PROFESSIONAL EXPERTISE

14

The Changing Pattern of Professional Influence on Local Housing Policy

BARRIE HOULIHAN

Abstract. This chapter examines the changing pattern of professional influence within the housing policy network in Britain. The pressures affecting professionals in the 1980s are identified with the cuts in public expenditure and the rise of ideological politics being the most significant. The character of the housing policy network is discussed and professionals are located within it. Three important developments in housing policy are considered and the influence of professionals is identified and evaluated. The chapter concludes with a discussion of the consequences for individual professions and the housing policy network of cuts in public expenditure and the strong intervention by central government in policy.

INTRODUCTION

The 1980s have proved to be a difficult, if not hostile, period for local government professionals in Britain, with pressures arising from a number of sources. First, during the last ten years or so, the professions have become the object of increasing criticism and challenge from clients, the media, and politicians. Pollitt refers to the "immensely appealing image of the professional which gained wide currency during the 1950s and 1960s" when he was considered to be an "expert . . . devoting his skills to fine public causes . . . with a combination of technocratic skills and his public service ethic [thus justifying] the high degree of occupational and individual autonomy" (Pollitt 1984, 29). This professional assertiveness and self-confidence came under increasing challenge in the 1970s. The planning profession, for example, suffered because of its limited success in containing urban growth and also because of the consequences of the delay in implementing urban renewal proposals (Hall et al. 1973; Davies 1972; Dennis 1972). Goldsmith (1980, 144) concluded that "far from being the powerful gatekeepers or urban managerialists identified by their sociological critics, planners now appear as rather weak, perhaps irrelevant, pawns in an economic and political environment which is much more hostile than it was twenty years ago." Other local government professions have been the focus of similar criticism.

Even the usually passive public-sector tenants began to organize and challenge professional wisdom (Short 1982). The change in attitude toward professions is best summed up by Laffin (1985, 8): "There has been a greater questioning of professionals' claims to expertise and an accompanying weakening of social deference towards them."

Second, this external criticism has been coupled with increasing self-questioning within professions. The normative and value consensus apparent in the 1960s in many of the welfare professions has substantially evaporated. While the consensus within the housing, planning, and social work professions has always been fragile, public disagreement within the profession has provided fuel for the external critics.

Third, the growth of external criticism and self-doubt has taken place within an economic context of declining resources, which has increased the pressure to defend existing programs. It has also resulted in a decline in the expansion of local government with a consequent reduction in the opportunities for career mobility among professionals. The net result has been a further undermining of morale within the professions.

Finally, many policy areas at the local government level have experienced forceful challenges to their established consensus regarding the scope, social purpose, and future development of the service. This is particularly true of housing, which has been an important focus for the application of Conservative policy regarding expenditure and privatization (see, for example, Forrest and Murie [Chapter 2] and Hamnett [Chapter 13] in this volume). The high salience of housing for the government and the radical policies it has introduced have contributed greatly to the politicization of the local policy network. Thus the last ten years have seen an increasing number of local authorities controlled by political parties with much firmer policy commitments than in the past. In addition to this growth of "manifesto politics" at both national and local levels, there has been an increase in the number of full-time members of the council and those wishing to be actively involved in policy making. As Laffin (1985, 9) comments, "this new breed of member has much stronger ideological commitments over a wider range of issues and often a suspicion of the motives of the professional officers."

It has been argued that these four factors have resulted in a retreat by professionals in the face of concerted pressure on their established "action space" within the various local policy areas. This chapter examined this hypothesis with regard to housing professionals.[1] The next section briefly considers the nature of local authority professions and the process of professionalization, together with the local organizational and political context. The chapter then briefly reviews the nature of the housing policy area and the professions that operate within it. The fourth section identifies and examines three major developments that have affected the policy network over the last ten years or so. The final section discusses the scope for professional and member influence on housing policy in the 1980s and the various strategies used by professionals to protect their "action space."

THE ORGANIZATIONAL AND POLITICAL CONTEXT OF PROFESSIONS

The characteristics of professions, the nature of professionalism, and the process of professionalization, though obviously important for the study of professional influence, are issues too broad in scope to be considered in detail here. However, as a necessary preliminary to an examination of the changing role of professions in the local policy process some definitions must be established.

The definition of a profession used in this chapter is one that sees a profession "not [as] an occupation but as a means of controlling an occupation" (Johnson 1972, 45). In other words, what professions aspire to is the power to control their own work—occupational autonomy, and a key aim of professional autonomy is an ability to define and defend their area of competence within the broad policy area—that is, their "action space." A consequence of this definition is that the achievement of professional status is the result of conflict where status is not absolute but needs to be constantly defended and reasserted in response to attempts by groups to challenge and undermine the position of the profession in a particular policy area.

Turning specifically to local authority professions, there are a number of ways in which they can be characterized, including their degree of dependence on state patronage (Dunleavy 1980), the basis of their expertise, and the extent of statutory support for their work. In general, the stronger professions at the local authority level tend to be private-sector dominated and be based on physical science expertise. By contrast, the weaker professions tend to be more heavily dependent on state patronage and possess an expertise based on social sciences. In addition some professionals, such as environmental health officers and to a lesser extent planners, work within a framework of statutes that, on balance, enhances their scope for the exercise of professional judgment.

Housing officers seem to be on the weaker end of each of these three characteristics, being strongly dependent on state patronage, possessing claims to expertise based on the social sciences, and, finally, working in a policy area that has few statutory defenses.

However, in order to identify the scope for professional influence it is necessary to complement the characteristics of the profession with an understanding of the organizational and political context within which they operate. Each profession must negotiate its eventual status locally.

They must therefore adapt to the existing organizational and political context or attempt to adapt them. As a result, the influence, status, and autonomy of members of the same profession may differ from one authority to the next. Thus when central government or public support is withdrawn, all professionals do not suffer to the same extent. It is therefore important to take account of how professional status is negotiated locally and to identify the strategies adopted to maximize their autonomy and influence on policy.

In order to understand the differing influence of professionals, and housing professionals in particular, it is necessary to identify the most common organizational and political contexts at the local level. Although there has been some pressure on authorities to create comprehensive housing departments (Bains 1972), there still is a wide range of patterns of allocation of function, with three seeming to be the most common. The first pattern results in a narrow-based housing estate management department that in general provides a weak organizational base for housing professionals. The second, and increasingly common, pattern of allocation combines housing and environmental health professionals in one department, while the third results in the creation of a broad-based comprehensive housing department that covers most aspects of the policy area. The different patterns of allocation of function between departments will have a variety of consequences for the housing profession with the first tending to isolate and weaken its role in the policy area, the second providing a stronger basis for influence and also muting rivalry with environmental health officers, while the third should result in a central role in policy and strategy development.

The variety of organizational settings for policy making is also important as it is one of the most frequently mentioned reasons given by housing professionals to explain their lack of influence over policy. Such problems most commonly take the form of disputes between departments over their respective action space. Thus rights of intervention in the policy process are often determined by departmental boundaries rather than professional competence. In addition, organizational problems arise concerning the relationship between departments and committees and the rights of professionals to intervene and provide advice for committees apart from their own. This most commonly arises with regard to planning and housing committees where there is often a complex protocol to be followed before a housing professional can contribute to a planning committee discussion or advise the committee chairman.

It is much more difficult to generalize about the local political context. There are clear signs of a trend toward a more confrontational and ideological style of politics in British local government. However, two tentative observations may be offered, with the first being that there is a tendency for a close relationship to develop between Labour majority parties and housing departments where the latter are thought to develop a "Labour Party ethos" (Young 1977). The second observation is that in general Conservative councils tend to be less interventionist in policy matters than Labour councils (Bains 1972; Collins et al. 1978).

THE NATURE OF THE HOUSING POLICY AREA

In this section it is suggested that the concept of a policy network is valuable in analyzing the pattern of influence of professionals. The section begins with a diagrammatic summary of professional involvement in housing, continues with a discussion of the housing policy network, and concludes by identifying the network's main characteristics.

One of the main problems in examining the role of professionals in housing policy arises from the nature of the policy area. First, it is extremely difficult to identify an agreed on set of boundaries with other policy areas such as planning, environmental (public) health, and social work. Second, it is also difficult to agree on the boundaries of professional competence within the policy area. As the housing policy area has expanded from its initial concern with slum clearance and building to include area-based improvement, homelessness, housing benefit, mortgages, private-sector improvement grants, and so on, a number of relatively powerful professions have joined the policy network. Figure 14.1 identifies the major professions concerned with housing and the service base of their involvement.

Figure 14.2 locates the professions within the policy network. The term "policy network" is used to describe the pattern of regular and established interaction within a policy area that involves actors and organizations that control resources. In other words the focus is on those actors and organizations that control the resources to turn policy interest into policy influence. At the heart of the network is the local authority, which contains a number of important actors in housing policy. The basic division is between professional officers and the elected members (councillors). Elected members sit on committees to which one or two service departments are responsible. It is common for departments to be single-service and single-profession, with most departments being led by a professionally qualified chief officer who is responsible to his department's committee and to the authority's chief executive. Thus within the local authority there may be a number of actors and organizations involved in housing policy dependent upon the pattern of allocation of responsibilities between committees and between departments.

Outside the local authority there are a number of important network organizations. Of prime importance is the Department of the Environment's (DOE) regional offices, which play a central role in the allocation of finance to local authorities for capital investment in housing as well as being closely involved in the development of local authority housing strategies. The Housing Corporation also has a series of regional offices that supply finance to housing associations. The main role of the corporation is to distribute the grant it receives from the central government to local housing associations, a task that frequently brings it into close contact with local authorities.

The housing associations are important network members in their own right, particularly in the larger cities where they often make a major contribution to the housing strategies of local authorities. Although almost completely dependent on public finance from the Housing Corporation, they jealously guard their independence, particularly from local authority pressure.

Although the network contains a number of powerful members, it is important

Figure 14.1
Professional Involvement in Housing Policy

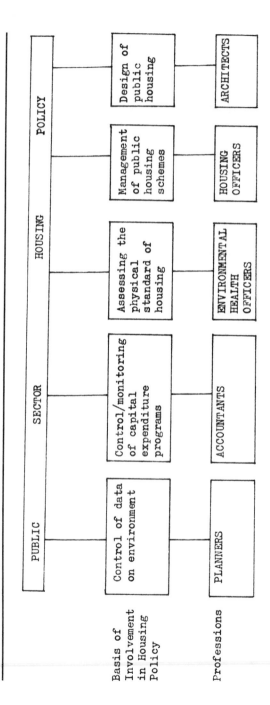

Figure 14.2
The Public-Sector Housing Policy Network

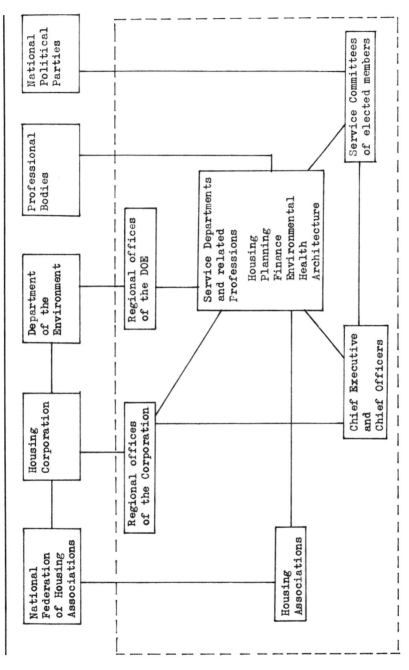

—————— Boundary of the network.

to take account of the pattern of contact within the network. It can be seen that while some members are involved in a strong network of links, others are only weakly integrated into the network. Bearing this qualification in mind, it is possible to identify three important characteristics of the policy network. The first is the mediating role of the regional offices of the DOE, with the extent of contact between individual local authorities and the headquarters of the DOE having declined substantially. Second, a variety of patterns of departmental organizations for housing services exist (Houlihan 1983; Malpass and Murie 1982). Third is the relative isolation of the elected members, who have only weak links with those members of the policy network outside the authority and whose perception of them is consequently substantially mediated by professional officers.

POLICY AND PROCEDURAL CHANGES IN HOUSING AND THE CONSEQUENCES FOR PROFESSIONAL INFLUENCE

Three important changes in the housing policy area have altered the balance of professional influence within the network. The first change is procedural and concerns the development of the system of Housing Investment Program (HIP) as the framework for allocating capital expenditure. The second change concerns the shift in emphasis in local housing policy from slum clearance and building to private-sector area-based improvement. The main consequence of this development, the rise of housing associations as an alternative source of new public-sector housing and as major elements in area improvement schemes, is also discussed. Finally, there is the present Conservative government's determination to cut public expenditure on housing partly by generating income by giving tenants the right to buy their council house. The next section discusses each of these changes and their significance for housing professionals.

Housing Investment Program

The HIP system was introduced in 1977 as a rational model of decision making and it included such features as the identification and prioritization of objectives, the development of a programmatic strategy for achieving them, and a medium-term projection of costs and resources. The HIP procedure initially involved the completion of three documents: a statistical analysis of housing; a strategy statement that outlined the authority's policies for housing for the next three to five years; and a request for capital finance for the coming financial year, together with projections of capital expenditure for the succeeding four years.

The HIP system was superimposed on an existing set of procedures that were fairly disjointed and ad hoc. More importantly, the new system had to be incorporated into an existing departmental structure and pattern of relations within the policy network.

The initial impact of the HIP system was to create within local authorities a focus for policy development. The annual cycle of the HIP imposed on local authorities a framework for policy making due to the need for interdepartmental negotiation over expenditure and the normal requirement of committee approval. In addition the HIP system gave the regional officers of the DOE a regular opportunity to visit authorities and discuss their strategy and financial bid, and consequently a structured point of access to the local policy-making process.

At the officer level the introduction of HIPs provided opportunities for the expansion of professional action space. Planners, in particular, found their role in the policy network strengthened by the high data requirement of the statistical analysis of housing need, but attempts to expand their role to include housing strategy development have met with firm resistance from other network members. Similarly, local authority finance officers found themselves expanding their marginal role to become increasingly involved in issues of housing policy. This was particularly noticeable as cuts in public expenditure became more severe. For example, finance officers favor a small number of large projects because they are easier and cheaper to monitor, thus tending to make more selective repairs or building schemes more difficult to establish. A similar example concerns the selection of housing associations to receive local authority support, with finance officers being more interested in their record as prompt and efficient builders and developers than as sympathetic landlords.

The increasing influence of professionals in the policy network is not simply reflected in the growing role of the recognized professional departments such as Planning and Finance but also in the spread of professional norms and values within departments, and among the weaker professions, such as housing officers. Among housing officers, attempts to retain the leadership of the HIP process in the face of challenges from finance officers and planners forced them to improve their expertise in financial and program control and also in data handling (Houlihan 1983).

Although the introduction of HIPs enhanced the scope for professional influence in the policy network, there is a marked contrast in terms of the basis on which different professions expanded their responsibilities. Planners, finance officers, and environmental health officers relied on the requirements in HIPs for their particular professional skills; in other words, it was a consequence of their professional expertise. By contrast housing professionals most commonly maintained their role in the policy area as a result of organizational and political factors. There are examples where the responsibilities of an authority were reallocated so as to establish a central coordinating role for the housing department. Similarly, particularly where the housing department is narrowly based, there are examples where there has been a reallocation of responsibilities at the committee level in order to give the housing committee the role of policy leadership—a role that is often devolved to housing officers. Thus the enhanced role of housing professionals, though sometimes the result of the absorption of the expertise of the planner or finance officer, is frequently the result of political sponsorship.

The professionalization of the policy network was given further impetus by the officers of the regional DOE for whom the statistical analysis included in the HIP was one of their main sources of information concerning the local housing situation (Leach et al. 1983). The annual visit by the region's officers has a heavy emphasis on examining the statistical summary as well as reviewing the quality and reliability of the arrangements for financial monitoring and project control.

As might be expected the professionalization of the housing policy process has generally been welcomed by local authority professionals. Indeed it was suggested by officers of the regional DOE that the source of professionalization originated with the local authority officers and reflected the tensions between officers and members with the former seeing HIPs as a way of creating a lay/ professional gap between themselves and councillors, thus enabling them to maintain a degree of discretion.

Economic uncertainty, public expenditure cuts, and the rise of ideological politics combined to undermine the HIP system with many of the rational elements of the process abandoned or downgraded. However, the structure of the HIP system remains and in many authorities the composition of the strategy statement and the completion of the statistical analysis of the local housing situation are still seen as important. In recent years an increasing number of authorities have begun using the HIP procedure as part of their internal processes of policy monitoring and evaluation. Thus central government's original objectives for the HIP have been adapted to meet local authority objectives and as such it is still at the heart of most authorities' housing policy-making process.

Recent years have seen a greater member involvement in HIPs with an increasing number coming to the Housing Committee for approval before they are sent to the regional DOE. However, the increase in member involvement tends to be at the elite level and outside the larger urban authorities there is little evidence of a serious challenge to professional definitions of problems and solutions. As one councillor commented: ''There is little scope for policy change or development at the moment . . . our priorities are long established . . . and even with additional finance from the sale of council houses to top-up our HIP allocations we are barely able to keep our essential programs ticking over.''

To sum up, the introduction of the HIP procedure has had a considerable impact on the pattern of network relations and still does despite a growing cynicism regarding the rationality of the process and the increasing politicization of housing finance. However, the nature of the HIP procedure supported by the role of the regional officers of the DOE enhances the professionalization of the policy area and makes political direction of policy more difficult.

The Development of the Policy of Area-Based Improvement

From the early 1970s the policy of private-sector area improvement gradually replaced that of clearance and building promoted at the central government level by the 1969 and 1974 Housing Acts, which offered high levels of grant aid. By the mid- to late 1970s most urban local authorities had, with varying degrees of enthusiasm, declared a number of Housing Action Areas (HAAs) and General Improvement Areas (GIAs). There are three local-level decisions that reveal the relative influence of professionals and elected members in the policy area. The first decision concerns the pace of policy adoption. The second decision involves the establishment of the procedure for identifying and prioritizing areas and the pace at which areas were declared, while the third decision concerns the role of housing associations.

The pace of policy adoption by local authorities needs to be seen against a background of strong promotion of the policy by the regional offices of the DOE, an increasingly attractive system of central government grants, and finally the rapidly rising cost of new building. Despite these strong pressures for early policy acceptance by local authorities a number resisted, particularly those Labour authorities who were committed to a policy of continued high levels of council house building and were suspicious of an improvement policy aimed at house owners and private landlords.

Among local authority professionals there was a division between those who perceived no clear benefit to themselves, most notably architects, and those who felt that the policy innovation would help to expand their involvement in housing policy. This latter group included planners and environmental health professionals for whom the extensive survey requirements of the policy were a key attraction. Housing officers exhibited mixed reactions to the policy with some feeling that area improvement was a temporary policy that was removing them from the mainstream of their professional career and consequently they were generally antagonistic toward the policy. By contrast there was another group of housing officers who welcomed the policy as an opportunity to broaden the basis of their professionalism. This group tended to be found in the comprehensive housing departments and was supported by a housing committee with an equally broad involvement in the policy area. Among this group the feeling was that other professions and departments could be treated as clients and that strategic direction of the policy would rest firmly with housing professionals.

As a result of the divisions between professions in most authorities, members were usually able to find professional support for their particular attitude toward the policy. However, where members, who resisted area improvement, were faced with an opposing coalition among the stronger professions, they found it very difficult to sustain their position.

Once the policy had been accepted by the authority, professional influence significantly increased. This was mainly due to the technical nature of the process of the identification and prioritization of potential GIAs and HAAs, but also because once the policy crossed the threshold and became "a policy of the authority" there followed a period of interprofessional and interdepartmental rivalry for policy leadership. Few members were concerned where responsibility for improvement was located so long as a satisfactory output was maintained.

Thus the issue of implementation tended to be settled at the officer level with little elected-member intervention.

The identification and prioritization of areas was normally treated as a technical exercise, which was led by, or relied heavily on, the social area analysis of the Planning Department and a physical housing survey by the Environmental Health Department. However, it was found that as members began to realize that area-based improvement was not a peripheral policy, but was rapidly becoming a central element in the local housing strategy, they began to take a much keener interest in the implementation process. Thus by the late 1970s the process of area identification, prioritization, and the pace of declaration was becoming more politically contentious.

The professional response was to stress the technical nature of the process and close out member involvement by keeping their survey material confidential and by publicly announcing the next set of areas for declaration together with their order of priority, thus tending to preempt debate. This procedure made it difficult for members and local pressure groups to argue for the promotion of their area without stimulating opposition from those already on, or higher up, the list.

Thus the typical pattern is for consultation with members to be limited as far as possible, usually to the chairman, and for areas to be announced in a block of anything from five to twenty-five HAAs.

On the final issue of the role of housing associations the pattern of events is in many ways similar to that on the issue of the adoption of area improvement, namely member involvement in the initial stage of policy acceptance giving way to greater officer/professional involvement. Professional views on the operation of housing associations as agents for improvement work vary with planners and finance officers being more favorably disposed than architects or housing officers.

In general, planners supported the role of housing associations partly because they were seen as more willing to contribute toward and to accept the need for environmental work in GIAs and HAAs. It was also felt that, regarding any newly built work, they were both more open to planners' influence on layout and more innovative in design than their local authority counterparts. The attraction of housing associations for finance officers lay in the fact that the complete cost of improvement work carried out by the association was borne by the central government. When savings in revenue costs were added to the capital cost savings, the clear financial advantage in using housing associations created a powerful ally in local authority finance officers.

Among housing professionals there was a clear ambiguity toward a greater role for associations. There was a general apprehension about their potential to encroach on the housing department's traditional role and pool of finance. However, this apprehension was overlaid with a number of other responses. In particular, many housing professionals saw the associations' role in area improvement as inevitable and of benefit as the department received nomination rights on 50 percent of vacancies. What seems to have been of major importance in influencing the attitude of housing professionals was whether they felt that would still be able to retain control over the broad improvement strategy. At the heart of their unease was whether they would be able to bring the associations under their sphere of influence or whether the associations would become allied to a rival department, particularly planning or environmental health.

It was rare for members to oppose strongly the involvement of housing associations, with most, the Conservatives especially, either expressing open support or at least tolerance. Thus the strong support from finance officers and planners was sufficient to give the associations a prominent and usually dominant role in GIAs and HAAs. However, once this initial decision had been taken, the relationship with associations and later decisions regarding their areas of operation, the mix and number of associations allowed to operate in the authority, rentals, and the type of improvement work undertaken became increasingly the preserve of professional officers.

In particular, as the policy matured there developed an important four-way relationship between local authority and housing association professionals, officers of regional DOE, and officers of the regional Housing Corporation, which became the forum for future decisions about the direction of improvement work. Entry by councillors into this network was rare and not encouraged and seemed to become particularly difficult as the local authority became progressively more dependent on the associations and Housing Corporation finance for success in area improvement work and increasingly for new building activity.

Public Expenditure Cuts, Privatization, and the Rise of Ideological Politics

Of all types of local government expenditure it has been capital expenditure that has borne the brunt of cuts and capital expenditure on housing that has been the most seriously affected. Thus while total local authority capital expenditure has declined by 47 percent in real terms since 1973/74, the decline for housing has been over 68 percent with a cut of 62 percent between 1978/79 and 1984/85 alone. However, it is not just the scale of the cuts that has caused problems for the housing service, it is also the application of cash limits within an inflexible annual framework that has put expertise in financial management at a premium.

In addition to experiencing severe cuts in capital expenditure the housing policy area has also been a key focus for the Thatcher government's commitment to privatization. The 1980 Housing Act, which gave council tenants the right to buy their dwelling, has resulted in sales valued at over £10 billion. The consequence of these policies has been to contribute to the rise of ideological or manifesto politics at the local level, which has led to a series of confrontations between a small number of authorities and the government—first over the sale of council houses and more recently over expenditure reductions.

What then has been the impact of these national-level changes in capital expenditure and housing policy on the balance of influence in the housing policy network? At first sight it would seem that the initiative in policy development has swung in favor of the elected member. To an extent this is correct with a number of authorities opposing the sale of council houses as a result of elected member decisions. A further consequence has been that the heightened political awareness arising from this conflict has spilled over into the HIP procedure and resulted in an increase in member interest and involvement.

However, the housing policy network does not involve a simple two-way relationship between members and a single profession but is rather a multi-professional network producing a complex pattern of interactions between professions, departments, and elected members. It is therefore important to examine how the pattern of interactions has been affected by the greater assertiveness of members and the salience of housing to central government.

Taking the sale of council houses as an example, those authorities who opposed the sale of council houses adopted, broadly speaking, one of two sets of tactics. They either fought the legislation at a public and political level or they fought the legislation at two levels—one public and political and the other professional and administrative. The leader of one authority referred to the latter tactic as "professionalizing our opposition." In other words the interests of the professionals in protecting their service were combined with the elected members' more overtly ideologically based opposition. As a result, professional advice was sought on how implementation of the act might be delayed and its consequences minimized. Thus a series of administrative subterfuges was developed by chief officers. For example, implementation was delayed by insisting that houses be valued by the district valuer, the sales sections of housing departments were deliberately understaffed, and conveyancing was transferred to local firms of solicitors who were not large enough to cope with the demand.

The allying of professional self-interest with members' political objectives is also evident in the response of local authorities to the government's pressure on capital expenditure. As noted earlier, the steady decline in HIP allocations has to some extent been offset by the inflow of capital receipts from the sale of council houses. As a result a number of Labour councils sold council houses because the capital receipts have allowed them to pursue other housing priorities without having to rely on the HIP procedure. However, the scope for using capital receipts has been steadily eroded by the government reducing the proportion of receipts available for use by the local authority from 50 percent to 40 percent and most recently to 20 percent.

Professionals have been involved in a number of aspects of the game of financial "cat and mouse" that many authorities have played with the government. First, finance and housing officers have been the source of many of the suggestions aimed at maximizing capital receipts, such as giving intending purchasers an ex gratia payment if they used a Building Society rather than the local authority for their mortgage. The second source of involvement of professionals concerned the circumventing of restrictions on the proportion of capital receipts that the authority could use.

Finally, finance professionals were also a major source of suggestions of other ways in which capital resources could be increased. Thus one authority draws on Urban Aid funds by "dressing up our main line housing schemes as 'special projects,' " while another has recently sold, to a consortium of London banks, its future income from mortgage repayments for an immediate lump sum.

While it is undeniably difficult to disentangle political from professional initiative, it would seem that many of these schemes and tactics were clearly suggested by professionals and justified in terms of protecting their services. Thus, while public expenditure cuts have greatly politicized housing policy and consequently enhanced the role of elected members in the policy network, it has also resulted in the increasing importance of the previously marginal finance profession.

CONCLUSION

At the beginning of the chapter it was suggested that many policy areas are witnessing a retreat by professionals in the face of external criticism, public expenditure cuts, self-doubt, and particularly the increasing assertiveness of elected members.

In appreciating the changing role of professionals involved in housing it is most important to acknowledge the complexity of the policy network where the multiprofessional character of the policy areas means that it is unwise to talk in terms of the advance of elected members or clients and the retreat of the professional. It is much more appropriate to conceptualize the changes in the policy network in terms of the constantly evolving pattern of policy coalitions that form and re-form as pressures on the policy network change, as policies develop, and as new issues arise.

Therefore, the main conclusion is that "the professional retreat" is at best partial and refers only to some professions on some issues, with there also being examples of "professional advance." Similarly, the change in the role of elected members in the policy area has not been uniform. Their prominence in some aspects of the policy area increased, but in others it remained relatively unchanged.

In the major professions, the greatest change has been in the role of finance officers. Their traditional role of internal audit, financial programming, and investment management has been altered as a consequence of successive cuts in public expenditure. This has resulted in a much closer involvement with substantive issues in housing policy shown by their role not only in protecting capital resources but also in affecting how they are used.

Establishing an accurate picture of the relationship between local authority finance officers and members is difficult but a number of tentative observations may be made. First, there is a high degree of deference toward finance officers by members, which arises partly from the jargon and mystique surrounding accountancy and partly from the knowledge that an external audit will be carried out. For a chief finance officer to comment that ''we may have problems with the auditors on that one'' is usually sufficient to stymie an unwelcome proposal.

Second, as finance moved to the center of the stage in the central-local government relations, finance officers were drawn, however unwillingly, into the political arena. Thus, the previously ''neutral'' profession of accountancy is now enmeshed in the game of financial cat and mouse with the government. It is significant that treasurers still attempt to distance themselves from the political stance of the council by referring to a set of professional values (maximize income, protect services, value for money, and so on), yet have a considerable impact on policy (Rosenberg 1984). Although it is increasingly difficult for them to retain their traditional detachment from substantive policy areas, particularly housing, it is too soon to draw any firm conclusions about the consequences for policy making. However it is clear that their potential for influence is considerable.

By contrast with finance officers, planning professionals and also environmental health officers have been forced to give ground to other groups within the network. In commenting on the position of planners in general, Underwood (1980) noted the establishment of a ''level of competence in land management [which] is firmly rooted in statutory duties'' as a ''fall back position'' for planners under pressure. Their involvement in HIPs and area improvement has seen a similar retreat behind their acknowledged statistical and technical expertise.

The final professional group is the housing officers themselves. In terms of the development of housing strategy their position is often weak, even marginal, and when they do achieve a strategic leadership role it is frequently the result of strong political sponsorship often achieved by a favorable structuring of departments so as to ensure them a central policy role.

It is not surprising that housing professionals have been most seriously affected by the rise of ideological politics and the financial pressures on their service. Professionalism as a defense of their occupation is therefore of only weak utility and as a result other tactics to defend the occupation have emerged.

The first tactic is that housing professionals ally themselves to another more powerful profession. Most common is a combined housing and health department with the chief officer qualified in both fields. Health and housing is a powerful combination of technical expertise and broad policy interest, though generally the housing profession is seen as the junior partner.

The second tactic is that housing professionals ally themselves to the dominant (usually Labour) party. Political sponsorship has its dangers, particularly when there is the possibility of a change in party control, but where political control is stable the close relationship between housing professionals and elected members provides a strong coalition within the policy area.

To summarize the changing role of members, first, much of the rise in manifesto politics has been stimulated by policy developments at the national level and consequently much member activity is directed toward the government rather than toward other participants in the local housing network. Second, member interest in housing policy is uneven, focusing mainly on capital finance, the organization of service delivery, and also short-lived issues such as opposition to the sale of council houses. It is only the second of these three issues that results in elected members impinging seriously on areas of professional competence.

Issues such as the sale of council houses or the increase in council house rents have resulted, in some authorities, in a spillover of member involvement into other aspects of housing policy, particularly concerning the HIP procedure, but the involvement tends to be superficial and toward the end of the HIP cycle.

What would seem to be of greater significance is that, important though members undoubtedly are within the policy network, they often need professional support in order to change or maintain existing policy. Professions are also important in mediating political influence, this being particularly clear when members seek to "take on" the government. It would seem that to talk in terms of professional retreat or professional crisis is oversimplifying the complex pattern that various procedural and policy changes have brought about in the housing policy area in the last decade or so.

NOTE

1. This chapter is a summary of research into the role of professionals in housing policy carried out in 14 local authorities in the West Midlands and North West regions of Britain. The sample of authorities contains a mix of urban and rural District Councils with varying patterns of political control and a range of housing problems.

REFERENCES

Bains, M. A.
1972   *The New Local Authorities: Management and Structure*. London: HMSO.
Collins, C. A., C. R. Hinings, and K. Walsh
1978   "The Officer and the Councillor in Local Government." *Public Administration Bulletin* 28, 34–50.
Davies, J. G.
1972   *The Evangelistic Bureaucrat*. London: Tavistock.
Dennis, N.
1972   *Public Participation and Planning Blight*. London: Faber
Dunleavy, P. J.
1980   *Urban Political Analysis*. London: Macmillan.
Goldsmith, M. J.
1980   *Politics, Planning and the City*. London: Hutchinson.
Hall, P., R. Thomas, H. Gracey, and R. Drewitt
1973   *The Containment of Urban England*. London: PEP/Allen and Unwin.

Houlihan, B.
1983   "The Professionalization of Housing Policy." *Public Administration Bulletin*, no. 41 (April), 14–32.
Johnson, T. J.
1972   *Professions and Power*. London: Macmillan.
Laffin, M.
1985   "Professionalism in Crisis." Unpublished paper, Political Studies Association Conference, Manchester.
Leach, S., C. R. Hinings, S. Ranson, and C. Skelcher
1983   "Uses and Abuses of Policy Planning Systems." *Local Government Studies* 9, no. 1, 23–27.
Malpass, P., and A. Murie
1982   *Housing Policy and Practice*. London: Macmillan.
Pollitt, C.
1984   "Professionals and Public Policy." *Public Administration Bulletin*, no. 44 (April), 29–46.
Rosenberg, D.
1984   "The Politics of Role in Local Government: Perspectives on the Role Set of Treasurers in the Relationships of Chief Executives." *Local Government Studies*, 10, no.1 (January/February), 1–23.
Short, J. R.
1982   *Housing in Britain: The Post War Experience*. London: Methuen.
Underwood, J.
1980   *Town Planners in Search of a Role*. University of Bristol, School for Advanced Urban Studies.
Young, K.
1977   "Values in the Policy Process." *Policy and Politics* 5, no. 3, 1–22.

15

Politicians and Statisticians in Conflict: The 1980 United States Census

HARVEY M. CHOLDIN

Abstract. The 1980 United States Census inspired a major conflict between mayors and census officials, struggling over urban statistics, which would have indirect effects upon the federal funding of local housing and other programs. In dozens of lawsuits, mayors alleged that the undercount of poor minority populations would have negative effects upon their cities. The central issue was both political and statistical: should the government adjust the statistics to correct for the undercount? Census officials effectively resisted the pressure to make adjustments. Nonetheless, the technical and political issues that were raised by the controversy promise to endure into the future.

INTRODUCTION

Ordinarily it might appear that national statistics and local housing programs are entirely disparate enterprises—one is situated in a national statistical office and the other is dispersed in the city halls and housing offices of towns and cities. The one seems to be a mundane operation in which administrators and technicians routinely produce books of numbers and the other is concerned with planning and providing shelter in communities. In the United States in 1980, though, mayors and census officials became entangled with each other, struggling over census numbers for cities and neighborhoods, which had indirect effects upon the federal funding of local housing and redevelopment programs.

With few exceptions, American communities have rarely engaged in neighborhood redevelopment or public housing efforts on their own; most municipal housing efforts in the United States are supported by the federal government. In recent decades, the federal government has increasingly allocated funds for various purposes including housing and urban redevelopment to states and communities by means of statistical formulas. Within some political limits, perhaps unstated, of who is to benefit and who is not, these formulas are designed to distribute federal resources to those places that most need them (Nathan 1983; Nathan et al. 1977). Government statistics, often derived from the decennial census, are used in the allocation formulas. Because many municipalities had become heavily dependent upon federal funds, their mayors strongly attacked the Census Bureau, a crucial agency of the statistical system, after the 1980 census, in an attempt to maximize their income or at least to minimize the losses that would follow a population loss when the new numbers were entered into the granting formulas.

Administrators and statisticians of the Census Bureau were shocked to find themselves in this imbroglio. Holding degrees in the social sciences or statistics, many census administrators are social scientists as well as civil servants. Except for those at the highest management levels, government statisticians are accustomed to working in a humdrum bureaucratic-scientific environment, but the events of 1980 shook them out of that comfortable situation. They were forced to operate in a contentious political arena, testifying before congressional committees, speaking to journalists, conferring with lawyers, and appearing in court. They had to make and defend difficult technical and policy decisions.

BACKGROUND

During the first century and a half of U.S. history, most governmental, economic, and social functions were considered to be the responsibilities of the states, not of the national government. Cities and towns as well were the responsibilities of the states. With few exceptions, mostly having to do with transportation, the federal government avoided local problems, much as it eschewed social welfare problems in general. The government began to make grants (known as grants-in-aid) to the states in the nineteenth century for a few purposes. Over the course of American history, the volume and scope of these grants expanded gradually until the advent of the New Deal, when they began to proliferate (Fossett 1983).

The New Deal radically redefined the scope of the federal government's involvement in social welfare concerns. The national government began to divert funds to the states for a variety of purposes, eventually including slum clearance and public housing. Several New Deal programs were implemented by means of grants-in-aid to the states. In the case of slum clearance and housing, the grants-in-aid were formulated so that the federal government would make grants to the states, which would in turn make grants to towns and cities. Grants-in-aid grew rapidly in the decades following the New Deal. Furthermore, postwar legislation for housing and urban redevelopment created a new channel that allowed grants to flow, for the first time, directly from the federal government to the cities (Fossett 1983).

Federal grants-in-aid grew enormously in the 1950s, 1960s, and 1970s, simultaneously with another major social trend, massive suburbanization, which had a number of negative effects upon most of the big cities. The suburbanization of major economic functions left cities with inadequate sources of local tax revenue to fulfill their ordinary and extraordinary services. For this reason, their mayors became increasingly dependent upon Washington's grants-in-aid for income to support their large budgets, including their redevelopment and housing programs. During the course of the decades, the federal government instituted and revised numerous programs for the cities, including urban renewal, public housing, and other programs administered by the Department of Housing and Urban Development. Furthermore, during the administration of President Nixon, the federal government began an expanded program, known as General Revenue Sharing, to send federal tax monies to localities. After incorporating this income into their budgets, the mayors were even more dependent upon federal funds. Looking at the years in the mid–1970s, Fossett (1983) analyzed the finances of 11 large American cities and their uses of federal dollars. He showed that most of the cities were having financial difficulties, led by New York City, which was running a deficit. Six of the largest cities were using federal grant monies to cover more than one-fifth of their expenditures on basic services, such as public safety and sanitation. The use of grants for basic services defines dependency. The cities' financial dependency set the stage for a conflict between localities and the central government at the time of the 1980 national census.

1980 CONFLICT

There is also a historical background to the census-takers' involvement in the controversy of 1980, which represented a new kind of issue for them. American statisticians and social scientists are proud of the nation's census, which has been taken regularly since 1790 (Eckler 1972). Nonetheless, the history of the census has been marred by a handful of controversies (for example, see Lee 1984). Privacy has been the major issue in recent decades, with legislators and others contending that the government has no right to ask questions about private matters like personal income (Taeuber 1967; Petersen 1972). In 1970, however, several mayors and black leaders attacked the census on a new basis, contending that it systematically failed to count certain categories of individuals living in cities, specifically members of poor minority groups. The mayors contended that this form of "undercounting" had been demonstrated statistically and that its effect was to deny full grants-in-aid to their communities (Mitroff et al. 1983). The mayors were convinced that statistical procedures were available with which the Census Bureau could readjust the results of the census so as to rectify the undercount and even in that year a couple of them sued the federal government.

In 1970 the mayors' lawsuits were ineffectual; the courts all ruled in favor of the federal government, saying in effect that the mayors' cases were insufficient. But in 1980 many more mayors were aggrieved and more than four dozen of them sued the government. This time two of the judges actually ruled in favor of the cities, in cases brought by Detroit and New York, and the judge of the Detroit case ordered the Census Bureau to prepare a plan by which it would adjust the results of the enumeration in order to correct for undercounting. That decision was overruled when census administrators appealed to a higher court, so they were not actually required to adjust the results. Even though the Census Bureau won the lawsuit, the first decision shocked them; it showed them that the judiciary had the power to tell them what to do.

In the lawsuits the first issue was accuracy: how complete was the count and was it possible to improve upon the accuracy of the enumeration by means of statistical adjustment? All of the mayors argued that census-takers had failed to count numerous residents of their cities, particularly in the slums. Some mayors charged the Census Bureau with incompetence by failure to count the citizens correctly. The more generous mayors admitted that it is basically impossible to count everyone. Some persons are fearful of the government, others have some-thing to hide, and yet others are not sufficiently literate to fill out the forms. American law requires each person to answer questions once they are contacted by the census-taker, but it does not require a person to come forth if he or she is not contacted. Both types of mayors agreed that the census's accuracy could be improved by the use of statistical adjustment. Census officials admitted readily that they had undercounted certain categories of persons, but they emphatically resisted the idea that they could improve the results by adjustment. They said that they were not legally authorized to manipulate the numbers and that even if they were they did not possess a scientifically proven technique for statistical adjustment (U.S. Bureau of the Census 1980a). Thus the statisticians and the mayors were in direct opposition.

Mayors framed the controversy as a matter of equity. They argued that the errors in the census, being systematically biased, tended to promote inequity in the distribution of grants-in-aid because the residents of communities where large numbers of persons were missed would receive less than their fair share of government benefits. They would also tend to be underrepresented in state leg-islatures and in the Congress because seats in these bodies are allocated to areas on the basis of census counts.

The issues looked considerably different to the administrators and statisticians of the Census Bureau. They relied upon the agency's record of producing high-quality statistical products to argue that they were best qualified to make re-sponsible decisions about statistical procedures. It was they who had discovered and documented the extent of the minority undercounts in a series of studies dating back to 1940. Preparing for the 1980 census, they introduced new field-work approaches in an attempt to count all individuals. This apparently reduced the black undercount from 7.7 percent in 1970 to perhaps 4.5 percent in 1980,[1] but it failed to eliminate it. Moreover, since the new procedures may have produced an ''overcount'' of whites, the census continued to have a *differential* undercount. Nonetheless, census administrators were strongly opposed to the idea of allowing the courts to make statistical decisions. They contended that judges are not qualified to make such technical decisions, which should be left to the professionals with their scientific expertise and access to the resources of their disciplines. Furthermore, as government officials who had for decades provided much of the data to document the conditions of disadvantaged minorities (data that frequently had been used to develop ameliorative social programs), they resented being portrayed as the "bad guys" who were supporting inequitable treatment of the cities.

In addition, the census officials suspected that the mayors were "playing politics" with the undercount issue. Suing the federal government is an easy way to get publicity and to appear to be helping certain segments of the community. Typically the mayors told the mass media that their cities were losing large sums of money, as much as $200 per year, for each individual missed in the census. Two political scientists who examined the formulas governing allocation of the major grants in light of the census result published a far lower figure. Maurice and Nathan (1982) estimated that an adjustment to correct for undercount might yield as little as $5 to $20 per individual missed. It is possible that a number of mayors did not want to face the consequences of the fact that the 1980 census would show that their cities had continued to lose people. Some relied upon locally produced erroneous estimates of current population. Others simply ignored the advice of their city planners who knew in advance of the census that the community had lost population.

The question of statistical adjustment was a difficult one for census officials. In order to assemble information and opinions about adjusting census results, they convened a series of conferences that drew together outstanding statisticians and demographers from the universities and elsewhere in addition to legal experts and political officials (U.S. Bureau of the Census 1980b). Inside the Census Bureau itself the administrative leadership group included highly qualified and experienced scientists and this group held endless discussions about statistical adjustment of census results. First and foremost, they argued that neither the Constitution nor the laws governing the census authorized them to adjust the results of the enumeration. They also contended that, while procedures had been proposed for adjusting census results, these procedures were untested and that a national census is too large an enterprise for experimentation. Also, they felt that the scientific community had not reached anything like a consensus on which was the best procedure or whether it would be wise to adjust the numbers. For all these reasons, then, the census administrators resisted the pressure to adjust the results in 1980 and they were able to prevail over the mayors.

Perhaps it is appropriate to end the story with an ironic point. The introduction of General Revenue Sharing in 1972 represented the greatest single expansion of federal grants-in-aid to cities and towns. This was probably the program that most sensitized mayors to the financial impact of national statistics and inspired them to challenge the census in 1980. At the time of this writing (1985) the conservative philosophy of the administration in Washington suggests that communities should become less dependent upon federal resources. For this reason and to help reduce the federal debt, the administration proposes to abolish revenue sharing. Thus, the device that may have triggered the crisis between the cities and the statistical office is about to disappear. In the statistical office, however, the technical issues that were raised by the crisis are still simmering and promise to endure for years into the future. In particular, the memory of the 1980s conflicts requires census administrators to continue to deal with the undercount, either to eliminate it, which seems to be impossible, to adjust for it, or to develop alternative or supplementary approaches to producing those statistical products that have traditionally emanated from censuses.

DISCUSSION

This episode shows that the statistical system is a crucial part of the environment of the local housing situation. In this sense, it is like the banking system, for example, insofar as events taking place within it may have real effects, in this case negative, for local housing administrators. More broadly, then, one may ask what other sorts of statistics, other than the census, are there that impact upon local housing authorities? What effects do they have? What are the effects of vacancy rates? What are the effects of demographic trends in marriage and divorce or in age composition? Shifting to routinely taken surveys, what are the effects of public opinion on community and housing satisfaction? What is known about how public officials use those statistics that pertain to housing?

More generally, what does this episode tell about the environment in which statisticians and social researchers work? This episode—which can be seen as a great and extreme case, insofar as it was widely publicized and reached the highest levels of national government—illustrates the potentially powerful effects of social science products. Insofar as these effects become visible outside of the ivory tower of the university or research institute, they may provoke reactions, not necessarily positive, even if statisticians and social scientists see themselves as well-meaning and blameless. Perhaps this is the price of not being irrelevant. If this episode shows that statistics and other research products form part of the environment for housing officials, it also shows that statisticians and other social researchers operate in a real-world environment that can impact powerfully upon their work as well.

NOTE

1. Demographic analysis of 1980 census data showed an undercount of 4.5 percent of all blacks. Analysis of the census in relation to post-enumeration surveys yielded estimates of a black undercount ranging between 0.7 and 7.2 percent. Use of either method shows a reduction in the black undercount.

REFERENCES

Eckler, A. Ross
1972   *The Bureau of the Census.* New York: Praeger.
Fossett, James W.
1983   *Federal Aid to Big Cities: The Politics of Dependence.* Washington, D.C.: Brookings Institution.

Lee, Anne S.

1984   "The Census Under Fire: The Press and the 1980 Census." Paper presented at meeting of the Population Association of America, Minneapolis.

Maurice, Arthur J., and Richard P. Nathan

1982   "The Census Undercount: Effects on Federal Aid to Cities." *Urban Affairs Quarterly* 17, 251–84.

Mitroff, Ian I., Richard O. Mason, and Vincent P. Barabba

1983   *The 1980 Census: Policymaking Amid Turbulence*. Lexington, Mass.: Lexington Books.

Nathan, Richard P.

1983   "The Politics of Printouts: The Use of Official Numbers to Allocate Federal Grants-in-Aid." Paper presented to a conference on The Political Economy of National Statistics, Washington, D.C.

Nathan, Richard P., Paul R. Dommel, Sarah F. Liebschutz, and Milton D. Morris

1977   *Block Grants for Community Development*. Washington, D.C.: U.S. Department of Housing and Urban Development.

Petersen, William

1972   "Forbidden Knowledge." In *The Social Contexts of Research*, edited by S. Z. Nagi: and R. G. Corwin. New York: John Wiley, 297–304.

Taeuber, Conrad

1967   "Invasion of Privacy: The Case of the United States Census." *Eugenics Quarterly* 14, 243–46.

U.S. Bureau of the Census

1980a   "Census Undercount Adjustment: Basis for Decision." *Federal Register* 45 (October 20), 69366–75.

1980b   *Conference on Census Undercount, Proceedings*. Washington, D.C.

Name Index

Subject Index

Contributors

PETER AMBROSE has taught at Sussex University since 1965. His research interests include many aspects of housing and planning. He is the author of *Analytical Human Geography*, *The Quiet Revolution*, *The Property Machine*, and *Whatever Happened to Planning?*

JAMES BARLOW has been a Research Fellow in Urban Studies at the University of Sussex since 1984. He has worked on major research projects on European housing provision and on economic and social restructuring. He has also carried out research on agribusiness and farming. He has published several articles on these issues.

TIM BRINDLEY lectures in the School of Architecture, Leicester Polytechnic. He has published reports and articles on housing values and choices, local housing policies and strategies, and most recently on aspects of housing renewal policy. Before moving to Leicester he held positions at Bath University and in the Department of the Environment.

HARVEY M. CHOLDIN is Professor of Sociology at the University of Illinois, Urbana. After studies at the University of Chicago, he did fieldwork on family planning and community development in Bangladesh. He then taught at Michigan State University where he conducted research on the Mexican-American community. He has contributed articles to *Annual Review of Sociology* and *American Sociological Review* and is the author of *Cities and Suburbs: An Introduction to Urban Sociology*.

GLENN DROVER is the Director of the School of Social Work at the University of British Columbia. He has previously been at Carleton, McGill, and Dalhousie universities. He has written widely on social planning issues, including industrial social welfare, social services, social security, and housing. His most recent major work is *Inequality: Essays on the Political Economy of Social Welfare.* He received his Ph.D. from the London School of Economics.

JOHN N. EDWARDS is Professor of Sociology, Virginia Polytechnic Institute and State University. Professor Edwards's main areas of interest are urban sociology and sociology of the family. He is the editor or coeditor of three books and the author of more than 40 articles.

PATRICIA KLOBUS EDWARDS is Professor of Urban Studies at Virginia Polytechnic Institute and State University. A specialist in evaluation research, she has published extensively in the area. Her work has appeared in such journals as *Evaluation Review*, *Journal of Applied Behavioral Science*, and *Public Administration Review*.

MICHAEL C. FLEMING is Professor of Economics, Loughborough University. He was educated at Oxford University and from 1963 to 1971 was a member of the staff at the Queen's University of Belfast. His major works include *Housing in Northern Ireland* and *Construction and the Related Professions* in the series of Reviews of U.K. Statistical Sources, both commissioned by the Royal Statistical Society and the Social Science Research Council. In 1985 he was appointed assistant editor of the series. Professor Fleming is codirector of the Applied Micro-Economics Research Group (AMERG) at Loughborough University, where he and Joseph Nellis were jointly responsible for the research and development of a new British house-price index for the Halifax Building Society in 1983. Reports on the index have been published by the Society and the United Nations Economic Commission for Europe.

RAY FORREST is a coeditor of *Urban Political Economy and Social Theory* and has published articles on housing in *Sociological Review*, *Society and Space*, *Environment and Planning*, *Journal of Social Policy*, and (with Alan Murie) the *International Journal of Urban and Regional Research*.

CHRIS HAMNETT is a lecturer in geography in the Faculty of Social Sciences, the Open University, United Kingdom. He has also held a variety of visiting appointments, most recently the Banneker Research Professorship, School of Public and International Affairs, George Washington University, Washington, D.C. He is an assistant editor of *Housing Studies* and in 1984–85 he was research director of an Independent Government Committee of Inquiry into the management problems of privately owned blocks of flats in Britain. He has written widely in a variety of journals on housing and social change.

SHERMAN HANNA is Professor and Chair of the Family Resource Management Department at Ohio State University, Columbus, and a past president of the

American Association of Housing Educators. He received a Ph.D. in consumer economics from Cornell University.

MICHAEL HARLOE, Department of Sociology, University of Essex, is the author of numerous books and articles based on extensive research in housing and urban studies. His present work includes an international study of innovative housing policies and practices as responses to emerging housing crises. He is also the editor of *The International Journal of Urban and Regional Research.*

BARRIE HOULIHAN, Ph.D., is Senior Lecturer in public administration at North Staffordshire Polytechnic. His main areas of research are the relationship between central and local government, housing policy, and public-sector professions. He has published a number of articles in these areas and is currently working on a study of the housing association movement in Britain.

J. DAVID HULCHANSKI is an Assistant Professor in the School of Community and Regional Planning, University of British Columbia, where he teaches courses in housing policy and the history of Canadian planning and housing. He has previously taught in the Urban Studies Program at the University of Toronto where he was a Research Associate with its Centre for Urban and Community Studies. He has prepared housing studies for the Ontario Commission on Residential Tenancies (on rent controls, 1984), the Ontario Ministry of Municipal Affairs and Housing (on residential land-use intensification, 1982) and the Canada Mortgage and Housing Corporation (on inner-city new neighborhoods, 1981). He earned his Ph.D. in urban planning at the University of Toronto.

JUDITH A. JONES is Experimental Officer with the Division of Building Research, Commonwealth Scientific and Industrial Research Organization of Australia. Her publications focus on various aspects of housing research.

SUZANNE LINDAMOOD is an Associate Professor of Housing at Kansas State University, Manhattan. She received a Ph.D. in housing from Cornell University.

DUNCAN MACLENNAN is Director of the Centre for Housing Research at the University of Glasgow. He has published extensively on all aspects of housing policy, and is the author of *Housing Economics* and *Housing Finance.*

BARBARA A. MISZTAL and BRONISLAW MISZTAL specialize in urban political sociology. They have published articles in *Urban Affairs Quarterly,* *Sociology,* and *British Journal of Sociology* and have contributed to several international volumes. Until 1980 they were, respectively, Assistant and Associate Professors of Sociology at the Polish Academy of Sciences. From 1980 to 1984 they taught in the United States. They currently live in Australia, where Bronislaw teaches at Griffith University.

ALAN MURIE is Senior Lecturer at the School for Advanced Urban Studies, University of Bristol. His research focuses on housing policy, and he is the author of *Housing Inequality and Deprivation* and a coauthor of *Housing Policy and the Housing Systems* and *Housing Policy and Practice*. His most recent article (with Ray Forrest) appeared in the March 1986 issue of the *International Journal of Urban and Regional Research*.

JOSEPH G. NELLIS is Lecturer in Economics in the School of Management at Cranfield Institute of Technology. He studied at the universities of Ulster and Warwick. He was formerly Midland Bank Research Fellow at Loughborough University and a Lecturer in Economics at the University of Keele. In addition to his work on housing markets, he is a joint author of *The Framework of UK Monetary Policy*.

ANTHONY J. O'SULLIVAN is a Lecturer in Economics at the University of Glasgow. His major research interests are econometric modeling of housing markets and the distributional impacts of housing subsidies. He has published several papers on aspects of inequality and housing.

MICHAEL J. OXLEY is Principal Lecturer in Urban Land Economics at Leicester Polytechnic. His major research interests are in the economics of housing policy. His work on housing policy in Western Europe has included a comparative analysis of the growth of home ownership, the consequences of rent controls, and the operation of housing allowances. Other publications include work on economic theory and urban planning, house and land prices, and the availability of land for house building in urban areas.

ELIZABETH A. ROISTACHER is Associate Professor of Economics at Queens College of the City University of New York. As a U.S. German Marshall Fund Fellow, she spent 1982 at the London School of Economics studying British housing policy. She has previously served as Deputy Assistant Secretary for Economic Affairs of the U.S. Department of Housing and Urban Development. Dr. Roistacher has published widely on housing economics and policy.

GERRY STOKER lectures at the Institute for Local Government Studies, University of Birmingham. He has published various articles and chapters on housing policy and local politics. Formerly, he lectured at Leicester Polytechnic and carried out research at Manchester University.

WILLEM VAN VLIET—, on leave from Pennsylvania State University, is a Visiting Associate Professor in the College of Environmental Design and Department of Sociology at the University of Colorado, Boulder. He is editor of the forthcoming *International Handbook of Housing Policies and Practices* and coeditor of *Habitats for Children, Housing Needs and Policy Approaches, Housing and Neighborhoods*, and the *Handbook of Housing and the Built Environment in the U.S.*